W9-CJU-031

Climb

Climb

Leading women in technology
share their journeys to success.

COMPILED & EDITED BY

Sandra Coffey Hofmann
Bonnie Bajorek Daneker

First published November 2010 in Atlanta, Georgia, by Women in Technology, Inc. (www.mywit.org)

Second printing Febuary 2011 in Atlanta, Georgia by Women in Technology, Inc.

Book design & cover design by West Reed (www.westreed.com), Atlanta, Georgia

ISBN: 978-0-615-40301-4

Printed in the United States of America

Dedicated to girls everywhere – our next generation of women in technology

"*Climb* eloquently reveals that we owe the success of our technology community to outstanding women leaders who have provided the direction and inspiration for our technology growth and innovation – they are the inspirers of success!"

— JOHN YATES, *Chair of the Technology Group of* Morris, Manning & Martin, LLP

"The women involved within the Georgia IT community are a remarkable collection of professionals. They have developed their focused community while also adding value and serving as role models within the larger technology community. They are making a gift to the future by capturing and sharing many of their stories here. I consider myself very lucky to have been able to support and serve these pioneers."

— MIKE ADKINSON, *Pointman*, TechLINKS

Contents

Preface

October 2010

Dear Readers,

Compiling and editing a work like *Climb* was exhilarating, emotional, and exhausting! Most of all, the experience was humbling. I am so in awe of these remarkable women. With eloquent insightfulness, humor, humility, and great self-awareness, the authors were captivating storytellers.

The book had simple beginnings. On June 18, 2010 the Women in Technology Board of Directors endorsed the book project that delivered *Climb*. Net proceeds from the sale of the book would be designated for WIT Foundation to sustain and create programs to get young girls interested in technology careers.

So many individuals could claim credit for the idea of compiling a book. Indeed, the annual WIT *Women of the Year in Technology Awards* typically generated great interest in capturing the stories of the phenomenal honorees and award recipients. Parents wanted to share the stories with their daughters; managers wanted to use the stories to coach aspiring leaders; and women were inspired. Lessons in life and leadership, cautionary tales, hindsight perspectives – so many stories that were begging to be captured.

The time was right for telling those stories. The year had been a difficult one with economic pressures often brutally impacting businesses and careers. Even in 2010, fewer women are graduating with degrees in science, technology, engineering, and math. Women are still paid at lower salaries than men. In spite of definitive research supporting the positive impact women have on company financial performance, there are still few women at the top or on corporate boards. So why not turn the focus away from the negative and focus instead on the positive. Why not highlight the good that happens? Why not celebrate the wisdom gained and the lives impacted by exceptional leaders? Why not celebrate the impact women have and the difference they make in our community? Why not?

Shortly after Independence Day 2010, a request was sent out to all the past presidents of WIT and past award recipients of WIT's *Women of the Year in Technology Award*. Atlanta has a wealth of talented women who serve as role models and it wasn't long before others joined in this ambitious undertaking. There were even a handful of men invited due to their unique and unwavering support for WIT's mission.

Contributing authors were asked to share their story and speak to their experience as a woman in executive leadership roles. They were asked to provide insights that might be of value to other women aspiring to the level of career achievement that they had reached. The call to action was: write about your mentors, what impactful advice you received, what the workplace was like for a woman, why you chose technology, what leadership truths you learned, how being a member of the WIT community made a difference for you or write a letter to the next generation. And what a beautiful and special tapestry they wove!

By the middle of October, almost exactly four months from endorsement, these stories, these rich threads of brilliance, were ready to be pulled from the loom. Certainly the contributing authors (*) deserve accolades for each thread contributed to the rich tapestry, but there is also a concurrent humble bow of the head for those extraordinary master weavers who threaded the heddles, loaded the bobbins, moved the treadles, and threw the shuttles! For those master weavers, I am grateful to have shared this experience:

BONNIE BAJOREK DANEKER* – for capturing the energy and joy of the WIT Foundation and the Next Generation programs at the heart of WIT's mission. You went behind the scenes to engage the participating girls and volunteers. You heard their stories and brought their experiences to readers. Even more, you were there during those hectic days of final editing and served as a real-time style guide! You earned co-editor credit over and over. Thank you.

CONNIE GLASER AND VIRGINIA MEANS – for validating *Climb's* vision and so graciously adding your support to bringing these stories to others. Your help mattered.

MARY LOU HEASTINGS* – for bringing process and passion to the project – you made sure there were no dropped threads! You and the Executive Alliance team were wonderful partners from the beginning. Thank you.

MYRA MCELHANEY* – for compassionately crafting those stories that might not have been told without your help. Thank you.

BEN REED – for perfectly capturing the book's vision. You and the West Reed team created a compelling book design and then went above and beyond by moving the draft from my MacBook to beautiful pages. Thank you.

ANDRÉ SCHNABL* – for providing a decade of enablement, encouragement and enthusiastic sponsorship for all things WIT. You and Grant Thornton, LLP model the way for so many others. Thank you.

HEATHER ROCKER* – for serving as WIT's Executive Director and ensuring both operational excellence and passionate advocacy. WIT's success is due in no small measure to your commitment. Thank you.

WIT BOARD OF DIRECTORS – for inspiring and promoting the creation of *Climb* and for your passionate advocacy for advancing women in Georgia's technology community. Your leadership and wisdom allow other women to soar and young women to dream. Thank you.

WIT, INC. 2010 BOARD OF DIRECTORS:

Helen Berg*
Denise Billups*
Tricia Dempsey*, *Secretary*
Jamie Greene, *Past President*
Brenda Holmes, *Vice President*
Marianne Johnson
Marian Lucia
Cheryl King, *Treasurer*
Jennifer Sobocinski
Terry Trout*
Judi Vitale*, *Chair*

WIT FOUNDATION 2010 BOARD OF DIRECTORS:

Vickie Albee*, *Past President*
Henrietta Barnes*
Helen Berg*, *Chair*
Lisa Clancey
Vicki Hamilton*
Margot King*, *President*
Marian Lucia
Denise Reese*, *Secretary*
Emily Suppe
Jannet Walker Thoms*, *Vice President*
Lori Turbé, *Treasurer*
Judi Vitale*

WIT PAST PRESIDENTS – for almost two decades, the vision of a small group of committed women has sparkled in the Atlanta technology community. You are fearless leaders. You are all 'a piece of work'. Thank you.

1993 Jan Wyche, Buying Time, Inc
1995 Valerie Crelia-Shaw, eLoyalty
1996 Luba Brock*, Technology Law Associates
1997 Betsy Cagle*, LoneStar Collaborations
1998 Shawn Grover*, Brain Works Ventures Inc.
1999 Sonia Lucas*, LucQue Group
2000 Sue Miller*, Sue Miller & Associates
2001 Marci McCarthy*, Lancope
2002 MaryLou Heastings*, Worldspan
2003 Dawn Patrick*, Deloitte
2004 Kasie Scott Palmer*, Computer Associates
2005 Sarah Bajc*, Questcon Technologies
2006 Marsha Calfee*, NetBank
2007 Judi Vitale*, AcuityCFO
2008 Judi Vitale*, AcuityCFO
2009 Jamie Green, Kilpatrick Stockton
2010 Sandy Hofmann*, ATDC

WIT PROGRAM CHAIRS AND VOLUNTEERS – for enthusiastically serving the organization and for sharing your talents to advance women. You are too numerous to list here, but you are invaluable to WIT's success. Thank you.

WIT WOMEN OF THE YEAR IN TECHNOLOGY AWARD RECIPIENTS – for being recognized leaders in business, visionaries of technology and women who make a difference in our communities. Thank you.

2000 Karen Robinson*, Prime Point Media
2001 Joan Herbig*, XcelleNet
2002 Elizabeth "LeeLee" James, Synovus Financial Corp.
2003 Sue Powers*, Worldspan
2004 Mylle Mangum, International Banking Technologies
2005 Pam Pure, McKesson Corporation
Bonnie Herron*, Intelligent Systems Corporation
Elaine Mitchell Norman, United Way of Metro Atlanta
2006 Susan Grant, CNN
Wendy Reed, InfoMentis
Jannet Walker Thoms*, MARTA
2007 Marie Mouchet*, Southern Company
Anna Convery, Nexidia
Terry Trout*, Cbeyond
2008 Marianne Johnson, Equifax, Inc.
Theresa Brunasso*, EMS Technologies
Nadia Butler*, ESi
2009 Amy Brady*, Bank of America
Shannon Johnson*, Points of Light
Linda Greer Braddon, Ph.D., Secure BioMed Evaluations

TO ALL THE CLIMB CONTRIBUTORS – for providing your humble testimonials to achievement and continuous learning as well as your willingness to share incredible personal stories of your journeys to success. You inspire us all.

— SANDRA COFFEY HOFMANN
President, Women in Technology, Inc., Atlanta, Georgia

WIT donates all net revenues from the sale of this book to WIT Foundation for providing the programs at the heart of their mission.

Climb

Hold True to Your Values

by Ginger Ackerman

Vice President of Marketing & Sales
Jigsaw Meeting

GAINESVILLE, GEORGIA

Hold True to Your Values

HAVING GROWN UP AS ONE OF NINE CHILDREN living in rural southern Indiana, you could say I was just a bit naïve about the world. With that many kids plus Mom, Dad and your grandma, living in a two-bedroom house, you quickly learned things like sharing, patience and helping others. But the most significant lesson I learned was that your morals and values are the most important thing to protect and hold true to, if you're going to succeed in life.

As kids we were serious about our games. We played what we got to watch on TV – shows like Hogan's Heroes, Cowboys and Indians, Barnum & Bailey Circus. And we were serious. We dug escape tunnels and hid them from adults. Boy was God looking out for us since we had no cave-ins. We had circus acts that rivaled the real thing. I broke my little brother's arm when we developed our act – I had him stand on a board that jutted over a two-tier barn; I climbed up on the rafters and then jumped on the other end of the board in order to propel him to the rafters where he was supposed to grab on to the rafters for that "ta-da" moment. My part of the act was perfect; his part – not so much as he hit the rafters instead of catching them. And then there was the serious cowboy and Indian games where the Indians, my big brothers, caught you, tied you up, and then roasted you at the stake. Yes. There was real fire on those stakes.

These games normally resulted with no one getting hurt, but once in a while we did. Then it was time to explain to Mom and Dad exactly what happened and who had done what to whom. Now, if you've got a big brother or two, you know how threatening they can be if you tell the truth about what they did. For those of you who don't know, the threat goes like this: "I'll kill you if you tell Mom that I caused this. I'll track you down and wait until you aren't paying attention and then I'll kill you". As an eight year old I didn't want to die so I lied to Mom about what had happened. Of course that lie would only last about two hours until she found out the real truth. And no matter how much I pleaded with her, telling her that I would have told her but my brother threatened to kill me, she didn't really care. I got it with both barrels for lying to her. Lying was never okay.

These lessons set the groundwork for how I conduct my life today. No matter what the consequences, I am true to the truth and hold strong to the values that my parents instilled in me when I was just a child. Holding true has not always been easy. I've been passed up for promotions, have resigned from positions, have experienced the "outcast" syndrome at work and have fought with bosses to do the right thing. Even so, I am true to the truth.

I started out my career working in nonprofit companies in Pittsburgh, PA. There I learned how to run a business on a dime, how to effectively "beg" for money and also how blessed I really am. It was during this time in my life that from a business perspective I got my first real test in values. I was asked to present information that wasn't quite true to the Board of Directors. This information made my boss look good but covered up what was really happening in the organization. The request was made in such a way as to say, present this information or you might not be here tomorrow. When I refused to present it, I was quickly excluded from the Board meeting. The next day, I walked in and gave my notice. I didn't have money, I was going to college at night, and I was fully supporting myself so I was frantic over what was going to happen to me financially. But, I couldn't sacrifice who I was and what I believed in for money. I knew that once I had sacrificed my beliefs for money, then I would always sacrifice my beliefs for money. Thanks Mom and Dad for that lesson.

My next big test came in the form of a male boss who believed you got promoted when you proved yourself through offering more of yourself than doing your job. His secretary made more money than most of the directors of the organization and she was willing to provide certain favors to keep her salary. During a long drive back from a business trip, my boss decided that he wanted to spend more time with me, so he pulled into a motel and asked me "do you want to get the keys or do you want me to". Shocked and shaking, I demanded he get back on the road and get me back to the office. I ran in, collected my things and went home to call a friend. This was the days before cell phones so the agony of not having an immediate support system was unbearable. In tears and frightened, I found myself facing a dilemma: do I continue to work here as though nothing has happened or do I go public with the incident and most likely lose my job? I went public, gave my notice and then met with the secretary. As it turns out, she was a single mom who struggled daily to support her family. She was terrified of losing her job. Fortunately, she kept her job, but he lost his.

I've worked with many good people during my career and have done many fun things, but the best work experience I've ever had was working with an international healthcare company in their genetic disease division. This company's community commitment and corporate morals and values were something that I've never experienced before or since. They actually paid me to spend time with families impacted by genetic diseases and to help them financially. They supported families when there was nowhere else to turn. And this commitment came back to them ten times over. In five years we grew this small division from $52M to $325M in revenue.

There were two most memorable things that happened during my tenure there. The first was fighting for a family who had lost insurance coverage for their ten year-old son. He had reached his lifetime maximum. The cost to treat him was $50,000 per month. I worked directly with our corporate CFO and fought every month for nine months for us to cover the cost of his treatment, pleading and explaining that it's the right thing to do. I promise we will get this money back from the insurance company, I stated, as I continued to fight with the insurance company to extend the lifetime maximum on this child. After eleven months of us paying the costs to treat him, the insurance company finally came through and paid us for every dollar we had spent and then increased the child's lifetime maximum to another $5M.

The second came in a heart-breaking meeting with a family who I was trying to help. The dad had abandoned the mom when he found out his son would never be an athlete. The mom was teaching in a small private school and could no longer afford the insurance to keep her son covered. At dinner one night, I was blessed to spend time with the little boy, who was six at the time. We talked about a lot of different things that evening. He was a "Make a Wish" recipient and was getting his wish for a covered/heated pool put in his back yard so he could have daily physical therapy. Out of the blue he said to me: "Did you know that I'm going to die?" I was taken aback so I responded: Of course, we're all going to die. He replied, "No, I mean I'm going to die soon. I'm okay with it, but I'm really worried about my mom. I don't know what she's going to do without me around. Can you please make sure she'll be okay?" Wow, what do you say to a six year-old little boy who has the courage of a hero? Unfortunately, he died 10 months later but the lesson is with me still.

This company gave so much to so many. My time there allowed me to experience so much of what life is really all about. This company provided a perfect example of how to stick to your values and how you grow as a result. I was incredibly blessed to be a part of it.

This wonderful experience set the stage for the next several years of working in corporate America. I was blessed to become part of several small businesses also living by solid values. I've had the opportunity to give back to others and help guide them as they struggle with challenges and decisions. As a result, the best advice I can give is be true to yourself and your values. What do you see when you look in the mirror each morning? What would your Mom and Dad say about how you conduct your life? Would there be a whipping or a hugging? Would there be tears of joy or tears of humiliation and failure? I can honestly say that I think mine would be proud of who I am. I definitely owe them a great deal for teaching me that very simple lesson – be true to yourself and your values.

GINGER ACKERMAN has over 25 years experience in the healthcare industry. She has worked in both profit and not for profit organizations gaining experience in sales, marketing, business development, administration and operations. Her interactive management style has led sales teams to consistently exceed their sales goals. Her primary focus and sales technique is to ensure quality customer service combined with identifying the customer needs and matching them to specific solutions.

Ginger's experience ranges from small company development through starting her own company and selling it to leading multiple sales and marketing teams for large companies such as Caremark International and NDCHealth.

JIGSAW MEETING is an online training and education delivery platform that works with online learning curriculums and learning management systems. JSM is the bridge between asynchronous education and live interaction between student and instructor. We help education expand beyond physical and geographic boundaries.

Only Rarely is Anything as Important as it First Seems

by Victoria A. Albee

President
Allset Consulting LLC

LAWRENCEVILLE, GEORGIA

Only Rarely is Anything as Important as it First Seems

WITH THE INVITATION TO PARTICIPATE in this book, came the suggestion that I might "write a letter to the next generation" to reflect upon leadership lessons and life changing experiences. So, with that charge, I write:

Dear Aspiring Leader,

If you aspire to be a leader in technology or in any field, my advice is written around four main areas – all of which rest on the fact that only rarely is anything as important as it first seems. We tend to live our lives attuned to the latest clatter (i.e. continuous rattling sound as of hard objects falling or striking each other) regarding what is important to our career, to our earning potential and to our leadership opportunities. I will leave those items to the experts, but invite you to consider my experience-based suggestions below (not backed by any stats or PowerPoint® [1] or blogs or committees of any kind.)

1. *Try to make good use of your choices regarding your education, even if you made those choices for the wrong reasons. (Remember, only rarely is anything as important as it first seems.)* I say this because I arrived at undergraduate school with no clue of my future major. (You're surprised, I know.) On registration day, I visited the business department. As it was lunchtime, they were all attending power lunches, paving their way for future leadership opportunities. So, I made my way to the math-science department, discovering they were all still in-house because "math people" don't go to lunch. It was settled. Based on the fact that they were there while others were not, I became a math person – good for my weight, if

1 PowerPoint® is a registered trademark of Microsoft Corporation

not my career. I probably should have walked a little further, to the English building, because my career has been made in writing. The math and science served well in training me for logical and technical things – but no one has ever walked up and asked me to derive the quadratic equation, while they have asked me to write concise representations of their plans and desires for their company. So, with that in mind, make the most of your choices. Don't spend too much time worrying about what you didn't major in – knowing that most majors will train a good mind to think critically, be creative, and take a disciplined approach to problem solving.

2. *If you don't know how to follow, you won't know how to lead.* I keep waiting to see a book by this title, but so far no luck ... everybody wants to lead; few want to follow. We tend to actively train our aspiring leaders to always jockey toward "leading." "Leading" is the mark of success, so get out of the gate quickly, we say. But, remember, only rarely is anything as important as it first seems. In fact, I have found that leaders who have never taken time to be attentive followers make very poor leaders. There is something about the perspective and emotions that go with following either a good or a poor leader that teaches the aspiring leader a great deal about leading. As a follower of a poor leader, we learn how it feels to receive indecisive, unclear, ever changing instructions and directives. We learn how it feels to be asked to accomplish something without the resources to do it. And, sadly, we often learn how it feels to be unappreciated or even maligned – all the fruits of poor leadership. With the privilege of following a good leader, we gain perspective on how to lead and how to treat our leaders well. If we learn those lessons, from the follower's unique perspective, we can only be better leaders when leading becomes our responsibility

3. *Learn to communicate and PowerPoint may not be the best way.* I am not picking on PowerPoint as a software program. It definitely has some great uses. Rather, I am pointing toward the "PowerPoint" mentality – which says that everything in life and business can be explained in a sans serif font, in six bullets, with an

appropriate color scheme. In fact, few things are explained well in our "hurry hurry", "summarize" perspective of communication. At one time, we used email; now we have even figured out a way to shorten that into a text message or a twitter. Even the word "twitter" should give us cause for pause, as in our zeal to "save time and summarize," we have very often sliced out that very piece of data or insight that could give a more experienced eye an almost revelatory perspective of our particular situation. Remember, only rarely is anything as important as it first seems, and saving time by summarizing, graphing, coloring and "powerpointing", as I like to call it – those things are not nearly as important as forming a basis of trust for good old fashioned conversation. Communication starts with relationship and trust; don't forget.

4. *The "net-work" may not be all it's cracked up to be.* I am leery of the word "network" for a number of reasons; two reasons mainly – the word "net" and the word "work." If we are not careful (i.e., have not heeded the advice of items 2 and 3 above), to "network" begins to mean, "working" the room to put all of the attendees' collective contact information into a net. The net is then used to serve different purposes … we work it, when it serves our purpose. Electronic gadgets help us in this work. We can put all of the contact information in our computer or cell phone, slice it, dice it and get so "personalized" that we can easily send birthday greetings to that gal we met once three years ago at that 8:00 AM meeting at the downtown Marriot. If we keep the greetings going, we can then "work" the net at an appropriate time, to maybe get an interview or maybe even a prized job, with great earnings and leadership potential. Those who are the best at this game have hundreds and even thousands of contacts in the net that they work. But remember, only rarely is anything as important as it first seems. And while networking as I have described is not very important at all, people are very important. They make life and work enjoyable and worth doing. So, while building your life and having your career, be sure that your network includes a core of people that are not

just in your net, but in your heart – whose birthdays you remember not just because it beeped on your FaceBook or iPhone® 2, but because they are in your heart. Then you will have made a life and not just a career, because only rarely is anything as important as it first seems.

Sincerely,
Victoria A. Albee

VICTORIA A. ALBEE is the president and principal consultant for Allset Consulting. Albee also serves as an adjunct professor at the Shorter College School of Business. She has worked in the executive office of the Georgia Technology Authority, where she was a member of the team that developed statewide strategies and policies and managed engagements related to the implementation of the State of Georgia's enterprise portal project.

Previously, Albee served the University System of Georgia for nearly ten years. Her career began as a mathematics faculty member. She also worked in various administrative positions, which had strong technology components, culminating in her appointment as director of business and educational services at Georgia Perimeter College, the third largest institution in the system. In this role, she established a technology focus in continuing education, including the online course program and highly successful technology-based marketing strategies.

Albee holds a Bachelor of Science, magna cum laude, with a dual major in biochemistry and mathematics from Mercer University. She is also a graduate of Georgia Tech, with a Masters of Science in Engineering Science and Mechanics, and served two years at Emory University as a Clare Booth Luce fellow in mathematics.

ALLSET CONSULTING LLC is a technology and business consult-

---

2 iPhone® is a registered trademark of Apple Computer, Inc.

ing company delivering expertise in technical and communication strategies for governance and integration of large, multi-tiered enterprise systems. Specific services include aligning projects, programs, and organizational structures with business goals; designing and implementing technology strategies to assist in moving the organization toward a unified approach to technology, and consulting on business development strategies which include technology assimilation issues. Main practice areas are: individual executive presentations, government, college & university systems, small business, and nonprofits.

The Year that Changed My Life

by Mary Carol Alexander

Regional Vice President
salesforce.com – HQ San Francisco, California

ATLANTA, GEORGIA

The Year that Changed My Life

As I look back on my career, probably the year that made the most impact on my life and career was 2001. There were a lot of things I learned about myself that year, and hopefully I can share some of my experiences to help other young women who are starting a career.

I had been working for a large technology company since 1997, and in 2001 I was given the opportunity to "shadow" an executive for a year. The job was created as a development opportunity to learn the business from the head of a very large global sales organization, while being mentored by one of the geniuses in the industry. This was a coveted position, but it meant a move to California, and I was living with my family in Atlanta. It was one of those plum assignments you can't pass up, but with three children, the youngest being in kindergarten, and a husband who had an equally demanding job, I felt I couldn't relocate my family for my own gain. I worried about the move to a new school and the impact on my oldest daughter, who was in middle school, and on my son, who was in fourth grade. My youngest child would have to leave her beloved nanny who she had known for five years. They would all have to move to a new part of the country for the year, and I wasn't sure how this would impact them. My husband would have to commute each week to make this work, and we were not sure if he would need to relocate with his job or find a new one. There were huge implications to this decision.

To say I struggled with this decision is an understatement. This was a stepping-stone to an executive position with the company, and a lot of people inside the company wanted me to go for it. But my family comes first in my life and I hesitated. However, my husband convinced me that this was a once in a lifetime opportunity and I should take it, with his full support. I remember thinking at the time how glad I was to have married someone who could make such an unselfish decision for us. Times like these magnify the kind of person you should spend your life with. So for any young woman considering life with a partner, here is lesson #1: Choose a life partner who really views you as an equal partner, and would sacrifice for you, as you would for them. This is probably the most important lesson I can teach you.

So, with a decision reached, I headed out West to start the new job on September 10, 2001 in California, leaving my family back in Atlanta. My family would come out as soon as we were able to find a home there, and they'd spend the year with me in Menlo Park. Then everything changed.

On September 11, my husband was scheduled to fly out to do some house hunting for us, and his flight was cancelled when the tragic events of September 11 began to unfold. I got up in the morning and at 6:00 AM, some of my East coast friends started emailing me to turn on the TV. I did and the feeling that I had was fear and helplessness. I really just wanted to be with my children. We really didn't know if the country was being terrorized, if there would be more attacks, and where was safe. I was about 1500 miles away from my family and without them I watched the tragedies unfold. In the midst of that horror, I knew I had to go on and find the strength to start a brand new job.

The world changed forever, and I found myself in California without my family, starting a new job in a new place, worried about not only my family, but also the many families who were in New York. The tragedy was personal since the company had an office with 400 employees in the World Trade Center. Fortunately, all of our employees got out of the building successfully, but the raw emotion during this time was pretty awful.

In my new role, my boss put me in charge of some of the logistics for helping our customers work through some of their business issues relative to the disaster. I had no idea how to get some of requests fulfilled in this new position, since I was new to corporate headquarters, didn't know anyone, nor how to get anything done. I also knew a lot of the New York office employees, and it was overwhelming hearing the emotion from them in the first few days following the disaster.

So as I look back on all of the chaos in my job in those first few days, I impart lesson #2: Trust your instincts when you are overwhelmed by the events around you. You will be surprised by how much you can accomplish if you just stay calm and try to focus on the task at hand.

In my new role, I was to travel globally with my new boss, but initially I was afraid to fly given the uncertainty of new terrorist attacks on airplanes. Fortunately, I learned that the man I worked for was not only brilliant, but also very compassionate. He too had a family, and while I spent four weeks without my family in California, not knowing when they would be able to be with me, he understood. He did not make me travel until I was mentally ready. He also allowed me enough personal time to go out and find a place for us to live and schools for my kids to attend. Lesson #3: If you are really honest and open with your manager about your personal needs, they will generally respond favorably. We are all human beings with issues in our lives that need to be addressed and you have to develop an open relationship.

Gradually things settled down, my family moved out with me, and the year of development began. Professionally, I learned about our business, attended CEO level meetings with customers, spent sessions with my boss after meetings to talk about what I learned. I didn't just shadow him or just observe. We discussed strategy, I handled his communications, and I learned about "brand". He taught me that each of us has a personal brand in business. Lesson #4: The ways we communicate reflects on our "personal brand", so you should be aware that everything you do or say reflects on you and on your organization. In other words, it matters how you act, what you say, and how you present yourself. This brand could be applied to not only your business life but also your personal life.

I travelled globally in my new position, learned about business in different cultures, and I had the good fortune to learn from someone whom I had the utmost respect for.

It was a yearlong struggle for my husband who had to commute to be with his family. He left every Sunday night for his bi-coastal commute. Fortunately, my kids flourished in their new schools. They still regard the experience as one of their fondest childhood memories, and it gave them the opportunity to see a different part of the country.

I look back on that year as the year of growth for me, personally and professionally. I had to learn a new job in a very trying situation, while working through my family issues. There were many times in the first month I didn't think I was going to get through it, especially alone, without my family. There were many days I wanted to get in my car and drive back to Atlanta and give up the new job. Frankly, I spent a lot of time by myself in church where I reflected on what was going on in the country and praying for the families who had experienced much greater tragedy.

Through this experience I learned that I can survive a very tough situation, and while it's hard, I can rise above it. I hope that I can pass this insight on to my children, because I know life will have its many challenges for them.

For all new women in business, the lesson I can impart is that you have to go for it. You have to understand that the decisions you make will not be easy, and there will be some consequences to those around you that you have to consider. Weigh carefully the impact of your decisions, and the affect it will have on your life and the lives of those around you. Take the time to list out the negatives and positives in any big decision. Consult with the people you trust the most in your life, as I did. Lesson #5: You can do anything if you put your mind to it, and give it your all. When tested, you will be amazed how you can rise to the occasion.

MARY CAROL ALEXANDER joined salesforce.com in January 2005. She has led the Mid Atlantic, Southeast, and Southwest regions during her career at salesforce.com. Her current team covers large enterprise accounts throughout the Southeast region.

Mary Carol has over twenty years of experience in sales and sales management at global Fortune 500 companies. Prior to joining salesforce.com, Mary Carol worked for Sun Microsystems for seven years, where she held several sales leadership positions in the Southeast, as well as California. She worked in an Executive Assistant role under the EVP of Sales for Sun Microsystems from 2001–2002. Before her tenure at Sun Microsystems, she worked for AT&T and Eastman Kodak, as well as several small start-ups.

She graduated Magna Cum Laude from Bradley University in Peoria, Illinois, and has had the opportunity to work in six different cities throughout the US and in various sales positions.

She currently lives in Alpharetta, Georgia, with her husband, Ken and their three children, Lauren, Ryan, and Lindsey. Lauren and Ryan attend the University of Alabama and Lindsey attends Alpharetta High School.

SALESFORCE.COM is a leading provider of enterprise cloud computing applications. We provide a comprehensive customer and collaboration relationship management, or CRM, service to businesses of all sizes and industries worldwide, and we provide a technology platform for customers and developers to build and run business applications.

Ignore the Glass Ceiling; Build Your Own House

by Evelyn A. Ashley

Managing Partner
Trusted Counsel (Ashley) LLC

ATLANTA, GEORGIA

Ignore the Glass Ceiling; Build Your Own House

I HAVE A FRIEND WHO SAYS, after 15 years of business ownership, he is "unemployable". What he means is that he will never again be able to be someone's employee. He says I have that "problem" too. We laugh about it regularly. He is absolutely correct. I'm not even sure I could "play nice" with a co-owner anymore. I like operating my business by my own rules of the road – it's my way or the highway. But then – it can be that way – it is my business. I only have a glass ceiling if I choose to put it there – and you know, I'd rather everyone see the sky, sun, the stars and moon without all that glare!

I've known since high school that I would be a business lawyer. I also knew that having a law degree would allow me, assuming I used it to my best advantage, to have independence and flexibility – both personally and financially. I soaked up knowledge from everyone and anyone who decided I was worth their effort (and, thankfully, there were many!). I've worked to keep my "learning curve" a vertical straight line throughout my career. Environment was (and is) critical to my personal success; the traditional model of law firms did not (and does not) fit with my personal philosophies (nor did the idea of making other people rich from my work, beliefs and innovation). Even given that knowledge, I did not know until 10 days before resigning from Morris, Manning & Martin that I would ever be a business owner.

I did know I would do everything in my power, while maintaining my passion for law, business and ethics, to make my business and myself successful. I also had an all-encompassing, passionate belief that technology companies and their founders needed great counsel and representation at predictable and consistent rates. I also understood that being a woman in technology law, with great business expertise, who could hold her own intellectually and substantively with the best technical and business minds, had great opportunity to make a mark. And so, I did.

In February 1998 we formed Red Hot Law Group as the result of the breakup of my predecessor corporate technology law practice. When I told the four lawyers who came with me that our name would be "Red Hot Law," they immediately drove me into a conversation about slowly introducing that name; they were terrified of its impact and what people would think. They tried to bring me to that safe place with them: Let's start with "The Ashley Law Firm" (or some other mundane, boring lawyer-like name!). Eventually, I took control and told them to believe. We didn't have 100 years to develop a law firm brand that people recognized. Technology companies would understand a marketing name and be immediately drawn to us – and that was what mattered, not what other lawyers or people not in technology would think.

Even given that drive, no one (certainly not me) predicted that we could garner the national and international attention to our name, our philosophy and our law practice – just on a sexy, cool name tied with the delivery of substantive, practical representation. But we did – without ever having an actual marketing budget! At Red Hot, we did a lot right and some things wrong – but we learned from everything that happened there. At Trusted Counsel, we still do this. It's less splashy, with only private referrals as our marketing. It's still all about substantive, consistent and practical service and practice. It works well.

Here is some of my learning from the journey:

1. *Be a "piece of work."* I am forthright and opinionated about what I require for my people and myself and how my law practices will be operated. Always have been; expect I always will be. Most of the time (I think, anyway), I'm diplomatic, but it's true – I'm direct – and relaxed about being that way. This often makes people who are less confident in themselves, nervous and/or uncomfort-

able. After we sold Red Hot, one of the lead partners at the Firm commented to one of my Red Hot partners "She is a piece of work, isn't she?!" (Ah, the "man to man" thing!). He, of course, was being derogatory. When this got relayed back to me, it hurt at first. But after thinking about it, I realized had the upper hand with him. His comment told me that my negotiations and requirements in the sale of the firm had really shaken him up. And in reality, time revealed that he had no ability to deliver half of the items he contracted with me – but he just didn't know how to deal honestly and openly. He knew if he admitted that to me; he would have no deal. To this day, I actively work to be a "piece of work" for my clients and my people. Calmly, unemotionally, but passionately, advocate for your beliefs, what you can and cannot live with – and execute on them. Hold people to their commitments. If they don't deliver, you will know what is right for you. To me, working in an untrustworthy environment is degrading – I won't give others the opportunity to bring me to their level. And never second-guess your beliefs because someone is a detractor. Know yourself better than anyone else in the room.

2. *Take 100% responsibility for yourself.* Never assume you will be rewarded for great work. If you work in someone else's system, you *must* work it to your own career advantage. Negotiate and *ask*. Women assume they will be treated fairly and rewarded greatly for great work. Wrong – if you don't ask, you will likely never "get". Remember that. Business is not your custodian. Trust no one to "take care of you." Ask for what you want: know your "deal breaker" requirements; what would be "good to have"; and what would be gravy. Then, negotiate logically, systematically and strategically and then get it in writing. *And please*, get professional assistance if you cannot do this for yourself (this is not a failing, in fact, no one likes to negotiate for themselves!).

3. *Invest in yourself.* From what I have seen and experienced, women do not believe that investing dollars and time into their knowledge base and growth is their best investment! Why?! I un-

derstand family obligations, budgeting and limits. However, most of us get our financial strength, retirement and independence from our careers; it is our greatest investment. So, why doesn't that translate into, a dollar wisely invested in "me" is probably worth thousands on the other side??! Do *not* expect this is your employer's responsibility and expense. I can say that I invest my "education dollars" wisely – I have focused on expanding my business knowledge (through Vistage and reading), my legal knowledge through national conferences (various events), my personal journey/spiritualism through coaching, friends around the world, seminars and workshops, and my expertise through additional legal licenses (New York and I'm considering others). I pay others lawyers to help me in my business and personal life. Life is learning; investment in you is the best investment you can make.

4. *Learn from your teachers and push beyond them.* I have been fortunate to have a mentor, guide, journeyman, coach and teacher at every stage of my career (and life). You have them, too – you just might not be conscious of them. All of those people saw something in me that inspired them to work closely with me – and I'm eternally thankful for the wealth of knowledge, experiences and learning they have given me. I have always worked diligently to take the gifts they bestow on me and extend them beyond their teachings – whether that is through mentorship of others or just taking their learning and spinning it into something "more" – and I hope I always will. Know who your teachers are and learn from them. Do them proud by extending that knowledge and power to others. No one has time to learn everything from the beginning!

5. *Listen to your "gut".* Red Hot was a gut instinct outcome and it was right that I pushed forward with those instincts. The same for Trusted Counsel – it has delivered me great challenge, success and independence. Listen to your heart and your soul and follow it. Do not allow others to diminish or make you other than who you are. Leave them if they try.

6. *Fly.* The first time you jump from the cliff is the hardest.

The more you do it, the more instinctual it becomes. Empower yourself. Know yourself. Be proud of yourself. Be fearless. Trust yourself. Praise your successes and learn from your failures. Set goals and the path to their execution and then act. Go around obstacles. Be honest. Be fair. Carry no baggage. Take your journey on the high road and let no one pull you down, regardless of how hard they try. Most of all, *enjoy* and appreciate the journey – it is where all the learning is!

EVELYN ASHLEY has been a member of the Atlanta Technology Community since 1990, when she became the Chief Legal Officer at Computations USA, the US subsidiary of an Australian employee benefits software company. Since then, she has practiced in large, medium and boutique legal practices, finding that the latter gives her the most professional and personal satisfaction and flexibility. After practicing with Morris, Manning & Martin and Balboni, Ashley & Schoenberg, Evelyn founded and grew Red Hot Law Group, which quickly became a nationally noted technology boutique law firm focused on start-ups and private companies. She was co-founder of Red Hot Venture Consulting, a strategic consulting firm and incubator for technology start-ups. McKenna Long & Aldridge acquired Red Hot Law in 2001 and Evelyn served as a Partner heading the Firm's technology practice. She left McKenna Long & Aldridge at the end of 2003 to form Trusted Counsel.

Evelyn advises private company clients on matters such as mergers and acquisitions, financing and investments, intellectual property protection, licensing, manufacturing, distribution, entity structure and related issues, corporate spinouts and international transactions. She has wide ranging experience and brings results focused, pragmatic business approach to the practice of law. She is licensed to practice law in Georgia and New York.

She was a founding Board member of TechBridge (which was "incubated" at Red Hot Venture Consulting) and is a founding Board member of Who Ha Da-Da, Inc. a Georgia non-profit working to create a "community" that supports "outsider" folk artists in the Southeast through assistance in applying for research grants, participation in art shows and similar events, as well as group health and dental benefits (www.whohadada.org). Evelyn loves and collects art, choosing on the basis of what she likes, not what everyone says is art,

Since 2003, Evelyn has been an active member of Vistage (formerly, The Executive Committee) where she participates in a monthly CEO roundtable with 16 other CEO's and business owners. She is regular speaker on business legal issues and leadership. Evelyn and her husband, Alan McKeon (www.alexanderbabbage.com) are avid travelers to both exotic and "usual suspect" locales.

Trusted Counsel is a high touch, boutique corporate and technology law firm and certified woman-owned business. We typically work for highly demanding, highly selective companies and individuals. Many of our clients have worked with us for many years (including predecessor law firms) and through multiple companies; they are our best references and referral sources.

My Mother, My Mentor, My Legacy

by Marva R. Bailer

Business Unit Executive
Industry Software Solutions Communications Sector
IBM Software Group – Armonk, New York

ATLANTA, GEORGIA

My Mother, My Mentor, My Legacy

My mother died at the young age of 61 from pancreatic cancer. At her funeral hundreds of women twenty-five to seventy, came up to me and shared story upon story of how my mother was a mentor to them. They gave examples like how my mother helped them pass college, establish their own practice, get into another role, and find a new love. They said how positive and encouraging she was and how the network of people she knew, including men, helped them immensely.

She entered a career path where women needed to stand out. She was the Chairwoman of the Dental Hygiene school at a major university. She was the first woman on the American College of Dental Board. She established relationships with women and men through her intelligence and grace. She elevated herself and those around her to higher positions and equal pay. How fortunate was I to have a mother who grew up in the 1950s, went to college, was valedictorian of her class and had a strong career in mind.

When my parents divorced she stood on her own and worked to elevate herself from a practicing hygienist to a professor at an esteemed university. Though her network she was invited to speak at major conferences. Later in her career, she worked for a large pharmaceutical company where she was paid expenses plus $1500 per hour to speak – which was a week's salary for a hygienist! As a teen and in my early college years, I attended many conferences with her and had the opportunity to interact with her colleagues and students. They had high praises for her work and always made mention of how she had personally helped them either directly or indirectly.

When I started my career, I had many mentors. My first job was managing a chain of women's health clubs. My mentor was one of the owners who took me under her wing when I was 17. I was promoted over people twice my age. I started as an aerobic instructor and six months later I was managing 200 employees and $6 million in sales. I was still in high school! It was my job to do all of the hiring and firing – which included many single moms who worked there. My mentor challenged me on finance, sales, and getting the job done.

My next mentor was also a woman. I sold typewriter and word processing maintenance. This was a high tech job at the time and all of the technicians and all of management were men. She gave me advice on human resources related situations. This was my first professional job and being young and naïve, I needed a strong mentor. Sadly, she too left this earth too early; she had a heart attack in a hotel room on a business trip.

When your role models leave this earth, you need to seek others to fill the role. I started attending women's affinity groups in DC when got my first vice-president promotion. I thought it would be a great experience to meet other women. I can say I met a few women, but I was more focused on meeting people to get business done. That meant I was focused on meeting people in federal businesses and they were all men! I recall that at the time, there was only one female CIO.

I was busy with my small children and frankly, I considered the time spent with women spare time I did not have. When I came to Georgia, I still focused on getting the deal done but I reached for experiences that I was missing. I wanted those things that my mentors of the past had given me: support, encouragement, cheerleading, constructive feedback, goal setting and setting realistic expectations. I began taking an active role in the meetings and really got to know and then respect the amazing women I met. Mentoring is a key value of the leadership competencies at IBM and I was encouraged to seek out a formal mentor for myself and become a formal mentor to others.

I believe that my mentoring is an important legacy for my daughter. Over the last two years I have made a commitment to mentoring, to encouraging women, and to networking with both women and men to advance their careers. I mentor two students, one in college and one fresh out of college. I learn just as much from them as they learn from me. In this connected world with boundaries of age and gender being broken down, it is important to stay fresh and understand what our newest generation of workers thinks and how they respond.

Instead of golf events, I take my female customers to women's conferences, decorator show homes, high tea at the Four Seasons, and art exhibits. I introduce my commercial customers to executive women in the nonprofit community. I make a point to ask how I can help. I have found that these different venues provide a fun atmosphere to break the ice and to talk about things we have in common. Women normally find it easy to share information about their families, shopping, hobbies, etc; I try to have the balance of personal and how we can help each other in business.

I truly believe leadership is not given but earned. Serving as a mentor is a way for each of us to set an example for others. Being recognized as a mentor is an affirmation of our success, our uniqueness, and our leadership. It is how I work to create a better world for both men and women.

MARVA BAILER has worked in technology for over 25 years and is known as a leader and team builder and for achieving bottom line results. Her current role with IBM is as Business Unit Executive for Industry Solutions for Communications Sector, NA. Her past roles include software manager for Integrated and Invest accounts for Georgia serving Delta, Travelport, Coke, THD, Macy's, CNN Turner, Norfolk Southern and Cox and serving as Business Unit Executive for Tivoli's Netcool Channel Programs. Ms. Bailer joined IBM as a result of IBM's acquisition of Micromuse, Inc in 2006.

At Micromuse Ms. Bailer held several key management roles including Vice President of Channels and Vice President of US Federal Sales. In the Federal Sales role, Bailer oversaw and managed sales growth from $1M annualized sales to $20M in a two-year period. She was part of the management team for the Micromuse acquisition of Quallaby, a performance management company, and Guardednet, a Security company.

Marva has served as a featured speaker on many trade group and publication panels and forums including several *Washington Technology Magazine* panels. She has also been a featured presenter and host for IBM Tivoli/Micromuse customer and partner conferences and events; and was nominated for Women in Technology's 2003 *Women of the Year in Technology*. She was appointed to the Techbridge Board of Directors July 2009. She participated in the 10th anniversary production of Techbridge's CIO Digital Ball. She is co-chair of the Digital Ball for 2011.

She actively supports Atlanta Telecom Professionals Association, Possible Women International Foundation and Women in Technology, Inc. She is a mentor for the Georgia State Robinson College of Business, as well as internal in IBM. She is passionate about networking, and is the sales leader for the Atlanta Executive Women's network events. She has also served as a facilitator for the New Taking the Stage Program.

FOR NEARLY A CENTURY, IBM has created and applied technology to make the world work better. Today, more than 400,000 IBM employees around the world invent and integrate hardware, software and services to enable forward-thinking enterprises, institutions and people everywhere to succeed. In the process, IBM is helping to make our planet not just smaller and "flatter," but smarter.

Let Fate Lead – It's a Surprisingly Good Dancer

by Sarah Bajc

Senior Vice President
hiSoft Technology International Limited

BEIJING, CHINA

Let Fate Lead – It's a Surprisingly Good Dancer

MINGLE BUSINESS AND PERSONAL INTERESTS: I graduated from the University of Michigan Honors College with a degree in Chinese Language and International Business. That was in 1988. There were only two others out of a graduating class of almost 8,000 who also chose Chinese, and neither of them was studying business. Most of my friends thought I was weird. Nevertheless, the seed of my relationship with China, the most powerful emerging market in the world, was planted. In the spring of 2007, I moved my whole family to China to help Microsoft develop their domestic partner program. Now my three children speak Mandarin and my two Atlanta cats have two Beijing dog sisters, and there are no plans on leaving the Middle Kingdom any time soon. You never know what life will look like when those seeds you planted years ago are exposed to a suitable environment.

The path I took is not traditional. After college, I worked for a famous management consulting firm. Then I decided to become an entrepreneur. Actually, I started four different companies. The first one was the Southeast franchise for a corporate research company. It was small, but when my partners bought me out, I used the money and the experience to start my own employment process consulting firm. Innovative Search worked with multinational corporations, improving the way they handled the recruitment and retention of people. With 30 full time recruiters and consultants, we become one of the largest recruitments firms in Atlanta in just five years.

My passion for new challenges never stopped, though, so when the opportunity arose, I sold that business to an investor and used the capital to build a SaaS company that deployed software over the internet together with a services component for human capital recruitment, development and retention. It was during that time that

I first became involved with WIT, which soon became an important resource for building contacts and confidence. Unfortunately, ThinkWorks closed after three years when the market crashed in 2001 and a huge portion of my "dotcom" clients went out of business at the same time that enterprise customers cut back on contracts. Not to be deterred, I started my fourth company, which is a manufacturing and wholesale distribution firm of specialty products for the sports industry and for children. We manufactured offshore in China, which was my first time re-connecting to China since college. After several years, I realized that manufacturing moved far too slowly to keep my interest, so my long time employee, turned partner, took over the business and I returned to the technology industry. Be sure to visit www.kideapolis.com if you want a Cuddle Cape, Sleep Silkie or Team Wrap!

I then joined an Israeli software quality company to take over their North American operations. That company was seeking to expand its international operations but was weighed down by its US subsidiary. They needed someone to help them either close or fix the business. In less than a year from my starting, the company was running smoothly and we had a successful public listing on the London AIM exchange. As part of my role, I visited China to assess vendors to outsource software testing and test automation. I was totally fascinated by the growth that I saw here, and returned home from that first trip to tell my family: "Let's move to China. I studied it all those years ago, but the time wasn't right. Now it is!" My family responded to this "crazy" decision by saying: "OK! You find a job there and we will go." A chance meeting with an executive from Microsoft sealed that deal.

I have since left Microsoft to join hiSoft, a China based information technology outsourcing company, as part of the senior leadership team to drive their global business expansion and bring the company public on the NASDAQ global exchange, which is another very entrepreneurial role.

Focus on the things you love most

Part of the reason why I moved to China is because I love to travel. As a child, my family didn't have enough money to send four kids to college, much less to travel, but I always yearned to see other places and achieve a better life. So, when I was in high school, I earned a scholarship to study in Sweden for a year. After that experience, I decided I really liked experiencing other cultures. I knew that if I wanted to go to college, I would have to pay my own way, so throughout high school, I was always in the top of my class and I went to the University of Michigan on a full scholarship. I did still find a way to see the world, in a very low cost way. By working over the summers I was able to take a semester off in my junior year to backpack in Europe by myself. I slept on trains and in youth hostels, and toured almost every country in Western Europe.

I have always had the opportunity to travel in my work, though sometimes it was more than I wanted once I started to have children. When the kids were a little older, however, we began to travel more as a family. I believe that having interesting experiences is a very important thing. So my family tends to visit new places instead of buying new things. When you look back in your life, you don't remember how it felt to wear a new sweater, or what each new car was like to drive, but you do remember the trips you took and the friends you had over for dinner! My family now has the best of both worlds in China, as our daily life and my quest for new experiences happen at the same time! With Beijing as a base, we have traveled to over a dozen cities in China, mostly by train, as well as to Vietnam, Indonesia, Malaysia, Thailand, Japan and the Philippines.

When confidence is more important than competence

I met my first culture shock when I arrived in Beijing to manage an all-Chinese team. I quickly learned that it was a mistake to expect people to be comfortable with the "be accountable for your own decisions" policy I had always used in the US. I found that Chinese were so concerned with making a mistake that it was sometimes hard to get them to come to me with opinions or decisions on their own, even though they were completely qualified to do so. In true entrepreneurial spirit, I have always followed the model that I would rather make 10 decisions in a day and have an even split of bad, neutral and excellent, than to end the day with just a few neutral decisions. There may be fewer bad decisions made, but there are also fewer excellent ones, and less gets done. I believe even bad decisions can be an opportunity to improve overall progress. You can only know what a mistake looks like, how to fix it, and how not to make it again once you have already made it once. But this mentality is totally foreign to the average Chinese, so it takes a *lot* of confidence building with people to get them to be fully effective.

In addition to the difference in decision-making styles, the Chinese management style is quite different from that of the U.S. The traditional approach is a mixture of telling people what to do and then yelling at them if it is not done. One of the unique aspects of working with hundreds of volunteers in WIT over many years was the opportunity to hone my leadership skills. Volunteers cannot just be told what to do. They need leadership that coaches how to do things, builds consensus around decisions and deliverables, and then holds people accountable. Although this approach is novel in China, it does work very well once people get used to it. Interestingly enough, women are adapting to it easier than men. It took a little while in the beginning for them to feel comfortable, but now they are thriving. Most people now feel secure to say "You know what, I do not agree with you on that." Or, "I've made a mistake and I need your help with it." There has been a dramatic improvement in performance, and it was all about improving confidence.

A window that is stuck open

Although the original plan was to return to the US after a few years, the experience of living overseas has so utterly changed my outlook on life that it is unlikely I will repatriate for many more years. Beijing has proven to be an excellent place to raise teenagers; it is safe, inexpensive, interesting and the academic environment is outstanding. The new plan is to stay through my youngest child's graduation from high school in 2014, and then to try something new. The Latin culture has always interested me as well, and no question Spanish will be easier to learn than Chinese, so perhaps a tour in South America will be next.

It is hard to guess what fate will allow next, but I will be sure to follow. I do love to dance!

SARAH BAJC – For over 20 years, I have been driving revenue generation and operational excellence in the professional services and technology industries. As Senior Vice President of Marketing and Alliances for hiSoft Technology International, I focus on significantly accelerating growth through marketing, sales process and alliances.

Before joining hiSoft, I was the Business Director for the Strategic Partnership Group of Microsoft in Beijing. There I worked with emerging and high growth Chinese companies towards the development of a robust technology ecosystem in China across software development outsourcing, hardware and device manufacturing, digital entertainment systems, independent software developers, and the venture capital community.

Prior to that, I ran the North American operations of Tescom, an Israeli software quality firm, where I helped to take the firm public on the AIM exchange in London, and drove the evaluation of outsourcing options in China. Before that, I founded four companies: a manufacturer of specialty textiles; a venture capital backed enterprise software company; an employment process consultancy;

and a corporate research firm. I began my career in management consulting with Deloitte & Touche and Cap Gemini.

I serve as an Advisor to the Board of Directors of Women in Leadership, the leading executive women's business organization in China, and am on the Advisory Board of Future Generations, a globally applauded Chinese NGO dedicated to environmental protection. I hold a seat on the Global EXEC Women Executive Team, and was the founding council member in China. I was selected to chair the *Global EXEC Women Magazine* "International Women of Influence Awards™" held in Beijing. I also served 2006 to 2007 as Vice Chair for Strategic Branding for the Zhongguancun Software Association.

Prior to moving to Beijing, I was an active participant in the US philanthropic sector. I was an Executive Delegate on the American Electronics Association trade mission to China in 2006, and was a Founding Ambassador for the Georgia China Alliance. I began my tenure on the Board of Directors for Women in Technology in 2000, and then served in 2004 as Vice President and in 2005 as President for WIT, as well as in 2006 as President for the WIT Foundation. I also served on the Board of Directors for the Technology Association of Georgia and on the Advisory Board for the US Government Technology Council.

I graduated from the University of Michigan with a degree in Chinese Language and International Business. I enjoy deep sea diving, yoga, salsa dancing, downhill skiing, hiking, cooking, music and spending time with my three children, two dogs and two cats.

SINCE 1996, HISOFT has delivered world-class information technology, research and development, and business process outsourcing services to customers globally, with particular focus on Fortune 500 firms. Our 16 offices in the US, Japan, Singapore, and China allow the perfect balance of high-touch and low-cost through flexible on-premise and off-shore options. (NASDAQ: HSFT)

Dream, Believe and Never, Never Quit: No Matter What!

by Henrietta Barnes

Chief Financial Officer
Qcept Technologies Inc.

ATLANTA, GEORGIA

Dream, Believe and Never, Never Quit: No Matter What!

DREAM & BELIEVE: As the third child in a family of seven children, I was always in search of something. I just wasn't sure what that "something" really was or how to go and get it. I spent countless hours dreaming and living in my imaginary world while sitting alone in the forest behind our NC home or just hanging out in the attic.

When I played with my two sisters, one of my favorite games to play was called "Business" which was a game I had created. We each would pretend to be married with children and our own business. We would then present our products to each other, talking for hours about our business, the type of car we drove, our spouse and the home we lived in. I always ended up with more "play money" than my sisters and I could describe my dream home in detail.

When we stopped playing games and became teenagers, I never stopped dreaming about the imaginary life that I had created for myself. In my imaginary world, money was never an issue. The roof didn't leak, the bills were always paid on time and the lack of money was never the reason you couldn't be a girl scout or take piano lessons.

Growing up in a family where the lack of money was the reason given for most of the limitations put on my life, I promised myself that one day I would be financially independent. I wanted to live my imaginary life so I needed to figure out how to earn some money … lots of money!

I started working my first public job at the age of 15, purchased my first car at the age of 16, and then began searching for a career that would make me financially independent. The realities of growing up in a small rural town in the mid '70s gave me more challenges than I ever could imagine, so I learned to use the rejections and non-support from friends and family as fuel to build my determination to make my dreams a reality. I stopped sharing my dreams with my family and treated all the "no's" I heard as an opportunity to prove to them just how strong and independent I really could be.

The lesson: It doesn't cost anything to dream or to believe in yourself, and if you really want to turn your dream into reality, then you must make a commitment to yourself. Though encouragement from others is a motivation, don't be afraid to motivate yourself. Write down your goals with estimated target dates. Then measure your accomplishments on a regular basis. Be your own cheerleader.

Never, never quit: As a child, I was always asked by some adult, "What do you want to be when you grow up?" I would say, I want to be financially independent. I didn't know how I was going to achieve this status; I just knew I wanted to control my own destiny. There are those who know at an early age what career path they plan to take. Then there are those like me who don't have any idea what they want to do with their life. This just means that you need to search a little more and a little deeper.

No one on my mother's side of the family had ever received a college degree. Only one family member on my father's side had successfully completed a four-year degree, but they weren't working in their field of study. As a result, there was no one in my immediate family or community that could provide me with any guidance when it came to going to college. But that's just part of the journey.

During my senior year, our high school sponsored a one-day visit to North Carolina State University in Raleigh. I was full of excitement as I toured the campus and I imagined living in the dorms and being a college student. I always knew that I would have to seek financial assistance to pay for my college, so you can imagine my excitement after speaking with the admissions department and learning of all the financial aid that was available. I could hardly wait to get back and let my parents know that I had selected a school and found a way to pay for it myself.

After my parents heard my wonderful news, they refused to sign the necessary papers because Raleigh was six-hours away for our home and in their opinion, too far away. They recommended that I attend the local community college and get a two-year degree. Given that I was seventeen when I graduated from high school, I reluctantly decided to attend the local college, work part-time and live at home so I could save my money.

During my early college years, I would seek out those friends who were home for college break to learn from them firsthand how college life really was. One evening, I ran into a friend who was considered to be a gifted and talented student. He informed me that he had just quit college because the classes were too hard. When I learned that his major was in accounting, I told him I had thought about taking some accounting classes at the local college. He laughed, and said "you'll never be able to get a degree in accounting. If it's too hard for me, you know it's too hard for you." His comment was all I needed to hear to motivate me to seek an accounting degree.

After achieving my three associated degrees and landing my first accounting position, I began working at a small private investment firm. I performed all of the accounting functions for two private corporations, a partnership, an s-corporation and a non-profit organization. All of these entities were part of the private firm. One day my boss identified me as a bookkeeper instead of an accountant because I only had a two-year degree. He went on to tell me that even though I was doing the job of an accountant, I needed a four-year degree to get the status of an accountant. My boss had his CPA license and I asked him what it would take for me to achieve the title of a CPA. He stated, " Well you're a very sharp person, but you don't have what it takes to become a CPA.

Years later, after completing a B.S. in Accounting, a B.A. in Interior Design, obtaining a NC Real Estate Broker's License, and passing the CPA Exam, I called my old boss to let him know of my accomplishments.

The lesson: Turning your dream into reality is a process and the process has many steps. Don't allow delays, the lack of funds, lack of support from others, or your heritage keep you from believing in who you are and what you can accomplish. Let the negative comments from outsiders be your stepping stone to your dream. Commit to achieving your goals honestly without cheating, stealing or pretending to be something that you're not.

No matter what it looks like: My career path was never clear. The path seemed to unfold only as a result of another choice that I had to make. No matter what type of job I held, I worked to be the best and give more than what was expected. Whether it was helping my mother clean houses, or working as a cashier, a waitress or bank teller, I worked to give my very best.

After having my own accounting business for five years, I decided it was time to try my hand at being a member of an executive team. I was accustomed to having to prove myself, so I decided to seek a position as controller at BETA Systems and begin my journey toward becoming part of the executive team within the organization. It only took ten days before I was promoted to CFO of the USA division. This approach has been successful in my career at ServiceCentral and my current position with Qcept Technologies. No matter what my title says, I perform my duties with integrity and take pride in my work.

If you find your career path taking you in another direction or it appears that your path has been halted due to an event or situation that's out of your control, just re-connect with your goal and be willing to take steps into the unknown. Push through the fear of failing or the disappointment of delays and keep believing.

The lesson: If you find that you're exhausted and you've fallen face down, find enough energy to roll over and look up. Lay there for a while. Give yourself a minute to review your options. You can lay there and give up or you can give yourself permission to have a 5-minute pity party and then re-work your plan. Take a breath and get up. Dust yourself off, but leave a little dust so you will remember where you've come from. If you aren't ready to take the next step, then just stand still; stand on your belief in yourself. Sooner or later you will regain your strength to take one more step. But no matter what it looks like … never, never quit!

Be assured that one or two or even more things will happen when you take that next step … trust that you have built a solid foundation to stand on and you will be taught how to fly.

HENRIETTA (HENRI) BARNES has over fifteen years experience in diverse financial operations and management of high technology companies. Henri embraces the challenges of implementing appropriate financial polices, accounting practices and creating relationships with lending institutions and the financial community for early stage companies. She plays a major role in the private funding transactions. In her present position, she serves as Chief Financial Officer of Qcept Technologies Inc., a semi-conductor services business. She has worked with Qcept since 2004, where she has led the company through multiple rounds of equity investments.

Prior to joining Qcept, Henri served as Vice President of Finance and CFO of ServiceCentral Technologies for five years and CFO for the US subsidiary of BETA Systems Software, AG for four years. At BETA Systems, Henri comprehensively managed the financial growth and profitability of a foreign-owned, rapidly emerging international software development and marketing company that specialized in the production and distribution of IBM mainframe software throughout North America and Mexico. She reported directly to the Board of Directors in Berlin, Germany and served as an officer of the US subsidiary.

For five years, prior to joining the high tech industry, Henri was owner of a financial consulting business where she secured a broad base of clients ranging from real estate construction to international distribution. Her experience includes the performance of financial and managerial accounting, participation in acquisitions and IPOs and implementation of accounting software systems and internal controls. She has a strong hands-on background in start-up companies on a fast pace of emerging growth.

Henri serves on the Board of Directors for Women In Technology and was a 2009 Woman of the Year Finalist for Small Businesses.

Henri earned a B. S. in Accounting and Business Administration from High Point University in High Point, NC and a B.A. from the American Intercontinental University in Atlanta, GA. She also earned three A.A.S. degrees from Wilkes Community College in Wilkesboro, NC. In addition, she maintains a current license as a Certified Public Accountant.

QCEPT TECHNOLOGIES is the world leader in the Non-Visual Defect (NVD) inspection category for surface chemical defects delivering a new inspection capability with its patented ChemetriQ® inspection technology.

Find the Opportunity

by Pam Beckerman

Vice President Human Resources
Metro Atlanta Chamber

ATLANTA, GEORGIA

Find the Opportunity

In the course of our careers, there are ups and downs and unexpected turns. There are great bosses and lousy bosses. There are plum assignments and thankless tasks. There are offers we wanted desperately for ourselves, but they went to someone else. There are promotions, which materialized when we least expected them and opportunities we never knew about. We have headily lived through growth cycles where we raced to hire new talent. And we have slogged through recessionary troughs where, with heavy hearts, we furloughed valued colleagues.

All these situations ultimately bring opportunities: to learn about our capabilities, to make or support a friend, or to explore new dimensions of ourselves. When we are done wringing our hands, wiping our eyes, or basking in a moment's glory, our next step should be to ask ourselves to find the opportunity.

Early in my career, I read, *Composing a Life* by Mary Catherine Bateson. In the book, she talks about how our diverse experiences weave the rich tapestry of our lives. Using this metaphor, an unexpected thread, like a job loss or caring for a sick parent, may yield a new learning that adds a new thread of bright yellow and brightens the tapestry of our life. So staying vigilant to the opportunities or threads to enrich our unfolding tapestry may be heartening and give new meaning to unfolding events and overall life experience.

Last summer I encountered my own new thread when I was unceremoniously fired from a position that had formed a large portion of my identity. The position had provided job satisfaction and a sense of community for over a decade. Ouch. I was embarrassed, scared, and disoriented. After mourning for a few days, I knew my financial demands required that I find employment pronto. I threw myself at finding the next opportunity. I invested in building the network I had neglected while heads down at my job. I befriended people on LinkedIn, had coffee with new acquaintances, and lunch with potential job leads.

Unexpectedly, I found tremendous satisfaction in my new regimen. What I anticipated being a chore turned out to be rewarding. I met bright, interesting comrades who offered rich observations, ideas, and empathy. I learned about how generous, talented, and committed the business community of Atlanta really is. I widened my circle, my understanding of my city and its needs, and my sense of what is possible.

True to the adage of when a door closes, a window opens; I found a refreshing breeze coming through my window. Through a colleague and within six weeks, I found a job that is intellectually stimulating, emotionally satisfying, and paid within my ballpark. Within months of starting my new job, I was markedly happier and felt more appreciated than during the last two years of the job I was so hesitant to leave.

When I counsel job seekers and those seeking their next career move, I confidently recommend they find the opportunity, as it often comes unexpectedly.

PAM BECKERMAN is a seasoned Human Resources executive who partners with business leaders to advance strategic objectives by unleashing the talent and potential of employee communities. She has worked in the banking, education, and consulting industries. Currently the Vice President, HR, for the Metro Atlanta Chamber, Pam has led programs encompassing the complete employee life cycle. She has designed and implemented hiring, performance management, rewards, retention, leadership development, employee reduction, and organizational development programs in the consulting, banking and education industries.

Pam holds a B.S. in Industrial and Labor Relations from Cornell University and a Master's in Organizational Communication from the University of California at Santa Barbara. A member of SHRM, she lives in Marietta and enjoys volunteering, hiking by the Chattahoochee River with her family, and reading.

THE METRO ATLANTA CHAMBER mobilizes and connects the business community to drive economic development and public policies that promote sustainable growth. The board draws from Atlanta's top business leaders and serves 4,000 member companies who employ one million workers.

Are You Leading the Life You Want to Live?

by Helen Berg

Vice President
Hitachi Consulting Corporation

DALLAS, TEXAS

Are You Leading the Life You Want to Live?

I HAVE A CONFESSION TO MAKE – there have been times that I've encountered what seemed to be insurmountable problems at work and I've felt really beaten down and have wanted to just walk away from it all.

Some of those situations that come to mind are: a) people who would look you straight in the eye and tell a flat-out, damaging lie; b) business meetings where women were referred to as 'dogs', presumably as a form of humor; c) unwanted romantic advances by subordinates; d) coworkers who publicly attacked your personal integrity because they didn't agree with your decision; e) high-ranked corporate officers who committed egregious unethical behavior. I'm telling you these things because I want you to be aware that life in Corporate America has its ups and downs, its wonderful days and awful days, its joys and its sorrows. Your ability to deal with difficult situations, to remain calm in the storm, to think clearly when all around seems chaotic – will be important as you progress through your career. Most importantly, through both the calm and the storms, is to be committed to following the path that brings you happiness and fulfillment.

Something to think about – you're likely to spend roughly the first fifth of your life in school, and the remaining 70%–80% working. Are you doing what you truly love? Are you able to integrate all the dimensions of your life – career, family, community, spiritual, personal, etc. – into a cohesive whole? Are you *proactive* about working toward your happiness? I believe one of the worst mistakes we can make is to expect others to define and balance our lives.

A few years back I got a call early the morning from a program manager who was leading a very large-scale systems integration project as part of the merger of two large corporations. The project had been going on for about nine months, and nearing implementation of the first major milestone. The lead solution architect on the project was a very bright man who had been identified as high potential for senior leadership within the new corporation. The call was to inform me that this solution architect had abruptly resigned with a short note, which was left with his badge on his desk. The note only said, "I want my life back."

After a moment of anger and then panic, I realized that person had found a deep source within himself of courage and truthfulness that precipitated his resignation. He had reached a breaking point, having waited too long to negotiate a different solution, perhaps feeling it wasn't 'manly' to say publicly that the whole life of integrated family, community, spiritual, career was more important to him than just career. Society can put all kinds of expectations on us if we allow it.

My mother knew from the time she was a little girl that she wanted to be a nurse. She maintained that vision throughout her adolescence and went on to graduate from nursing school. In 2011 she turns 80 years old and is still doing volunteer nursing through various programs at the church to which she belongs. Yet, most of us do not have the good fortune of having that clarity of vision. Instead we wander aimlessly hoping that the right combination of events, words, or just serendipity will steer us in the right direction. Then we wonder why we are not fulfilled in our lives. We do not take the time to figure out what 'centers' us, how we define ourselves, and what principles we are not willing to negotiate. We don't reaffirm that we are leading the life we want to live.

I have a dear friend who recently turned 42 and has decided that she wants to have a baby. I've known her since she was in her early twenties and never before have she and her husband spoken of a baby. I'm not exactly sure what precipitated this change of heart, but I am feverishly hoping for a successful pregnancy, delivery, and healthy child. We are all up against time and mortality, and some decisions cannot be postponed indefinitely.

I had a boss once who told me that every Friday afternoon he moved his weekend clothes to the front of his closet and his work clothes to the back so he wouldn't have to see his work clothes over the weekend. On Monday he reversed it. He needed total separation between his work self and his weekend self in order to manage the stress. I think leaving the day's work issues on the front doorstep before coming into the house is a good idea. However, when we resort to having a 'self 1' and a 'self 2', it may be time to think about changes.

Another time a senior level employee with whom I had worked for almost a decade suddenly began coming in late, taking excessively long lunches, and leaving early. After a little time had passed we sat down and discussed the situation – trouble at home … or was it dissatisfaction at work? The company we worked for had recently been acquired by a much larger one and our jobs were extremely stressful and our future careers uncertain. By talking through the situation we were able to see quite clearly how the work situation was affecting his family life and vice versa – they were actually so intertwined that it was hard to see exactly what instigated the crisis.

As much as we'd like to believe it, we do not consist of dual or split personalities – you bring yourself to work each day. I believe the ones who are most successful at self-fulfillment are those who embrace the meaning of the word 'vocation', derived from the Latin verb vocare, meaning 'to call'. They treat their occupations as their callings.

I began this article by talking about situations that challenge our journey – situations that make us question whom we are and where we are going. We all have different circumstances to deal with, but it's what we do with our circumstances that define us. Do quietly accept our fate? Do we challenge head-on and fight? Do we "stand up and be counted"? Paul of Tarsus wrote a good deal of the Christian New Testament while in prison. FDR was president while fighting debilitating paralysis. George W. Carver went from a slave to an accomplished scientist, botanist, educator, and inventor.

To wholeheartedly follow your passion may well take everything you have to give. But, then again, isn't it worth it?

General Norman Schwarzkopf is reported to have said, "Self-fulfillment is the most important thing of all. Being happy with what you do, feeling good about what you're doing is probably the great secret to life."

Are you resolute in leading the life you want to live?

HELEN BERG has a proven track record of transforming IT to help companies achieve increased growth and profitability. She has more than ten years experience in executive leadership and IT strategy development. Her background spans several verticals, including the entrepreneurial and innovative IBM Internet Security Systems, global hospitality market leader InterContinental Hotels Group, and technology powerhouse Lockheed Martin, where she worked on the F-22 Next Generation Fighter and numerous other large-scale technology integration initiatives. She has a deep background in systems engineering, system architecture and design, data communications, software development and integration, and information life-cycle management.

Helen earned an M.B.A. degree from The Citadel and a B.S. from the University of South Carolina. She has also completed advanced leadership development programs at Carnegie Mellon University and the Georgia Institute of Technology.

Helen is active in the Atlanta technology community, serving on the board of several non-profits and providing leadership mentoring to young professionals. She is heavily involved in encouraging young girls and women to pursue careers in science and technology.

AS HITACHI, LTD.'S (NYSE: HIT) global consulting company, with operations in the United States, Europe and Asia, Hitachi Consulting is a recognized leader in delivering proven business and IT strategies and solutions to Global 2000 companies across many industries. From business strategy development through application deployment, Hitachi Consulting is committed to helping clients quickly realize measurable business value and achieve sustainable ROI.

Lessons Learned from the School of Hard Knocks

by Denise L. Billups

SVP, Business Development/Executive Coach
C Robinson Associates, Inc.

ATLANTA, GEORGIA

Lessons Learned from the School of Hard Knocks

As I contemplated what personal leadership lessons I would want to share with the next generation of leaders, the reflection took me back to all of the things I didn't like hearing from my mother.

As I was growing up there were many things my mother use to say that drove me crazy and I swore I would never say to my children, "Don't ask me why, just do it because I said so."; "Your friends don't live at 6016 Menlo Avenue so I don't care what their parents let them do!"; "It's not how a person looks, but how they act that really matters"; "When you have a house of your own you can do anything you want to do, but as long as you live under my roof you'll do it my way."; and "You need to use some elbow grease to get the job done right." And then there were a major line of comments all around the same theme: "The best lessons are from the school of hard knocks, lessons you learn won't all be fun, it's not important that you get knocked down it's important that you get back up."

I can still remember the way some of those statements rubbed me the wrong way in my youth when I didn't want to hear them, but I also came to understand and truly value (as she told me I would), the many lessons my mother was determined to teach me. It's truly amazing how smart she became the older I got and the more of life I experienced. That younger (know-it-all) Denise would never have believed how many times that, as a parent and as an executive leader of people at IBM for 30 years, I would open my mouth to hear my mother's words being spoken.

I'm happy to state that I finally listened and my mother's very basic teachings, along with other things I learned along the way (many from the school of hard knocks) formed the very strong foundation for the way I live my life today, how I approached my career at IBM, and now my career as an executive coach. In sharing the following lessons learned I hope I will help others as they move through their careers and their lives.

Know and stay true to yourself

If I had to choose just one piece of advice to give the next generation it would be this one. Truly knowing yourself is a critical requirement. Who are you? What are your values? What are your priorities? What drives and motivates you? What are you willing to give and what are you willing to give up for your career? As you grow in your life and your career you will have to make decisions that will have significant impact on your direction and your future. Decisions become much easier to make when you are very clear on what is important to you, what you want to accomplish, where you are willing to compromise and where you must stand firm. It is also much easier to accept the consequences, sometimes negative, of your decisions when you know that those decisions are best for you and they are grounded in how you want to live your life.

A successful career takes management

It is important to know that a successful career doesn't happen by accident – it must be actively managed. Even doing a great job does not guarantee a successful career. The following items are just some of the basic, but vital requirements: Build strong relationships at all levels; constant and effective communication is critical; make sure you bloom where you're planted before you start looking to be promoted (perform well in your current job – apply that "elbow grease" to set yourself apart); demonstrate leadership outside of your day-to-day job; don't let your fears limit you – take risks, be willing to take a non-traditional (and sometimes unwanted) path; be willing to learn from anyone (any age, race, gender, position or education level); create a plan for your personal and professional development; focus on continuous learning and building of relevant skills; take on difficult tasks; know and be able to articulate your value to your team/department/company; don't confuse a high quantity of work with high quality work; understand your manager's view of your performance, not just your own (perception is reality); realize that career advancement is not just a promotion up, but can also be lateral; and lastly, maintain a positive attitude.

It's how you respond to setbacks that makes the difference

No matter how well you plan for and manage your career, failures or setbacks can and will occur. It's how you respond to those setbacks that will show what you are made of. It is important to be resilient. You can recover and continue to move forward. At one point in my career as an executive at IBM I took on a very challenging sales role. I was confident that I had the right leadership skills, knowledge and experience to drive the organization's immediate success. Was I ever wrong! I was not able to drive the results that were expected and I ended up being replaced. While this wasn't my only professional setback, it was definitely one of the most painful and humiliating experiences of my career. I was determined to keep my head up, stay positive and honestly acknowledge the fact that I had not performed as expected and I had learned some valuable lessons. I also freely shared my experiences with others to help them avoid some of the mistakes I made. The value of that lesson to me and to others was that no matter who you are, you can have failures and setbacks, but you can recover. The key is that you get up, brush yourself off and get back in the game. As my mother said, it's not the getting knocked down that's important, it's important to get back up. It's easy to be a positive leader when things are going well, but the true measure of a leader is how they respond when things don't go well. Others will watch how you respond to adversity to understand and assess your resilience.

Focus on your values

Stand up for what you believe is right – lead and live with honesty, integrity and ethics. This is very simple for me. I was raised with some very basic beliefs grounded in my religious and what might be considered to be "old fashioned" upbringing. I was taught from an early age to know right from wrong, to abide by the Golden Rule – "Do unto others as you would have them do unto you" and that living my life with honesty and integrity was a requirement, not a choice. These foundational beliefs served me well in my life and as I led teams and influenced others. But even with this strong foundation I must admit as a young and ambitious manager there were times when I didn't stand up for what I believed or I let others' views override my own. I soon realized there will be times in your career when it will seem much easier to go along with what everyone else is doing, to take a short cut, or to simply be quiet and look the other way, but staying grounded in your values and doing what's right will make your choices very easy.

Whatever you call it … work/life balance or integration or harmony, it's important

There continues to be a lot of focus on the importance of work/life balance and how to achieve it. All work and no play can lead to burnout and poor health. And while I know it is important that you find work/life harmony in order to be the best you that you can be, I don't have any rocket science answers to share on how to make it happen. What I do know is that there is no one right answer. The answer is personal and depends on each person's situation. Creating your own sense of work/life harmony requires that you give some intentional thought to understanding yourself and your priorities, your definition of happiness, the needs of your family and any other things that will influence the quality of your life. Working 80 hours a week may be fine for some people because they love what they do and they don't have other obligations, but that balance might not work for others. Whatever it is you want to do – have more time to exercise, spend time with family and friends, work in your child's school or volunteer in your community – you simply have to create a plan and take action ... just do it!

Give back and share your gifts

One of the enduring lessons I learned from my mother which was then reinforced through my work at IBM is that I am my brother's and my sister's keeper. Even though we were poor when I was growing up, my mother taught my sister and me that there was always something we could do to help others at our church and in our neighborhood.

And just as we were helping others, there were agencies that were helping our family when my mother was ill for an extended period of time. As I grew older I realized the deep satisfaction that I got from helping others and I continued to volunteer. I also included my children in many of my volunteer activities. When I moved with IBM to Atlanta in 1986, I was proud of our company's obvious focus on giving back to the community. Not only is volunteering for non-profit or education organizations a "good" thing to do but it is also a good way for businesses to build strong relationships and to develop leadership and other industry skills. There are many ways to give back. You can be a mentor. You can volunteer in your community to help one person or hundreds of people. Giving back is an imperative.

I have lived, and continue to live, a wonderfully fulfilled and truly blessed life. While I have achieved more in my life and career than I ever knew would be possible for me, my road to career and life success has not always been an easy journey. There have been times of great achievement, opportunity, happiness and both forward and upward movement. I have also faced times of insecurity, disappointment (in myself and in others), unfairness, hardship, failure and sadness along the way. But through it all, what I have found is that is has been both the ups and the downs (those hard knocks) that have woven the rich tapestry that is my life.

DENISE BILLUPS is the SVP, Business Development and an Executive Coach with C Robinson Associates, Inc. In her current role Ms. Billups has the privilege of being able to focus on her passion for partnering with individuals and organizations to deliver business consulting and professional development services and coaching to drive optimal performance. Prior to joining C Robinson Associates in 2009, Ms. Billups built a 30-year career with the IBM Corporation, advancing through Customer Service, Business Operations and Sales executive leadership roles where she led teams of 300 to 900 employees, to her final role with IBM as Director, Sales Learning, Americas and Worldwide ibm.com. In her Sales Learning role Ms. Billups was responsible for enabling the success of over 4000 field and teleweb sellers, sales teams and sales leaders through the deployment of effective learning and training initiatives.

Ms. Billups serves on the boards of Women in Technology, The Civic League of Metropolitan Atlanta and Possible Woman Foundation International (Scholarship Committee Co-Chair), She, Cool Girls, Inc. (past Board Chair and current Strategic Planning Committee Chair) and the Atlanta Women's Alliance (past President). She serves as an advisory board member for Cool Girls, Inc., the Atlanta chapter of Women in Technology International and was a 2003 graduate of Leadership Atlanta. Ms. Billups is also proud to serve as a mentor for high-performing professional women through Pathbuilders, Inc. and the Manheim External Mentoring Program where she has volunteered for over eleven years and two years respectively.

For her personal and professional leadership and her many contributions to the community Ms. Billups was recognized with an Inspiria Award from Pathbuilders, Inc. in 2009, a United Way of

Dekalb County Legacy Award in 2008 and a Turknett Leadership Character award in 2007. In 2005 she was spotlighted by *Atlanta Woman Magazine* as one of the 25 Power Women to Watch and is on Women Looking Ahead's 100 List of Georgia's Most Powerful and Influential Women. Ms. Billups was also chosen as the finalist in the Enterprise Business category for the 2005 Woman of the Year in Technology award.

C ROBINSON ASSOCIATES, INC. is a leadership development and performance improvement consulting firm. We deliver coaching, leadership/professional development, customized consulting and workshops to a wide range of clients: Small and mid-sized businesses, Corporations, Non-profits, Educational institutions and Individuals at all levels: Executives, Managers, Non-Managers and Students. We work with clients to set the stage for growth, leveraging key leadership principles that empower individuals and teams to meet today's demands and to prepare for tomorrow's challenges to deliver leadership strategies for the 21st century.

Fail, Forward, Faster!

by Virginia A. Bradley

Founder, CEO, and Publisher
Global EXEC Women, LLC

ATLANTA, GEORGIA

Fail, Forward, Faster!

After hanging up the telephone, I felt that cool feeling that comes over you when the color disappears from your face, your jaw is hanging open, and the deep breath that you have taken is followed by an audible sigh. *Did that really just happen?*

Let me rewind the scene for you. I had created the first *Global EXEC Women* International Women of Influence Awards™, originally held in Atlanta. Now it was time to go abroad. Only a few months ago, I was elated. After a lengthy search, I found an overseas partner, and this partnership would allow the Asian organization to enjoy increased revenue, attendance at their conference, and global visibility via *Global EXEC Women* print and online magazine. The magazine could then focus on the selection and presentation of its awards. Both the partnership organization and the magazine could leverage each other's strengths and showcase the importance of diversity and *inclusion.*

Then I received *that* telephone call where I was informed that the partner organization was going to present its own awards, different from ours. They did not want to do both. I was disappointed. This would have been great for both of us. Had I not made things clear? Did the partnering organization not want global visibility? Project Status: Failed.

Though this was not the outcome that the team at *Global EXEC Women* had planned, we would move on.

I went to the four sponsors that I had secured to support our awards, explained the situation, and informed them that I would return their funds. While three of the sponsors were ecstatic to find that someone was actually willing to refund their money, the fourth sponsor informed me that the funds had already been committed to help provide visibility for the businesswomen in China and that I needed to host the awards as planned. Project Status: Forward.

LESSON I:
When money has been authorized for a specific purpose, it is up to you to deliver, no matter what the obstacles.

Having just published *Global EXEC Women* magazine and distributed it at the Asian women's conference, how in the world was I going to host my own awards on another continent, in a month, after Thanksgiving and before Christmas?

The questions started coming: Is our database strong enough to fill an overseas conference ballroom with attendees? How can we concentrate on the awards process if we have to focus on so many other areas? How will we produce another magazine in such a short period of time?

LESSON 2:
If you want to have a better life, ask yourself a better question.

Rather than asking questions that give you negative answers, ask, "If I *had* to, *how* would I…?" The marketplace is global; Christmas and Thanksgiving are not. Tap into your global in-country contacts and remember, some people who claim to have international experience may not. One way to obtain a quick insight is to ask them how many overseas air miles they have logged in the past few years and for what purpose. In most countries, especially developing ones like Brazil, Russia, India and China (BRIC Countries) face-to-face contact, matters.

If you can't, then you must was a lesson I learned very early in my career as a heart and kidney transplant nurse at Emory University Hospital. Solving problems is what nurses did. Creating excuses was loser talk. So, back to my mantra: *How things get done is none of my business. Why we do them is everything.* Project Status: Faster!

One month later, after buckling down, I was amazed to have 28 qualified female nominees (five from the USA), whose titles were director level and above, who agreed to attend the China awards event. The awards would be held as planned, and I would publish another issue of the online and print magazine. Filling the hotel conference center? Well, one crisis at a time!

LESSON 3:
Sam Williams, President, Metro Atlanta Chamber of Commerce, a panelist at one of our recent Global EXEC Women organization's educational forums, stated, "Eat the elephant, one bite at a time."

The next challenge we faced was when several of the Asian women, who had agreed to be featured in the newly created edition of the magazine, pulled out. They said that they were not worthy of being in a global publication. Believe me, they were significantly worthy! However, Asian women have a history of not promoting themselves for thousands of years and now the time was drawing near, they started to postpone the interviews and explain their difficult feelings. No matter how much I reassured them, several of them felt too humble to be highlighted in a global magazine.

Disappointed, I reviewed my options. I could make the magazine smaller, though it would not be the same as what I sold to advertisers. I could find other women to feature yet, finding the same caliber of Asian women would not be easy. I could use filler articles and disregard the quality of the magazine. Or I could try to get more advertisers overnight. But that was difficult and would take time.

"Ask a better question." I told myself aloud. "I have to make it bigger. How? There is always a way." Rather than making the magazine less than the original vision had been, I asked myself what I had learned in healthcare. There is a way. What is it? If I can't, then I must. It was then that I came up with the idea of translating the *entire* publication into Chinese and making it bilingual.

LESSON 4:
Your skills are transferable, and there is always a way if you are committed.

Delta Air Lines was so impressed with the magazine that they wanted to distribute the publication to their internal women's group, which of course, I agreed to! I also had convinced the first U.S. female Consul General of China to be featured in our cover story. She had previously been reluctant due to her cultural heritage, yet after a few conversations with others, and myself, she took the lead and established the foundation for other Asian women to feel more comfortable with visibility in the media. Using the *there is always a way* approach, I asked the male Japanese Consul General to write an article for the previous issue of the magazine, which is also quite rare in the Asian culture, and he agreed.

LESSON 5:
When one way fails, create a contrasting situation. In this case, I selected someone else who did feel comfortable with the request.

With the female Consul General of China on the cover, I asked the Delta representative if the magazine could be placed in the airplane on the inaugural flight to China. Delta politely said no, they, like most other airlines, do not put external publications on their flights.

LESSON 6:
The past does not equal the future. Not knowing all of the rules may be an advantage.

Well, okay. I then asked, "What if I secure the Consul General to take the Inaugural flight to China, then can we have the magazine on the flight?"

" … Maybe." The Delta representative said. "Doubtful, but maybe."

The Consul General agreed to take the flight, and then Delta consented to put *Global EXEC Women's* bilingual magazine on the flight and in every single seat pocket. At our request, Delta also flew Lani Wong, President of the National Association of Chinese Americans, to Beijing where she was to be honored as the first *Global EXEC Women* Luminary Recipient. She was recognized for 30 years of promoting bilateral US-China relationships, most of which were built at a time when few people were interested.

As I headed to China, I asked my Delta contact, "If you had one request for me, what it would be?"

"Find an Asian based executive with at least 15 years of airline experience, who speaks fluent and understandable English and completely understands the global market as well as details of the American airline industry and who is willing to relocate to Atlanta."

Got it. I'll just whip out my magic wand on that one! However, I did take her request seriously and found an Asian female airline executive who could order off the menu at Fat Matt's Rib Shack. And yes, Delta hired her.

LESSON 7:
Always ask your customers how you may serve them. Allow them to tell you what they really want. The more specific the request, the better it is. When asking for flights, or other perks, remember your objective. In this case it was to make the recipient feel honored, not get something free for myself.

Former WIT Women of the Year in Technology finalist, Joan Lyman, Partner at LMG, Corp., and Co-founder of SecureWorks, provided our International Women of Influence and Luminary Awards™ keynote address, and Jacqui Chew, President of iFusion Marketing and past chair of the WIT Women of the Year in

Technology, joined the other China-based panelists to kick-off our Asian awards event.

LESSON 8:
Reach out to women and give them unique opportunities for visibility. Look for new and experienced talent. Avoid those who don't share the spotlight.

In thinking about how to make our magazine more valuable, I decided to add some well-known, impressive talent by including great leaders like Stephen S. Roach, former Chief Economist and subsequent Chairman of Morgan Stanley Asia, as well as Professor at Yale University's School of Management and the Jackson Institute for Global Affairs as well as Randi Menkin, Global Director of Workforce Diversity and Sustainability at UPS. The magazine was honored with an award from the Magazine Association of the Southeast (MAGS) for Best Service Journalism.

LESSON 9:
If you don't ask, you don't get. Go for top talent and let unbiased third-party experts evaluate your results.

I was motivated as well by the support of many women, including Rebecca "Becky" Blalock, Chief Information Officer at Southern Company and Karen Robinson Cope, Managing Partner of Atlanta Technology Advisors, both of whom were recognized as WIT Women of the Year in Technology. Karen also supports Opportunity International, an organization that provides microfinance loans to women in Africa. It has been my pleasure to donate ongoing ad space in our magazine to Opportunity International, CARE and the Hispanic ad version for "Go for Red."

LESSON 10:
Corporate responsibility and cause marketing are everyone's responsibility, not just the responsibility of large companies.

Rather than say that you *can't afford to*, think that you *can't afford not to*. Some days, this strategy will give you a sense of contribution. On other days, it may motivate you to keep going, knowing, as in the Opportunity International case, that you are helping one more woman in Africa acquire a $60 investment and start her own business. Be the hand-up and the hand-off to another opportunity!

Had I listened to myself initially, listing all of the reasons why the original plan should have worked and not quickly accepting the fact that it had failed, I would have been delayed in moving forward. Focusing on the matter at hand allowed us to highlight the women's successes via the awards and magazine and give them the global visibility that they deserved.

My skills in healthcare and hospice have transferred to business and technology. I know that ... life is exciting and short. Time is not a renewable resource and it waits for no one. Do all you can, with all you've got. *When in doubt, fail, forward, faster!*

VIRGINIA A. BRADLEY is the founder, CEO and publisher of *Global EXEC Women*, LLC – a media company that produces the only award-winning, globally distributed multi-lingual, print and online magazine for female entrepreneurs, corporate executives and women business owners who conduct international business.

In addition, she oversees the membership-based organization that connects female business leaders with other women of influence for peer-to-peer education, training via live and web-based forums.

It also provides best business practices with a focus on process and solutions for generating innovation, revenue, and sustainability as well as business introductions. These executive leaders exercise billions of dollars of purchasing power. To unite forward thinking global minds, Ms. Bradley created the International Council, which is comprised of female Consuls General, trade commissioners, and country representatives. Each year this council recognizes outstanding women executives with worldwide interests via its *Global EXEC Women* International Women of Influence and Luminary Awards™. These awards have been presented in: Atlanta, Beijing, Cairo, Istanbul, San Francisco, and Toronto.

She partners with other business organizations who want to honor women from their host country as well as other countries, who are committed inclusion and giving their constituents global visibility. These organizations believe that awards should be decided upon by a visible, independent panel of judges and that monetary exchanges do not influence the selection of the recipients of the awards. Supporters and sponsors of these diverse initiatives include Accenture, Alcatel-Lucent, AT&T, CA Technologies, The Coca-Cola Company, Delta Air Lines, Heidelberg, IBM, ING, InterContinental Hotels Group, KPMG, UPS, and Walmart.

Previously, Ms. Bradley was a marketing executive for a start-up, venture-backed global business-to-business technology company that automated commodity trading. She spent 15 years as an executive in the healthcare industry in both entrepreneurial and corporate environments, and she co-founded six professional organizations. During that time, she won many awards and served on several ethics committees. She was an initial employee of a pioneering healthcare company that was later acquired by a Fortune 500 company. There she served as a district sales manager responsible for five subsidiaries, and was ranked the number one sales person in the USA.

She was recognized by the U.S. Department of Commerce for creating an international multi-day training and mentor exchange program. Recently, she was selected to be on the advisory board for the 2010 Governor's International Awards Recipient – Center for International Business Education and Research (CIBER) Program in the J. Mack Robinson College of Business of Georgia State

University. This initiative was created by the U.S. Congress, and is one of only 34 in the country created to improve competitiveness and provide services that assist businesses in the United States succeed in global markets. With twelve locations internationally, Ms. Bradley was chosen to participate on the founding United Nations Institute for Training and Research (UNITAR) CIFAL gender equality task force. She was on the founding board of the National Latina Business Women – Atlanta Chapter, and holds a seat on the Global Business Committee of the Women Business Enterprise National Council (WBENC).

Originally from the United Kingdom, Ms. Bradley is a frequent speaker at national and international conferences. Her range of presentations include keynote speaker for Microsoft in Shanghai, panelist for the MIT Entrepreneurial Forum in the USA, as well as small group presentations in cities such as Tbilisi, Republic of Georgia. In 2009 and again in 2010, she presented at a global conference in Cairo, Egypt that partnered with eight other alliances and included executive representatives from more than 30 countries.

GLOBAL EXEC WOMEN magazine is the only award-winning globally distributed, multi-lingual, online and print publication that features women who conduct international business. *Global EXEC Women* presents the International Women of Influence and Luminary Awards™ in partnership with other organizations who want to showcase their commitment to inclusion. *Global EXEC Women* is also an organization that connects female business executives for interactive forums and a perspective for regional, national, and international business. These executive leaders exercise billion of dollars of purchasing power. They also provide best business practices, with a focus on process and solutions for generating innovation, revenue, and sustainability as well as business introductions.

A Letter to the Next Generation

by Amy Brady

Global Transition, Quality & Change Delivery and
Global Integrated Business & Technology Services Executive
Bank of America

CHARLOTTE, NORTH CAROLINA

A Letter to the Next Generation

I ALWAYS FEEL HUMBLED when asked to give advice about careers, working as a woman in technology, or achieving a work-life balance. To me, my life feels more like a disorganized sock drawer than a smoothly run piece of machinery. I always feel there's so much more I could be doing to improve and to learn.

So while I am glad to suggest some thoughts for the next generation of professional women, the impression I do *not* want to give is: "I've got it all nailed."

We are always a work in progress, both professionally and personally. When we are young, we think we will reach a point when we know it all. In truth, the world, the economy and business dynamics will change so much in the course of our careers that we will never be able to know everything or see the complete "big picture." Our lives will be a continuous journey of knowledge, understanding and growth.

Maintain your learning agility

Going to university and having one or more degrees is important. But a degree just demonstrates that you had the ability to learn at one point in your youth. To be successful long term you must keep practicing the skill and never lose it.

Take for example the challenge for programmers. In my job I meet many experts who have been working on the same technology, using the same programming languages, for many years. Now, as their technology nears its end of life, they face the dilemma that their professional lives may end along with their technology – because they weren't willing to keep their skills current and learn new programming languages.

On the other side of the coin, the people I see who have successful long term technical careers are those who are constantly learning, who are passionate early adopters of new ideas and new technologies.

Pay attention to diversity

Throughout your career, seek out and respect the value of diversity in thought, religion, gender, ethnicity, age and experience. But be sure to add regional and global diversity to the list. I wish I had learned that lesson early on in my career. I think I knew instinctively what I was missing, but could never pinpoint it.

Different cultures respond to change – and to each other – in distinctly different ways. That's important to understand in an increasingly global economy, especially if you work for a global organization.

In technology, it's no longer acceptable to be globally ignorant. To value diversity means being globally aware and globally educated. So you don't expect colleagues in Singapore to join you for an afternoon conference call in the United States. And you understand that a piercing analysis from a client in England is not a personal attack.

Results speak louder than words

The ticket price for career progress is good execution. Do what you're asked to do very well – and preferably exceed expectations – before seeking your next opportunity. Promises fade quickly: what matters are delivering results, not once but over and over again. Build a personal brand with a reputation for excellent execution on every assignment.

Become a good leader

Leading means different things to different people, as everyone has their own style. Personally, I focus on empowering others.

I've learned that I have to demonstrate my own confidence and vulnerability before I can expect the same from members of my team. I also try to create an environment that welcomes candor – with feedback that is both constructive and positive. I'm genuinely curious about what others have to say, so I make sure I get everyone's input. And I've learned that the best teams are diverse teams, where constructive conflict empowers everyone to collaborate.

I try to prevent hierarchy and status from entering teams and the workplace. Otherwise it will destroy collaboration. Trust is the key ingredient for a productive, satisfying and fun work environment. Suspicion corrodes working relationships and undermines team members' confidence in themselves and their colleagues.

Accept that change is inevitable

You are inevitably going to see a lot of change during your career. So how you perceive change and how you manage it are very important. Change is never easy, especially when you are the subject of what is being changed. And it's not that easy to be a catalyst in creating change, either.

Change is actually an everyday part of what we do and who we are. It's in everything we do. But that still doesn't remove the reality of having to confront personal change. For some people, their first such encounter can be dramatic, even traumatic.

Turn change into an opportunity

Most changes actually offer the opportunity to be part of a solution. No organizational change is ever delivered fully defined – there's always room for us to further refine it within our own sphere of influence. And as leaders, we have the opportunity to engage all our teammates in refining it some more.

See turmoil as enriching

We all experience bad situations in our careers that may or may not be of our own making. Again, the trick is to turn that bad situation into an opportunity. Taking stock of where you stand can be a healing process. It can also turn into a pivotal opportunity to find work that's more in keeping with who you really are. So it's very important to recognize – and understand – when and how you do your best work.

Throughout my career I've found that unexpected turns of events have proved to be the most rewarding. So be open to new opportunities, new channels and new experiences.

Keep the faith and stay courageous

It took courage to be the only girl in school who was interested in computer programming, robotics camp or engineering. And as an IT professional, it still takes courage to be the only woman in the room.

Remember that diversity is important. You bring a perspective to the table that no one else owns. Speak up and make sure that perspective is heard.

Leverage the experiences of other women

Network, and do it smartly. Research shows that more than 80 percent of positions are found through networking. So get away from your computer: Get out and meet people!

However, be strategic in how you network, and with whom. Build a diverse range of contacts so that you continue to learn and grow. And for the same reason, reach outside your professional discipline.

When you network, make sure you are bringing things to the table and not just looking for the mentor to do the work or have all the answers. Mentors don't always have to be more senior than you are, either. Some of my best mentors are my peers.

As you meet people, make connections and build relationships, you'll be in a position to land new opportunities much faster, and you might even create some great, long-lasting friendships and relationships along the way.

Find your balance

I have had the privilege of mentoring many young men and women. And the question I hear the most is how to achieve a work-life balance. Well, I am not sure I've ever found mine!

What's important is that you have a choice about what work-life balance means to you. And equally important is that you remain in control of your own destiny. Only you can make the choices that are right for you. Don't ever let anyone else judge or dictate those choices. And while change may be inevitable, make sure your response to it makes sense for you.

So don't just take a promotion because it's offered to you. First make sure the opportunity is challenging enough, that you're moving to more challenging work. If you are not stretched, then you are not learning and growing professionally, regardless of your position in the hierarchy. And that's not satisfying.

In fact, the most 'non-traditional' lateral moves I made – the ones that made me most uncomfortable – turned out to be the best for my career.

So make sure you define your workplace and that it doesn't define you. We all have days when we get knocked down and things don't go well. Just don't let those days define you.

Have fun

I tell my daughters to choose a path that's exciting and challenging and to expect to have to work hard. But I also tell them not to get hung up about their destination. The point is to enjoy the journey.

Accept that no journey is uneventful. Accept that the road will be unpaved occasionally and that you will sometimes find it difficult to make progress.

Be patient with yourself. Take the time you need to invest in yourself and learn and grow. You'll be the best version of yourself when you enjoy your work and enjoy personal life in a balance that works for you.

So in work or in play, my advice to you is: have fun!

With every best wish for a happy and prosperous life, Amy

AMY BRADY is the Global Transition, Quality & Change Delivery Executive for Bank of America, overseeing the company's transitions and critical business change initiatives. She also leads the company's Global Integrated Business & Technology Services division, which is responsible for technology and business services like program delivery, business controls and technology transitions. She is the Executive Sponsor for the Atlanta LEAD Chapter, Bank of America's Women's Networking Group, as well as for Bank of America's Women in Technology and Operations organization, which has 12 active chapters around the world. Amy lives in Atlanta, Georgia.

BANK OF AMERICA is one of the world's largest financial institutions, serving individual consumers, small- and middle-market businesses and large corporations with a full range of banking, investing, asset management and other financial and risk management products and services.

Happy Accidents

by Melanie Brandt

Chief Operating Officer
Technology Association of Georgia (TAG)

ATLANTA, GEORGIA

Happy Accidents

My "climb to the top" occurred via a series of happy accidents. That is the best way I can explain it. While the harder I worked the luckier I got, as the expression goes, I certainly didn't have a roadmap that led to my position here at TAG despite the fact that everything I've done prior seems to have perfectly converged into this role for an organization that I truly love. In college I was pre-med at the University of Colorado, Boulder and quickly realized I didn't really want to become a doctor. However, I had made it through all the hard science classes intended to weed people out so I decided to stick with the major. Unfortunately, an undergrad degree in Molecular Biology isn't all that valuable in the real world. I didn't want to go to grad school at the time, so I decided to be a pharmaceutical sales rep. I went to work for Minolta Business selling copiers downtown Chicago to get a year of sales experience, or so I thought. It was great training, but the most irritating people I sold to were doctors – they were very protective of their time and didn't follow any of the business rules. Plus, once you get a customer to "sign on the dotted line" and get a big commission check, it is hard to envision yourself delivering focaccia bread sandwiches and branded notepads and calling it "sales," which is basically what pharmaceutical sales reps did back then. I was a closer.

So I kept selling – copiers in Chicago, software and telecom in Denver and then telecom in Atlanta. ICG Communications hired me to work national accounts in the southeast but pointed out I didn't have much of a network in Atlanta yet, so I got involved with the Atlanta Telecom Professionals, first as their Director of Events, then as Vice President, and then as President. I got married. I got pregnant.

I loved being at home with my son Will for the 12 weeks I was entitled to, and when I returned to work I noticed for the first time that my job required me to leave the house before seven o'clock in the morning and I got back home after seven o'clock at night – my commute was too long and it quickly became clear the company I was working for didn't really get the "mom" thing. So, I put the word out to a select group of people that I was "looking" and Tino Mantella, the President of TAG, was on my Board of Advisors at ATP at the time. He created a position for me. He hadn't really budgeted for a new position but was willing to give me flexible hours and let me work from home part of the time, so it was a good deal for both of us.

I got pregnant again. When my daughter Farrah was about eight months old I met a recruiter at Sandy Hofmann's Christmas party, and was contacted by Nick Masino with the Gwinnett Chamber's Economic Development Department. The job description he sent me was so perfect my father, also a recruiter, thought someone had created it based off my specific background. We lived in Gwinnett and the preschool I wanted the kids to go to was five minutes away from the Chamber, and Nick and I clicked. I hadn't even heard of "economic development" before, but it seemed to be all about improving the community and creating jobs.

I was able to take a lot of the great things I had learned from Tino at TAG to the position in Gwinnett, and learned so much from the Gwinnett Chamber as well – local government etiquette, effectively navigating through a multi-faceted organization (who to ask and in what order), and of course the whole world of economic development – I had, like many people, always read about companies moving their headquarters or opening up an expansion facility and thought "oh that's interesting," not knowing anything about the immense wheels that are in motion to make these things happen, or the intense, high stake sales campaigns that are constantly going on to bring jobs into one's community. Most importantly, working for the Gwinnett Chamber was where I developed a deep sense of pride about Georgia and all of the people at the Chambers, the cities, the counties and at the state who are working so hard to improve our quality of life.

And then Tino called. He was hiring a COO, he said, and wanted to know if I would interview for it. I said yes, never thinking I would get it or that I would take it if I did; I had a job, a boss – a life – that I loved. He tells me now there were 150 qualified applicants who submitted their resumes – it would have been a competitive process in a normal economy, and of course we were in the middle of a recession. When I learned I was one of three final candidates I couldn't sleep. I had recently completed my MBA but had no real operations experience, or management experience, but TAG wanted to diversify into economic development and I had become pretty well known in the community as someone who was genuinely committed to making a difference. He also knew I could fundraise, that he and I worked well together and that no one would work harder for him, but I wasn't sure what background he would choose.

I finally went in and talked to Stephen Fleming, who is a leader in the Georgia technology community who had become a mentor to me. He had recently taken the position of Vice Provost for Georgia Tech's Enterprise Innovation Institute. His process had been even more competitive, and entirely public as is the norm with those kinds of positions. He told me, "Look, Melanie, he knows you – he knows what you bring to the table, and what you don't. If he doesn't want you, then the job isn't right for you." That helped me sleep, but I still desperately wanted the job at that point. TAG is such an amazing organization – it is hard to say that without sounding banal, but it really has incredible scale, scope, and the most elite group of people actively engaged on the board. And I was and am again at my best working for Tino – he is a great leader and brings out (demands!) excellence in the people around him.

After I was hired I met a kind of casually dressed woman who told me "oh, I applied for that job – it sounded like so much fun!" and I smiled to myself – I have eight pages of performance standards! I think a lot of people think working for a non profit is mellow, but TAG is every bit as demanding as any quota I've ever been given, and because we are representing our board, our members, and the state of Georgia, everything we do – which is a lot – must be done exceptionally well. Tino has a plaque on his desk paraphrasing a proverb that says, "Those who say it cannot be done should not interrupt the one who is doing it," and, well – we have all learned not to interrupt.

I think the key to me being where I am is the people I've been surrounded by along the way. Minolta Business was a fantastic place to learn how to sell; the Atlanta Telecom Professionals was comprised of great, committed volunteers who are some of my closest friends still today; Nick Masino is phenomenal at the art of managing people, and he and his team at Gwinnett are setting the standard for economic development and marketing excellence; and of course Tino Mantella is the very best at, well, everything he does! I've appreciated being given the opportunity to work alongside all of them, and feel so fortunate to get up every day with the primary goal of improving the community. Honestly, it doesn't really even feel like a job.

MELANIE BRANDT serves as TAG's Chief Operating Officer. In this role, she manages a select set of TAG's key strategic functions which include the annual State of the Industry Report, the GRA/TAG Business Launch Competition, TAG's Statewide impact initiatives including Economic Development support and an Economic Gardening pilot project in Savannah, and the TAG Leadership Council.

Before joining TAG, Brandt was part of the Gwinnett Chamber's Economic Development team, implementing the Partnership Gwinnett initiative as their Business Development Manager for Information Technology and Advanced Communication. Prior to joining the Gwinnett Chamber, Brandt served as TAG's Director of Information and Community Resources where she led the creation of TAG's first and second *State of the Industry: Technology in Georgia* reports.

Brandt is currently on the executive advisory board for the Atlanta Telecom Professionals (ATP), where she served as president in 2004 and 2005, an executive advisory board member of Digitainment Georgia, and a founder and board member of StartupChicks, an organization dedicated to connecting and inspiring entrepreneurial women.

TAG is a leading technology industry association dedicated to the promotion and economic advancement of the state's technology industry. TAG provides leadership in driving initiatives in the areas of policy, capital, education and giving, and also brings the technology community together through events, initiative programs and networking opportunities. TAG serves as an umbrella organization for 27 special interest groups, or societies, including Women in Technology (WIT) and TAG's charitable arm, the TAG Education Collaborative, is focused on helping science, technology, engineering and math (STEM) education initiatives thrive.

A Journey Recalled

by Luba Brock

Technology Law Associates

ATLANTA, GEORGIA

A Journey Recalled

It was 1990 and men in dark suits dominated the industry meetings in the technology sector. Yes, suits! The few women that could be found amongst the suits wore hose! How things have changed in 20 years – and especially with respect to the role women are playing today – for the better, including the option to go hose-free (but not Spanx-free as we *do* want to support our good friend and local role model, Sara Blakely!).

Having joined a law firm with a visionary partner intent on building a technology law practice, one of my goals was to help generate clients by attending technology industry meetings. A "good ole boys" gathering was my initial reaction when I first began attending the meetings in the late 1980s having recently moved to Atlanta from California. Having worked for IBM in Silicon Valley and experiencing perhaps a more liberal and cutting-edge attitude toward promoting women in business, I initially felt like I had taken a big step backward in time when I entered the legal work force in the South. With a technology background (having worked for IBM as a systems engineer and product planner), I was convinced that focusing my legal career in the technology sector would give me a distinct advantage in the competitive ranks of newly admitted lawyers. Timing was everything and my move to Atlanta coincided with John Yates' initial plans to establish a technology law practice – the first of its kind – in Atlanta. It was a perfect match – few lawyers at that time had the "computer" background and could talk bits and bytes to clients in the technology sector.

Mentors? There were none, at least not one individual that could serve as the perfect role model! We were all trying to figure it out – Atlanta wanted to be "Silicon Valley" of the South – lawyers wanted to serve the burgeoning high-tech industry – and female lawyers trying to fit in, well there was only a handful and we were all newbies. Although there were no female lawyers running technology practices, I would be remiss in not crediting those individuals that helped me shape my practice and mold me as an individual: John Yates – the hardest working lawyer and most successful networker I have ever had the pleasure of working with, building what has become one of the most successful technology legal practices in the country; Penn Payne – the first female partner that I worked with who shared her experiences in working with an all-male firm of lawyers; and then my "GOGS" as we later dubbed our group – the "good ole' girls" – Barbara Stafford, Chris Coleman and Emma Morris – all successful women who have run their own businesses for the past 20 years.

From the time a lawyer starts practicing law, you quickly learn that success comes with "rain-making" – generating clients. To generate clients, you have to network and build relationships. One of the most direct ways to network in Atlanta's technology community at that time was to become involved in industry associations. In the early 1990s, only two existed that drew key executives from that sector: SSA (the Southeastern Software Association) and B&TA (the Business and Technology Alliance). "Networking" was a key benefit of each group's monthly meetings, where business executives mingled with each other and service providers. Slowly women began to join the executive ranks of the young technology companies in the Atlanta area, but the numbers were few and assimilation slow. One of the major contributors to the promotion of women into key positions and ultimately spawning many young start-ups was MSA. Largely due to the successful technology legal practice established by John Yates at Morris, Manning & Martin and the fact that I was part of his technology group, I quickly became a regular attendee and eventually active as a board member of the industry organizations.

However, even though the existing organizations provided opportunities for strategic relationships and helpful information for their members, there was a noticeable lack of female involvement, participation or support. By then, in the early 1990s, there was a growing number of successful, entrepreneurial women running their own businesses or occupying key positions in technology companies. Maybe because the SSA and B&TA members were still predominantly a male-centric culture, many younger women striving to succeed in their respective technology careers had nowhere to go to "network" with peers and role-models. Credit must go to Jan Wyche and Valerie Crelia-Shaw who identified the need for a women's technology-focused business organization that could provide the networking and peer-bonding opportunities that were clearly enjoyed by their male counterparts. It took more than a year of haphazard but enthusiastic participation for our small group of women to realize there was a real need for another SSA/B&TA-like organization, but one that emphasized the participation of women and focused on the challenges they faced as part of Atlanta's technology workforce.

Having been involved in B&TA and SSA for several years at that time, and being a lawyer I suppose, gave me the experience and logic to push our group to a more formal status. My coaching from my early mentors served me well and I was elected Women in Technology's (WIT) first president. Our initial board was small, our finances limited, but our enthusiasm, perseverance and get-it-done attitudes formed the basis of what is now one of the strongest technology organizations in Atlanta. The team of women that led WIT in its early days dedicated themselves to building an organization that would educate and support women in business – an organization that today is highly respected by its peer organizations. WIT's mission has not changed greatly in the years since its formation, but the number of members, its finances, its contribution to and impact on the community are immeasurable. The programs that have been initiated and honed over the years have mentored, supported and recognized successful women leaders – the list is long and impressive.

From a personal perspective, the women that have entered my life as a result of my involvement with WIT will remain friends forever. Those women who contributed time and energy to the growth and success of WIT through the years have gone on to found and run successful businesses of their own. I take great personal pride in the fact that many of our women leaders today have played an active role in WIT and many attribute their success, at least partially, to their connection to the great community of women – the Women In Technology.

LUBA BROCK is one of the founding partners, along with Ann Moceyunas, of Technology Law Partners. These two women partners originally formed the firm in 1993. Ann has continued her practice in both a corporate setting and her own private practice. Luba Brock has maintained her private practice and currently serves as part-time legal counsel for LeadLife Solutions and Firstwave Technologies. In addition to her practice, she has also served as Adjunct Professor at Kennesaw State University teaching computer law courses in the Computer Systems & Information Systems Department from 1993 through 2006. She has practiced intellectual property law in Atlanta since 1986.

Prior to her legal career, Luba worked for IBM from 1974 to 1982 as a systems engineer, development analyst and product planner in Vancouver, Canada and Menlo Park, California. She has served as an arbitrator for the American Arbitration Association since 1987. Luba has been active in the legal and technology communities in Georgia, and is a member of and has served as: Chairperson of the Georgia Technology Law Bar Section, President of Women in Technology, member of the Board of Directors of Business and Technology Alliance, member of the Advisory Board and Board of Directors of Technology Association of Georgia (TAG), Chairperson and member of the Board of Directors of the TAG Foundation, and member of the American Bar Association, Computer Law Association, Georgia Association of Women Lawyers and the Charitable Grants Committee of the Georgia Women's Foundation.

TECHNOLOGY LAW ASSOCIATES is a law firm dedicated to the practice of technology law focusing primarily on representing technology clients in general corporate matters, including contract negotiation, protection of intellectual property rights, structuring technology business relationships and general corporate matters.

Lessons for Success

by Theresa Brunasso

President
D&S Microwave

SNELLVILLE, GEORGIA

Lessons for Success

OVER THE COURSE OF MY THREE-DECADE CAREER I've learned a few simple lessons that contributed to my success. Some of the lessons I learned by watching colleagues that I admired, and others I learned from my own experience. Although my career is in engineering, these lessons are applicable to any field.

Be dependable

The first career lesson I learned was the simplest and the most obvious. I was the oldest daughter in a large family (six children), so I had many responsibilities when I was growing up. I fed, bathed, and watched my younger brothers and sister when I was a girl. Although I often resented the work I had to do, I liked knowing that my parents could count on me and appreciated my help. So, it seemed obvious to me that I should also be dependable on the job. When I was given an assignment I put in the time necessary to meet the due date. When I was having difficulty getting the work done, I asked for help so I could meet my milestone. In fact, I assumed that everyone had the same attitude. Unfortunately, I quickly learned that was not the case. I can't understand why others don't take their commitments seriously, but I can tell you that managers seek out those of us who are dependable because we get the job done. This trait, more than any other, will give you job security.

Be confident

Most of my career I spent with a company that did not have a product line. As a result our projects were custom designed hardware that required creativity and lots of engineering design. When I first started, I was intimidated when I started each new project. I'd think, "Why do they think I can do this? I've never done this before!" It was stressful and a bit scary. However, each time I learned what I needed to perform the work. I remember on one particular project, one of the engineers was struggling to complete his design work. Our technical lead, who was one of the smartest engineers I know, told me, "Theresa, I think you and I should take over the design of this device." My first thought was, "What?! I don't know anything about that!" Fortunately, I kept my mouth shut. The technical lead then asked my office mate, "What do you know about those devices?" My office mate said, "Not much. They have three ports, and they're 120° apart." Much to my surprise, the technical lead replied, "Yeah, that's all I know too." I was amazed. I just assumed he was so smart and experienced that he had years of experience designing those devices. Instead, what he really had was confidence that he could figure out how to design them.

I learned an important lesson that day. The successful engineers are confident that they can learn whatever they need to tackle a new project. As the years went by, my confidence naturally grew with each new project I worked on. At the start of each project I would remind myself of what I had to learn to complete the previous project, and tell myself that I would learn what I needed to be successful on my current project. And, a nice surprise was that I grew to love the beginning of a new project when I was frantically trying to learn the specifications, the challenges, and new technologies in a very short time. I found it to be one of the most exciting and rewarding parts of my job. Most importantly, managers and customers appreciated my confidence. It makes sense; when you have responsibility for a multimillion dollar project, your customers need to believe that you will be successful. If you aren't confident, they won't trust you or your work.

Be inquisitive

Like all engineers I know, I'm a naturally inquisitive person. However, when I first started working, I hesitated to ask questions.

I thought I was probably the only one who didn't understand why we were using one approach instead of another, and I didn't want to show my ignorance. That's not a very good approach for success, since I needed to understand the job requirements, and the reasons we used a particular approach. So, I started slowly. I'd ask someone else in the meeting, "Did you understand why we aren't doing it this way?" More often than not, he would respond, "Not really." That gave me the confidence to start asking questions as soon as I had them. Typically, it would clarify things for others too, it sometimes led to a different approach, and it always helped me. I've since noticed that the smartest people I know never hesitate to ask questions. They are confident enough in their intellect to ask when they don't understand. Only insecure people are afraid to ask questions. Over the years I've learned to embrace my inquisitiveness.

Be bold

It's easy to stay with what you know. If you've had the same responsibilities for years, you will be very good at your job, and it will be easy. However, you won't be stretching yourself, and you won't be growing. I always loved engineering, and was happy to continue working on design projects for the rest of my career. Fortunately, my manager had other ideas. He wanted me to take over management of the microwave engineering group. I resisted his request for months. I thought, "I like the technical work, and leading people is not one of my strengths." However, I knew that I should do what my boss asked. It's not very good for your career to turn down opportunities that your manager offers you. More importantly, I had a tremendous amount of respect for him, and I thought I should help him if I could. So, I took over the group. It turned out to be very good for me. I learned a new side of the business, and it forced me to work on my people skills. To be perfectly honest, after serving in the Navy, I *needed* to work on my people skills! I learned that

I did the most growing when I was outside my comfort zone and forced to stretch.

Be tough

By being tough, I mean have a thick skin and don't take things personally. We all have bad days. If someone snaps at you, it may not be about you at all. Maybe his daughter is sick, maybe her husband is out of town and she's stressed. Let it go, and for heaven's sake, don't escalate the situation. You can always stop the discussion, and pick it up a day later when everyone is calmer. Your colleague will be grateful that you forgave him or her, and someday you will be grateful when she returns the favor! You don't need to be friends with your colleagues, but you need to work together to be successful.

Be generous

Much of my success I owe to colleagues and friends who acted as mentors to me. They gave generously of their time and expertise, and I benefitted greatly from their wisdom. As my experience grew, I honored my mentors by mentoring others. I found that giving my time was its own reward. I enjoyed helping others in the way that I was helped, and I developed friendships that lasted long after we worked together. Moreover, my volunteering was instrumental in my winning the Women in Technology *Woman of the Year in Technology Award* in 2008. I was honored to receive the award, but the greatest gift I got from mentoring was the joy of helping others succeed.

Be frugal

This is financial advice, but it helped me in my career. Like almost all engineers I know, I've always been very financially conservative. I always lived below my means, and *always* saved money. Fortunately, my husband has the same attitude about money, and it allowed us to pay off our mortgage early. As a result, that gave me the financial freedom to start my own company. I had time to build a client base without worrying that I wouldn't be able to pay my bills. All your friends may have an iPhone®, an iPad®, satellite TV, beautiful clothes, and a really cool car, but if they have no savings and thousands of dollars of debt, they don't have the freedom to take the jobs or opportunities that present themselves. If we've learned anything from the great recession, it's that we should minimize our debts and maximize our savings. You will sleep better at night and have more opportunities if you live below your means.

THERESA BRUNASSO is a 30-year veteran in the field of Electrical Engineering. She currently is a consultant in the Microwave Aerospace and Defense Community. Previously, she spent over 20 years at EMS Technologies, Defense and Space Systems division. At D&SS, Theresa served as Microwave Engineering Manager, Director of Technology Development, and provided innovative design and development expertise for D&SS heritage programs such as JSTARS, DarkStar, NSTAR, Milstar, Advanced EHF, IntelSat and Mars Science Lab.

Theresa joined D&SS in 1989, after serving as a Research Engineer for the Georgia Tech Research Institute (GTRI), one of the nation's leading independent R&D organizations. Prior to joining GTRI, Theresa spent two years as an Engineer for Teledyne MEC, an international leader in the design, development, and manufacture of high gain broadband amplifiers. Brunasso began her career in the U.S. Navy as an Instructor at the Consolidated Naval Electronic Warfare School in Pensacola, FL. She was awarded a graduate fellowship through the Air Force Thermionic Engineering Research Program.

Theresa holds an Engineer's Degree and M.E. in Electrical Engineering from the University of Utah, and a B.S. in Physics from the University of West Florida. She is a member of Sigma Pi Sigma, the National Physics Honor Society. In September 2008, she was awarded a U.S. patent titled, "A Compact Beam Former with Low Side Lobes." That same month she was one of three Georgia area women honored by Women in Technology (WIT) as a winner in the ninth annual *Women of the Year in Technology Awards.*

D&S MICROWAVE is a microwave consulting company for the Defense and Space industry. With over 30 years of experience in the defense and aerospace community, D&S Microwave has demonstrated success in systems engineering, microwave design engineering, and technology management

Embrace the Tigress

by Nadia Butler

President and CEO
Emergency Services Integrators, Inc.

AUGUSTA, GEORGIA

Embrace the Tigress

POWER. STRENGTH. LEADERSHIP. These are subjects that fascinate us; that have been studied since philosophers first started thinking about social dynamics. And through history, powerful women have been complex characters in the play. Eve, Cleopatra, Elizabeth, Lady Macbeth, Hillary. Women in power or with power fascinate but also seem to repel us. Why is that? Power comes from many sources, but it is strength – strength of will and intellect, and even physical strength – that defines the individual regardless of position or credentials. Therein lies the irony. A strong woman with position and credentials can be a powerful leader, but one that down through history has been more often threatening than accepted.

In today's dialogue, when we speak of women in power, we hear of how women are more inclusive, how we seek consensus and approach leadership with a more gentle touch. How much of our dialog is about how women use power? How much is about our relationship with our own strength? It is time for us to acknowledge our strength and lead through strength. To lead, one must have both credentials and personal strength. It is that combination that gives people the confidence to follow you.

It is only in the last several years that I have come to recognize the elements of leadership in myself and to understand how to use them wisely. The WIT *Woman of the Year* process caused me to stop to acknowledge my accomplishments, and the myriad of challenges made me acknowledge my strength.

I was raised by my father, who had the same expectations of me that he had of my brothers. It was not "you can do this" but rather "you must." He believed that a society that excluded women from technical professions was losing half its potential. He instilled in me a sense of responsibility to contribute to society. He taught me to think critically, and to articulate my thoughts clearly. And he had high standards, even to the extent of saying that getting straight A's in school was "the least I could do" given my capabilities.

My father was a researcher in basic physics at Bell Labs. During his tenure there, Bell Labs was an amazing place, populated by brilliant scientists, all doing basic research. And yet these scientists all had the title MTS, Member of the Technical Staff, and none used the title "Dr.", although all had PhDs. I was raised in an environment where one didn't taut one's accomplishments.

As I progressed through school, college, and my career, I excelled at most everything I did, but never stopped to consider what I was accomplishing. I was always measuring myself against what I felt I could do, and always saw how much further I needed to go rather than what I had already done.

I have always been a strong woman, physically, intellectually, and emotionally. And yet I have always tried to hide that strength, reflexively reacting to the vague negative undercurrent of the phrase "she's a strong woman." I have consistently risen to positions of leadership, primarily by virtue of my drive and ability to work with the people around me to accomplish the most that we can. But I have come to realize that leadership is a position of power, and that one must acknowledge that power and understand it in order to lead well.

The WIT *Women of the Year in Technology* (WOTY) Award played a critical part in my coming to this realization. It was not the external recognition, but rather the process of applying for the award, that set me on a journey that led ultimately to acknowledging my accomplishments and, more importantly, understanding how important an objective sense of self-worth is to leadership.

I was an unwilling nominee for WOTY. It seemed to me to be a self-congratulatory process and, after all, I had not yet met my own standards of performance. Further, leading an entrepreneurial technology company that was in hyper-growth did not leave much time for reflection. I believe strongly that leading means helping and driving people to meet their own potential and thereby create the most value both for the individual and the company. Leadership was not about me; it is about the company and the people in it. I was finally convinced to participate, because the recognition would be good for our company.

Going through the process, completing the application, participating in the interviews, and thinking about the possibility of be awarded WOTY, I came face-to-face with my accomplishments. And I realized I was far more comfortable hiding them than having them highlighted. I wondered about this in myself and wondered if it other women experienced the same hesitancy to showcase their credentials.

I also started to watch powerful men with a different eye, to understand how they "wielded" their credentials and how others responded to them. I looked more closely at the employees of our company and how they responded to me. And I started to understand that rather than being somehow unseemly, establishing one's credentials is a vital element of leadership. I had taken one step toward embracing the tigress.

The next vital step came through a series of events that challenged my personal strength on every front. As I progressed through a year that took me from navigating the company through the economic downturn and conflicts with my board, to cycling across the US, and finally through illness, I found myself at the end of the year emotionally drained and physically weaker than I have ever been.

In meeting these challenges I had to look critically at myself, to understand my motivations, understand what I value and what is not so important, and to develop a clear sense of my worth. It was a difficult journey. Having re-established my core values, I set out to rebuild my strength. And as is often the case in life, it was in having lost that strength that I came to understand how much I cherish it and how important it is to leadership. In something as seemingly irrelevant as weight training, I find myself taking great pride in the weight I can lift and also noting the conflicted reactions I get from both the men and the women in the gym. But now, rather than feeling embarrassed, or feeling that I am somehow not being "feminine" I revel in my physical power.

All this has caused me to contemplate strength and power and its relationship to leadership, especially in women. I understand now that hiding one's accomplishments is not a positive thing, that it is important to everyone that looks to you to lead to know that you have the credentials for your position. There is a valid reason why military uniforms are covered with badges and ribbons. But more importantly, I understand now that allowing one's strength to be evident is equally important. You cannot lead effectively from behind the curtain.

And so I encourage all women to look objectively at yourselves – to stop striving for a moment and acknowledge how much you have accomplished. I urge you all to look uncompromisingly at your strength. If you want to lead, you must be willing to be strong and to allow your strength to show. You will find that it is in this strength that you will have the ability to draw the best out of others. In true strength, you will not react out of insecurity, but rather will respond with clarity of vision and objectivity.

It is by embracing the tigress in us all that you can grow to be the true leader we all want to be.

NADIA D. BUTLER – Throughout her 30-year career, Nadia Butler has managed large organizations and created new businesses. As president and CEO of ESi®, Ms. Butler has provided the vision and direction for all ESi software products and technical support services that has brought the company to its industry-leading position.

Boundless Collaboration™, the tagline on the company logo, describes both Nadia's personal philosophy and ESi's corporate one. With her all-staff meetings, open-door policy, and receptivity to new ideas from everyone in the company, Nadia exemplifies boundless collaboration as she leads over 80 employees based in

12 offices around the U.S. At ESi, the concept of collaboration applies not only to the value of its products and its role as a solutions provider to its customers; it also drives the enthusiasm and commitment to excellence among ESi employees. In the 2008 edition of the popular business book *The Starfish and the Spider* by Ori Brafman and Rod A. Beckstrom, the authors have this to say about ESi: "From the outside, ESi seems like a normal business, but a deeper look reveals starfish DNA: company-wide meetings where everyone is expected to be frank; open collaboration; and, of course, a team leadership model."

Nadia is an advocate for physical fitness. She practices yoga daily and, last fall, completed a cross-country bicycle trip. ESi provides gym membership for all employees and their family members, and the company will sponsor, for the second year, the ESi IronMan® 70.3, a sanctioned half-marathon event, in Augusta. Nadia also believes in contributing to the community. She is the president of The Augusta Ballet Board of Directors and also serves on the boards of the Medical College of Georgia, the Metro Augusta Chamber of Commerce and the corporate leadership group Augusta Tomorrow.

ESI®, the global leader in crisis information management technology, pioneered the market with WebEOC®, the world's first Web-enabled emergency management communications system. ESi software connects crisis response teams and decision makers at more than 500 national, state and local agencies, healthcare providers, airlines, and Fortune 500 corporations worldwide by providing access to real-time information for a common operating picture during a crisis or daily operations. For the fourth consecutive year, ESi® has been named to the *Inc. Magazine* list of America's fastest-growing private companies, with a three-year growth rate of 63%.

Out of the Blue

by Betsy Cagle

Senior IT Recruiter
Brick House Resources

ATLANTA, GEORGIA

Out of the Blue

As a child I led a nomadic life, living in cities in Europe and the United States, never staying much longer than three years in one place. I went to a different school every single year until my eighth grade year. Consequently, it was challenging, to say the least, to develop friends, much less lasting friendships. During my growing up years I tended to stay pretty much to myself and instead I developed a passion for books. Reading a book didn't require companionship. My friendship skills tended towards the remedial level at best.

Now all this travel also had its up side and I really can't complain about my upbringing, but when I got to high school it was obvious I was out of my element when it came to finding my way into the "in" crowd. First, I didn't grow up with anyone in my school, second I was a minority being Caucasian in a Hawaiian high school and finally, even when I did have friends I was more comfortable in male company than I was in female company. I think that was because males just accepted me as is and females usually wouldn't let me in until I proved myself in some manner and on that point I was clueless!

Joining clubs, cliques or groups usually was not an option for me because I never stayed long enough in one place to make it worth my while, or their while really. Besides, on the rare occasions when I did join some group or other I just couldn't seem to break into the core group members. I was the outsider "wanna be." My role usually ended up being "head gofer." I suppose in a way it was a "leadership" position!

I always admired those in leadership positions in my high school and college. They projected such confidence and constantly seemed to be surrounded by friends. They were looked up to and they had seemingly endless energy. Leadership for them looked natural. It was simply an outgrowth of their basic personality structure. I, on the other hand, hadn't a clue as to how to become a leader nor did I know if I even had the qualities it took. Not because I didn't consider myself smart enough to be a leader, but because the opportunities for this role were basically non-existent in my life – or at least this was my thought at the time.

So it was quite the surprise when out of the blue, at the ripe age of 38, I found myself in a small group of eight women who joined together to form an organization in the technology sector that we eventually named WIT (Women in Technology). To this day I'm not sure exactly what circumstances serendipitously came together that put me on the original WIT Board, but my life was changed dramatically as a result.

For me, this was my very first foray into formally being in on the ground floor of an organization, any organization, much less one that was all female! But from our very first meeting our small little group created magic. Even at the time I marveled at how well we all seemed to get along. Our charter to become the place for women to network in their industry and give back to our community was in place almost from the first day and that charter hasn't substantively been altered to this day.

Fifteen plus years later, with strictly volunteered time and sweat equity, we've affected the lives of hundreds of women, given hundreds of thousands of dollars to charitable organizations, developed programs which some Fortune 500 companies use today to bring disadvantaged women into the technology sector, instituted school programs for young girls, created the largest and most visible annual technology special event in Atlanta, and were one of three organizations that combined to form the Technology Association of Georgia, one of the largest technology associations in the U.S., as well as so many other accomplishments. All because we saw a need and had a desire to do something about it.

In my 12-year tenure on the WIT Board I held almost every position we had, including President. Can I say I was the best president ever, no, however I can say with confidence that even though I had no training in taking leadership roles, even though it scared the heck out of me to even think about the possibility of becoming the WIT President, and even though I was following a few other wonderful and more qualified female leaders into this role, I couldn't have done it at all were it not for the support of all the other women on the board. This is finally where I learned that true leaders are really the glue of an organization, and that the daily operation, if allowed to run correctly, is handled by those in the other "management" positions in the organization. I learned a leader does not dictate. In fact by definition, if a leader is dictating you are not a leader, you are a dictator. Even as it pertains to direction, the leader is just one of many who have ideas on how things should be run. A true leader, in my experience, only steps in and makes a decision for the good of the organization if a consensus opinion of all interested parties can't be reached, and even then she has carefully considered the options before making her decision. I learned that people are much smarter and more creative when they are set loose to make decisions, develop projects and run their operation the way they see fit without too much interference from upper management.

This is the way WIT was run from its inception and its incredible success is due in great part to the fact that its early leaders all held to these beliefs about leadership. They were never stated in a handbook or taught to us in a seminar, but somehow, intrinsically, we all had the same beliefs about leadership. The friendships I forged, the professional connections I made and the respect given me in the marketplace were all the result of the magic we created then and the magic that continues today.

My sage advice for young women coming of age today would be to take a big leap of faith and find an organization that speaks to your sensibilities, your passions, and your skills (even if you think you don't really have any skills) and either volunteer or join up. It doesn't matter what kind of organization it is, be it a school club, a professional association or a group of people that come together due to a shared interest. I promise you, if you stay with it you will be rewarded in ways you can't begin to imagine. If you've ever played team sports then you have some idea of what I'm speaking about. I find it ironic that most people say they just don't have the time to volunteer. They say their lives are much too busy to cram one more thing in, but the reality is that your life shifts to accommodate your new interest and because you are doing something that speaks to your passion it doesn't feel like a burden. In fact it's usually just the opposite. You soon begin to wonder what you would ever do if you couldn't participate in the organization of your choice.

I was so blessed that WIT turned out to be my organization of choice. Its lessons continue, as do the relationships, both professional and personal. It was a great ride and the amazing thing is that it's not over yet!

BETSY CAGLE – Ms. Cagle began her professional career in the technology sector over 20 years ago. As a veteran of seven technology startup companies, she has experienced both the challenges and the excitement of managing one's career through multiple corporate cultures and new ventures. Betsy's expertise includes software sales, programming, and Internet Marketing.

During her tenure in technology, she has served on numerous local and national technology boards. In 1993, Ms. Cagle helped to co-found Atlanta's Women in Technology (WIT) association and served for 12 years in the roles of President, Vice President and the Director of Membership. When WIT, the Southeastern Software Association (SSA) and The Business & Technology Alliance (B&TA) joined forces in 1998 to form the Technology Association of Georgia (TAG), Ms. Cagle was selected to move up to the TAG board where she served as a director for two years.

Eight years ago Ms. Cagle bid the corporate world adieu and enjoyed her time as a consultant and entrepreneur, though recently she once again joined her eighth startup company as a full time employee.

BRICK HOUSE is a dynamic women-owned technology-staffing firm offering contract, contract to hire and full-time placement services. We focus on opportunities for IT talent from Staff to Executive level in the Atlanta area. Our areas of expertise include Software Development/Engineering, Database Development/ Administration; Web Development; Network Administration/ Engineering; Product/Project Management; Business Analysis and Quality Assurance. Our clients can expect us to deliver a high quality service that is built on strong recruiting principles and tactics combined with personal service.

Never Underestimate the Power of Passion

by Marsha Calfee

CRM/Marketing Consultant
Strategic Consulting Services

LAWRENCEVILLE, GEORGIA

Never Underestimate the Power of Passion

I HAVE LONG BELIEVED that the right sort of desire will break down anything that stands in the way of its fulfillment. This has never been as true as it has been with WIT.

You might think of WIT as a non-profit organization, but it is far more than that. The organization that began with only a few women who met to share ideas and support one another has endured for 18 years now and has evolved into something much more. Where many non-profit and for-profit organizations have come and gone during this time, you might wonder why it is that a small group of females have been able to grow the organization into one of the most widely recognized and respected networking organizations in Atlanta. As I sit and reflect on this marvelous group of women called WIT, there comes to mind two underlying values that I consider to be hallmarks of WIT's success: a willingness to evolve and the volunteers.

We all know stories of great companies who have plummeted into the bowels of the unknown or dwindled away until swept up by another organization. Take for example Sun Microsystems. For approximately 27 years, Sun was a recognized leader in network computing delivering to the world such innovations as Java, open standards and open source, and high-performance computing. But it seems that staying focused on doing what they always had done instead of evolving to what the market demanded was its downfall. Once software became more valued, Sun was unable to find a success formula that would allow it to charge for the software it developed. The company remained locked in to its old practices of being a hardware manufacturer and refused to evolve into a new way of doing business. After 10 years of declining revenue and profits, the end of Sun Microsystems came to be in January 2010 when it was acquired by Oracle.

On the other hand, WIT has continually looked to what the market is demanding while still remaining true to its core mission of developing and promoting women for success in Georgia's technology community. Take a look at the WIT Mentor program, which was first established in 1994. Designed to provide mentors to women who were up-and-coming, the program went through many iterations and sometimes even sat on the shelf, until it got to where it is today. Working off the foundation of a solid idea, the first evolution of the WIT Mentor program came with the launch of the Executive Coaching program in 2002. This program, much like the original WIT Mentor program focuses on women already in senior positions in their companies. But instead of just one-on-one mentoring, this program brings in several coaches to mentor and guide the women on what they need to do to further their careers.

In response to the requests of sponsors and members of WIT, the Careers in Action program was established in 2008. In order to advance women into executive positions, the pipeline needed to be built. Careers in Action helped do that by focusing on the women who had moved from a junior level position into a management role and were now looking how to develop their skills to be prepared for advancement into a senior role with the Leadership in Action program. And for those women interested in making a change in their career, the Careers in Transition program was added.

And WIT did not stop there. Knowing that the future of technology was dependent upon young girls making decisions to pursue a career in technology, Girls Get IT was launched in 2003. It too has evolved since its inception by adding to the Behind the Scenes workshops two new programs – Job Shadowing and Career Exploration workshops. So from the initial concept of providing support and encouragement to other women, the WIT Mentor program has evolved into five exciting programs that address the needs of girls and women pursuing and trying to advance their careers in technology.

Let's also take a look at how WIT has evolved with fundraising. Did you know that WIT's annual fundraiser, WIT Connect, started in 1995 as a fashion show event called "Reengineering Style?" Again keeping up with the demands of the market place, WIT evolved that first fashion-show fundraiser into what is known as the premier networking event of the year where time with executives of Atlanta's top companies are auctioned off to those in attendance. Now in existence for 16 years, who would have ever guessed that the first "Reengineering Style" fundraiser could evolve into an event attended by hundreds and raise $400,000 this past year alone in the process?

The success of WIT's ability to evolve would not be complete without addressing how the organizational structure has evolved as well. Those familiar with the history of TAG and the technology community in Atlanta know that three years after it was founded, WIT joined forces with Business and Technology Alliance and the Southeastern Software Association to create TAG. Even after that WIT continued on with its development of programs focused on the support and promotion of women in technology. Then in 2004, WIT, INC. and the WIT Foundation were formally incorporated as 501(c)(3) organizations giving it the ability to really focus its efforts on the fundraising necessary to support its programs. But one of the biggest changes took place in 2007 when WIT hired its first executive director. Always supported by volunteer efforts, the growth of WIT and the WIT Foundation was getting to be too much and required the constant eye of someone who could help the board manage day-to-day activities. WIT has always prided itself on being an all-volunteer organization, but having the courage to take this step showed great strength and determination to ensure the future and success of the organization.

And speaking of volunteers, that is the second hallmark of WIT's success. Anyone who is responsible for running a department, a division, or an entire company knows what I am talking about when I speak of what is involved with the running of an organization. There are budgets, staffing decisions, project management, creative processes, planning, execution, assessment, and meetings just to name a few of the things required to run a successful business. We all know that when Friday comes we are exhausted and ready for the few days of relaxation we will get over the weekend. But can you imagine what it would be like if you not only had your full-time job but the equivalent of another part-time job to handle? Well, that's what is it like for all the volunteers who help run WIT. These are women who willingly give of their free time to help schedule speakers, seek out event sponsors, manage the finances, find more volunteers to staff an event, do the marketing, and keep track of where things are with a project.

If you were asked why you thought the women did this, you would probably say for the networking contacts. Well, that is for sure a benefit that comes with the job a being a WIT volunteer. But for anyone seriously involved in networking, you know that the benefits of networking do not always come immediately, but sometimes take time to develop. So why is it that these women would give up so much time if there may not be an immediate reward in terms of networking?

Based on my experience, it is because of an underlying passion and desire to give back and to be able to say they made a difference. The volunteer experience at WIT is not for the weak of heart. There is a lot of work that is required to carry off the programs successfully. But if you are like me, when you are committed to and passionate about something, it does not seem like work. In fact, it becomes effortless and a joy. I have been awestruck over the years to see how many women have committed themselves to WIT. These are women who may have had an executive position with a company and yet were willing to sit at a registration desk or stand and direct people where to go. These are women starting out wanting to learn new skills and learn from more seasoned professionals. These are women who may be in transition and want to stay active by spending their time on something that matters to them. These are women who work a forty-hour week or more and still find time to volunteer with WIT. These are amazing women and without the support of all these hundreds of women, WIT would not even exist today.

So here we are, 18 years later and WIT is going stronger than ever. There have for sure been many stumbling blocks along the way that could have caused WIT to crumble into non-existence or to lose focus. But WIT has overcome them all. Even in times when other organizations or companies have failed to adapt quickly enough to the changing demands of the market, WIT has survived. It's not because it is a greatly capitalized company or that it has had great leadership (which it certainly has) that has allowed it to endure. But rather it is the underlying desire and passion of its volunteers that have broken down the barriers that stood in the way of fulfilling it mission. And instead of holding on to what is familiar and what worked in the past, it is their passion and desire to succeed and to make a difference in the lives of girls and women in technology that has allowed them to evolve into what WIT is today.

My glass is raised in salute to all these women for what they have taught me and how they have shown me what the true power of passion is.

MARSHA CALFEE – An 18-year veteran of CRM, Marsha has held several senior management positions with a variety of CRM software companies in Atlanta. Currently Marsha is a principal of Strategic Consulting Services (SCS), a CRM and marketing consulting firm. As principal in this firm, Marsha is responsible for working with customers to help them in the development and execution of the CRM and marketing strategies. Prior to SCS, Marsha was the Director, Product Marketing for Genesys Telecommunications where she was responsible for the development of messaging and branding for their Operational Performance Management suite of products. Other positions held by Marsha include roles in Product Management for Infor CRM Epiphany, Director of CRM for NetBank, and Vice President of Product Management and Development at Firstwave Technologies. Rounding out Marsha's extensive CRM background is her 10 years of experience as the President and Founder of VisionLink, a CRM consulting practice.

Marsha has also been active in various volunteer roles including serving on the board of WIT, WIT President, National Vice President of Membership for the CRM Association, board member of Atlanta Unity Church, and board member of the Atlanta's Arts and Business Council. She is also affiliated with the American Marketing Association and TAG.

Marsha is a graduate of Brigham Young University with a degree in Psychology and Education and resides in Lawrenceville, Georgia.

Marsha is a CRM and Marketing consultant with a focus of the development of strategy, demand generation programs, marketing communications and competitive analysis. With over 18 years of CRM and marketing experience, Marsha helps organizations translate market demands into successful CRM and marketing strategies and then assists them with the implementation of results-based programs including demand generation and marketing communication.

Never Underestimate the Power of Your Professional Relationships

by Nancy D'Amico

Senior Vice President & CIO
LeasePlan, USA

ATLANTA, GEORGIA

Never Underestimate the Power of Your Professional Relationships

In 1983, I started my career in technology in a small Ohio town with a company called NCR. Over the last 27 years, I have worked for only three great companies: NCR, Delta Air Lines and LeasePlan.

About five years ago, Delta Air Lines decided to consider outsourcing all of Information Technology. I was a Director at the time and I knew that this level of management would likely not have a position under the new organization arrangement. So I decided to explore other opportunities. I updated my resume and reached out to recruiting companies. As a result of my outreach, a Vice President level job specification was presented to me. The position was a perfect fit for one of my Director colleagues who was also considering other opportunities. I shared the information with her and she decided to take the next step. She contacted the recruiter, completed the interview process and got the job in Memphis, Tennessee. We kept in touch through an occasional email, but did not see each other on a regular basis.

About two years later, the same colleague received from a recruiter a job specification for a position that she thought was perfect for me. She reached out to me about it and I decided to talk with the recruiter. It took five months and six rounds of interviews to make sure that the position was a "win-win" for me and for the company. Finally, in September of 2008, I took the position and joined LeasePlan as Senior Vice President and CIO.

This was one of the best decisions of my career. As CIO in this medium sized company, I have the opportunity to make a positive contribution to the business every day. My commute is shorter, so I have more time to spend with family and friends. And, over the last two years, I have had the pleasure of working with great people who live LeasePlan's four values every day: Passion, Expertise, Commitment and Respect.

My experience is proof positive that you should never underestimate the power of your professional relationships.

NANCY D'AMICO – As Senior Vice President and Chief Information Officer, Nancy D'Amico is responsible for all of LeasePlan USA's project management, information and communications technology functions. She also serves as a member of the Executive Management Team.

Nancy's 27 years of experience includes 12 years at Delta Air lines and 13 years with NCR Corporation. Her background includes leadership positions in software development, systems engineering, database management, quality assurance, data center operations and program management.

She holds a Bachelor of Science degree in Information and Computer Science from the University of Pittsburgh and an MBA from Roberto C. Goizueta Business School at Emory University.

Nancy is a contributing author in the book *Data Center Insights – A Compilation of Leadership Thoughts, Views and Observations*, published by Executive Alliance in 2010.

LEASEPLAN USA, a subsidiary of LeasePlan Corp. N.V., is a global leader in vehicle leasing and fleet management solutions. The company, which manages approximately 1.3 million vehicles worldwide and has a consolidated lease portfolio of almost EUR 14 billion, offers clients customized plans for total fleet cost reduction through its technologically advanced products and dedication to customer service.

The Importance of Mentors and Friends

by Bonnie Bajorek Daneker

Founder & President, BD Donaldson Publishing, Inc.
Author, *The Compassionate Caregiver Series®*

ATLANTA, GEORGIA

The Importance of Mentors and Friends

When I joined MCI, its workforce of 25,000 people was larger than the population of my hometown and exponentially more productive. I joined as a "temp" looking for a "real" job, which I laugh at now: working for that company immersed me in the demanding world of technology and led me in a direction lasting nearly a decade.

My manager, Laurel King, saw my potential and hired me as an employee. She began pushing exciting projects my way. Her idea to create an internal MCI Company Store was one of my first business planning experiences; its success has become a standard to which I compare my other enterprises. Laurel also extended other opportunities for advancement to me, within and outside of her group – epitomizing mentorship. When promoted to business development in the Alliances and Affinities Group, I assisted with the Stentor Alliance and the Banamex Agreement, witnessing history-making changes as long distance calls became available between Canada, the United States and Mexico. Our dedicated team understood the commercial and political impact of reliable telecommunications, and we often joked that we "bled orange" – MCI's corporate color.

Moving forward from MCI, I met another mentor and friend, Woody Cannon, whose seasoned perspective from years with Motorola and other multinationals encouraged me to continue to think globally. Following his recommendation, I attended my first CeBIT show in Hannover, Germany. The largest digital IT and communications trade show in the world, CeBIT featured 26 *buildings* crammed full of innovation to explore. Clearly, this worldwide phenomenon was not going away, and I wanted to be part of it. Under Woody's wise leadership, I honed my skills to as a translator between engineer and customer, negotiating the relationship between business and technical specs. These cherished skills I carry with me today.

While at this company, I experienced the magic of microwave radio transmission, as we brought telephone service to remote parts of China without laying land lines (the standard at the time). One of the country's stumbling blocks in establishing their communications was that when the copper lines were ambitiously laid, they were usually stolen – dug up at some point in the night and headed to the black market by morning. Cellular technology had leapfrogged land-based, line-based telecommunications! What an interesting time; innovation was moving as quickly as CDPD (cellular digital packet data). But I knew it was the right moment to leave when the sale of the company was inevitable.

At the suggestion of Katie Wolter, a friend from MCI, I applied for a job as a project coordinator on one of the largest tech projects in the southeast at the time: A strategic objective for SunTrust bank was to standardize and upgrade IT operations in five states, over 300 locations. The hiring manager asked me "You're not an engineer or a programmer. Why do you want this role?" I convinced him that my interest in computer-telephony integration, my understanding of technical specs, plus my MCI-honed organization and planning skills were natural fits for the project management job. He hired me. We successfully scoped the project, and, at its completion, over 900 servers and 20,000 PCS were installed.

Shortly thereafter, Karen See introduced me to the Technology Association of Georgia and Women in Technology. After being one of only a handful of women on my prior project, I had wondered if women were interested in these fields. I got my answer as I entered the ballroom housing WIT Connect – there were *hundreds* of attendees. The Women in Technology represented many industries and occupations, universally smart and savvy: they were trying to propel technology while making a difference for their peers and for future generations. It was an incredible networking opportunity.

Through WIT, I connected to MATRIX Resources, contracting with Emily Ping and Shawn Donnell in project and product management roles. My career had progressively grown more technical. In one of my last contracts with them, our team managed certification testing for Y2K Compliance. My client, CheckFree, handled the majority of financial transaction processing then; we felt as though the trust of the banking public was in our hands, and we didn't let them down. It's easier to work all night (as we did on December 31, 1999) when you're with people you like and respect.

Months later, my father was diagnosed with cancer and my career direction took a radical turn. Though I'd always had an interest in medicine, helping him became my priority. Resources to help me were limited: the Internet was so young and books to help caregivers of cancer patients were so few. I found mentorship and comradeship in other caregivers as we waited in hospital lobbies and doctors' offices. With their wisdom and support from professionals who would become part of my Medical Advisory Board, I wrote and published *The Compassionate Caregiver's Guide to Caring for Someone with Cancer*. Later, I founded my own publishing company to reach caregivers faster, at their access points. Continuing to write, I covered heady subjects: *Understanding the Cancer Diagnosis*, *Handbook on Hospice and Palliative Care*, *A Cancer Patient's End of Life*, and *The Journey of Grief*. I learned one lesson very quickly: although you may be a competent individual contributor, you cannot do it all yourself.

Technology re-entered my life through a new road: national conferences in cancer research. I was fortunate to attend these as a guest of my medical advisors, and saw what a critical role technology plays in scientific discovery. Workstations and networks have supplanted beakers and burners, with a tremendous dependency on information access, storage, and security.

While promoting my books and spending more time as a grief counselor than business executive, I realized that I missed technology, and I missed the "business of doing business." It was time for a change. Remembering how fast innovation happens in some industries, I knew I'd need more formal training to compete. At Emory

University, I was fortunate to do a Directed Study with Charlie Goetz within my MBA program. The project was to commercialize a translational research program of Saint Joseph's Hospital and Georgia Tech, pooling talent from multiple departments including surgery, medical oncology, interventional radiology, biology, physics, bioinformatics, mathematics, and nanotechnology. Even after receiving my diploma (early 2010), we're still working to bring those efforts into the regular practice of medicine. My exposure to this revealed a natural marriage between technology and medicine, especially in the medical device, healthcare information exchange (HIE), and medical intranet spaces.

For a few years, I had been away from WIT, involving myself in healthcare-related initiatives. Through Emory, I found another mentor and friend, Romy Heylen, who reconnected me with WIT and introduced me to WIT BiblioBabes. Being involved with WIT's community has richly enhanced my view of women's roles in technology and with each other, especially through Sandy Hofmann and Margot King.

I always considered myself a self-starter, but looking back I see the invaluable impact these people have had on my accomplishments, my career path and me. I have to say, the background I developed working in telecom and IT has served me well as the foundation for comprehending more complex systems. But more importantly, my personal network has served me as the foundation for growth and development.

The message is simple: no one succeeds alone. Surround yourself with strong people: True mentors and friends challenge you. They lead you to surprising opportunities that can magnify your efforts. They point out things you don't want to hear but need to hear. They're there – maybe intermittently – to celebrate or share. Keeping in touch takes effort, but it's worthwhile, and something we all should spend more time doing. Mentors and friends are important because they sculpt you to become a leader, enabling you to be a friend and mentor to others.

BONNIE BAJOREK DANEKER – As President of BD Donaldson Publishing, Inc., Bonnie Bajorek Daneker oversees the strategic direction of the company as the team writes, produces, and distributes caregiving materials. She is a past member of the Board of Directors for the Cancer Survivors' Network at Saint Joseph's Hospital and Decatur Children's Theatre.

Bonnie's background features over 10 years of consulting, launching three successful startups and publishing multiple books and articles. Her experience includes product and project management, marketing and business development, program management and business communications.

Bonnie holds a Bachelor of Arts degree in Journalism from The Ohio State University and an MBA in Strategic Planning and Entrepreneurship from the Roberto C. Goizueta Business School at Emory University.

BD DONALDSON PUBLISHING, INC. creates and distributes healthcare-related information to caregivers and entities that support caregivers. Woman-owned since 2004, the company's mission is to reduce the negative impacts of cancer and other life-threatening illnesses by teaching non-medical caregivers to effectively manage common day-to-day situations, which change as the disease and treatment progress. With a special interest in research and technology utilization, BD Donaldson Publishing, Inc. provides tools and support for your caregiving journey.

What Should Leadership Look Like?

by Cigdem Delano

Chief Information Officer
Morehouse School of Medicine

ATLANTA, GEORGIA

What Should Leadership Look Like?

IN 1997, I WAS RESPONSIBLE for a $15M customer account. I was leading a two-year systems integration project with a team spread across two countries. The project was running so well, that I was considered for a similar engagement in Sydney, Australia. An engagement executive came from Sydney to assess my qualifications by interviewing my client, my team, and me. Shortly after we met, I offered to buy him coffee. He casually stated women didn't buy coffee for men and that he would buy my coffee. Recovering quickly from the shock of his response, I calmly expressed my disagreement with his comment and bought him a cup of coffee. The next day, my client informed me that during the interview the Australian engagement executive expressed his surprise that I was the leader running the project. He told my client that he expected me to be overbearing and intimidating based on the success of the project. Similar to his comment about coffee, I believe this was expressed as a casual and frank comment. By the time he left, we had established a positive and respectful relationship.

This incident has stuck with me since. I believe this was a reflection of what many expect successful leaders to look like. Although, there has been improvement over the years, I believe this perspective may still exist to some degree.

I believe being a woman influences my leadership style. Some women may feel that to be successful, one must adopt more masculine behavior. Although the pressures of the work environment and perceptions of others may at times cause doubt and lead to more masculine leadership styles, it is important to stay true to who we are as women, adjust for improvement without compromising one's values, and to keep one's eye on the ball.

My core belief system was brought to a conscious level with my first job. Straight out of college, I didn't understand why IBM felt the need to state that their first basic belief was respect for the individual. Over time and experience in the business world, I began to understand the importance of stating what most would expect to be the obvious.

The Challenge – Creating an Environment that Promotes Success

The characteristics of an environment that promotes success are non-threatening, encouraging, rewarding, challenging, and excellence driven. The goal is to produce successful results through everyone giving his/her best effort, contributing toward the accomplishment of the organization's goals, realizing continuous improvements, and growing one's skills and capabilities.

Three essential ingredients needed for this environment are *trusting relationships*, *nurturing environment*, and *stability*. These attributes are natural for most women, but may be underutilized in the work environment.

Trusting Relationships: Having gone to an engineering university and being trained to strengthen my analytical skills, it took some time for me to recognize the importance of relationships at work. A few months into my first job, my manager told me I needed to get out of my office more. He said it was important that I walk around and talk to others and not work at my desk all the time. I was confused. This was contrary to what I understood I should do to be successful. Although I heeded his advice to some degree, it wasn't until years later that I understood the full significance of his guidance and how crucial this was for a successful career.

To be clear, work has to get done. But to successfully accomplish one's work, it is essential to effectively communicate with others, get buy-in and support, obtain needed resources, and to understand and resolve the non-technical things that can get in the way of progress. These can be more easily accomplished with trusted relationships that are developed over time through respectful, sincere, and considerate interactions in work and non-work settings.

These relationships should extend throughout the organization. It is important to build relationships at all levels and have a credible reputation throughout. As a leader, trust is the foundation upon which everything is built. If a team trusts its leader's intentions and capabilities and trusts that they will be treated fairly and respectfully, they will follow the leader's direction. They will warn her of potential danger, help course-correct when needed, and tell her when they have failed and what is being done to avoid recurrence of the failure.

It is important to build trusted external relationships as well. Long-term success often depends on clients, vendors, partners, and colleagues inside and outside one's corporation.

My basic learning during the first part of my career was that doing a great job alone might not always lead to success and that with the right kind of relationships; one could perform his job even better. As one's career advances, relationship skills become a more crucial element of the job. As a CIO, my success is defined not only by the success of my team, but by my relationships with my customers, peers, boss, and business partners and their view of my team's contribution to their success.

Nurturing Environment: It is important for individuals and organizations to continuously grow. This requires an environment that values learning from failures.

Increasingly, an organization will take on more complex and risky projects. Inevitably, some will lead to failures that cause business impact, some quite substantial and serious. Prompt and appropriate action from leadership to assure accountability is essential during these times. Additionally, it is important to recognize each failure or "miss" as an opportunity to learn and grow. The goal is progress. If mistakes are not repeated, chronic problems are being resolved, individuals are learning, and the team is striving to deliver beyond expectations, it only makes sense to continue to nurture, support, and express appreciation. If there are no failures, the team is most likely taking the easy route and the business is probably at a stand still or falling behind.

Stability: In work environments abound with deadlines, competing priorities, and problems of various sizes and shapes in a sea of emotions and egos, it is easy to take one's eye off the ball and flow with the chaos to nowhere. This is when calm actions, reassuring communication, and reminders help refocus the team. Whether it is brushing the dust off someone's clothes after a fall, helping someone deal with another's fury, escalating an issue that is keeping a team from moving forward, or blocking verbal blows to the organization, these are essential roles for leaders. Often, it is just as important to step back, watch, and step in only if absolutely needed. During these situations, the team is watching and listening. Leaders must be role models for their teams when it comes to not getting wrapped up in emotions, not focusing on things that are outside their sphere of control, or finding someone to blame.

Failures can be painful for the leader and it is very likely that the failure could have been avoided. If the team is giving their all, they are learning and making clear improvements with each effort, and they are making quantifiable progress toward business objectives, without doubt, the team is headed for success. During times when failures occur, leaders should strive for calm and continue to encourage the team.

In closing, similar to most things in life, these are common sense ideas. However, during a crisis, common sense may be hard to remember due to outside pressures. It is during difficult times that I remind myself of the gentleman from Australia and what he initially thought that a leader should look and behave like. I strive to continue this dichotomy, as my goal is to lead teams that have the courage to grow and achieve extraordinary success rather than teams that achieve average levels of success because they are afraid to fail.

CIGDEM DELANO is the Chief Information Officer of Morehouse School of Medicine (MSM), a private, historically black institution with a largely public mission. She is responsible for developing and implementing an IT strategy for the school's academic, research, clinical, and administrative departments.

Previously, Ms. Delano served as the Deputy Executive Director of the Georgia Technology Authority (GTA), an organization responsible for governing and overseeing the effective use of IT in state government. Prior to GTA, Ms. Delano was with IBM for over 15 years, where her responsibilities ranged from telecommunications and data center operations to quality, project and account management.

She was a recipient of the 2006 CIO Ones to Watch award from CIO magazine. Ms. Delano was a finalist for Women in Technology's 2006 *Women of the Year in Technology Award.* She was selected one of 25 Influential Women in Project Management by the Project Management Institute. And she is a finalist in the Georgia CIO Leadership Association's 2010 *Georgia* CIO *of the Year Awards.*

Ms. Delano is on the boards of Hands on Atlanta and the American Turkish Friendship Council. Past responsibilities include Cobb County Industry Advisory Board, and TAG's Business and Technology Advisory Board.

Ms. Delano holds a Bachelor of Science degree in Information and Computer Science from the Georgia Institute of Technology.

MOREHOUSE SCHOOL OF MEDICINE (MSM) was founded in 1975 as a two-year Medical Education Program at Morehouse College. In 1981, MSM became an independently chartered institution and the first medical school established as a Historically Black College and University in the 20th century. MSM is among the nation's leading educators of primary care physicians. Our faculty and alumni are noted in their fields for excellence in teaching, research, and public policy, and are known in the community for exceptional, culturally appropriate patient care.

My Heroes

by Tricia Dempsey

Chief Executive Officer
Agile

ATLANTA, GEORGIA

My Heroes

When I opened my company in 2003, I vowed to spend my first year developing advocates by building a great network of technology leaders. At least three times a week, I would venture out to networking lunches or evening events in the active Atlanta technology community. Julie Purdie with TechLinks, a local organization that connected Georgia's buyers and sellers of technology products and services, introduced me to Women in Technology (WIT). Julie thought I would find what I was looking for at Women in Technology – a great network of women who were supportive of me, my own business and technology clients who were active in the organization.

After attending my first breakfast meeting, I could see why Julie felt so strongly about the organization. The President of WIT at that time, Kasie Scott Palmer, was a dynamic, confident communicator who got me instantly excited about what WIT had to offer. I was hooked … WIT was for me! Soon after at a TechLinks event, I introduced myself to Kasie and told her that I spent the last year seeking an organization to dedicate my time, money and resources to and WIT was it. Seven years later, I had the opportunity to serve as the Program Manager of Events and work side by side with Kasie who was the co-chair of the *Women of the Year in Technology Awards*. I reminded her of our encounter at the Ashford Club and that she was the reason I was dedicated to WIT.

My first introduction to WIT was as a volunteer for the nomination committee for the *Women of the Year in Technology Awards*. That year, Pam Pure from McKesson Technology won the Enterprise Category Award and I sat in the audience like a proud mama. I had worked hard to get McKesson to nominate Pam and after talking to multiple marketing executives, her executive assistant and her chief of staff, McKesson agreed to proceed with the nomination. I remember Pam's acceptance speech – she gave full credit to every man and woman in her organization for the recognition she received. I saw her after the speech and we shared a hug. She told me she had just called her kids to let them know she had won, and that they were psyched with excitement for her. I thought how cool ... here is a lady who testified on Capitol Hill (that's Washington, DC) in front of Congress earlier that year about the importance of electronic medical records, who was President of a Fortune 50 company, and hero to her kids. She was inspiring – I wanted to be like her.

The next year, I chaired the nomination committee and was part of the small business interviewing team where I met Wendy Reed, CEO of Infomentis, a global sales training company. Wendy was truly dynamic and I instantly felt a kindred spirit with her. She was feisty, not shy to share her opinion, and she was where I wanted to be – a $10 million dollar fast growing organization, whose accomplishments were recognized nationally. Her start-up story was inspiring – similar to mine ... two people with an idea that would put her company on the map. She won that year in the Emerging Business Category and I was smitten. Wendy Reed was my hero. I asked Wendy to lunch and we talked for hours. About growth ... the ups and downs of business ownership ... how to get the most of out of our people, protect our brand, grow a sustainable business, and how *not* to have CEO Syndrome. To this day, we get together once a year to share ideas, talk about how to take our businesses to the next level and share our stories.

Over the next few years, I moved up the volunteer chain and was chair of WIT's *Women of the Year in Technology Awards*. That year, I met Marie Mouchet, CIO of Southern Nuclear. I was part of the team that interviewed the Enterprise nominees that year and Marie stood out. Like me, she was a school teacher out of college. She entered Southern Company and climbed her way up the ladder. Recognition came to her – not by choice ... Marie was not one to seek recognition ... just the opposite, she always provided it to her own people. Marie was known as a "change agent" at Southern – this had become her personal brand. One of the things that stood out that year was the newsletter her team published each year recognizing every employee's anniversary, promotion and each departments' impact on the business. When she walked out of her interview I told the interviewing team jokingly that I would leave my husband for Marie Mouchet. She was amazing! At a minimum, I wanted to spend time with her, learn from her and soak up her wisdom like a sponge. After the event she graciously agreed to have lunch with me and for me, it was one of those lunches where we could have talked for hours. As I look back, she was one of the most down to earth, amazingly talented, people motivators I have ever met in my professional career.

In 2009, I called Bank of America to nominate Amy Brady. I had met Amy through business and knew she was special. I suggested that WIT pursue her to be a speaker at the monthly WIT breakfast meetings and she agreed to come. The crowd that morning listened intently to Amy's story – she started in the branch at the bank and had made her way through the entire business before moving into the technology division at Bank of America. Initially a fish out of water, Amy leaned on others to help her understand the technology arena, and in turn, she educated them about what it was like to be in the business, a user of technology, and someone who wanted to provide solutions to the bank's customers. Amy's message revolved around taking risks, not being afraid to do something you had never done before, and she used a fun David Letterman, "Top Ten Lessons of my Career" approach to share insights into her journey at Bank of America. That year, Amy took home the honor of the *Women of the Year in Technology* in the Enterprise Category. During her acceptance speech she thanked me for nominating her. Her two daughters and husband were there that night and came up on stage to hug their mom … their hero and mine!

My tenure with WIT is like a rich tapestry of women leaders like Kasie, Pam, Wendy, Marie and Amy. These women were first and foremost, moms and wives who raised successful kids – a job most women know is very difficult to do while working full time in a leadership role. These women were secondly, great business minds – all of them had climbed the ladder by doing three things: 1) taking risks, 2) being willing to take on new challenges and 3) inspiring others to be their very best. Each and every day I draw on their stories and their strength as I attempt to lead a business that brings value to its clients, employees and the communities we serve. This – most of all – is what I have learned most from the Women in Technology organization. Today, I am the Secretary of the WIT Board of Directors and Program Manager of Outreach. Each day I proudly tell the WIT story about the amazing women I pay homage to each and every day.

AGILE is an IT staffing and consulting company that helps technology leaders speed their time to top talent.

About Tricia Dempsey – an editor's perspective

What Tricia's story "My Heroes" fails to reveal is that she is "my hero" to women who face the challenge of cancer. As a breast cancer survivor, Tricia has shared her experiences on numerous occasions and throughout the community. Her personal strength, her bubbling enthusiasm in life, and her courage provide an enduring model. Tricia is a WIT Hero and here is her personal journey:

Life With and After Breast Cancer … 5 Lessons of a Survivor

"I am 99% sure you have breast cancer. We will send your biopsy to pathology, but if it is negative for breast cancer, we will biopsy again … because I am 99% sure you have breast cancer." These words took my breath away! After two false negative mammograms and ultrasounds, I was sure that my visit would re-confirm the first two results. Unfortunately, they did not. After I received my biopsy results it was confirmed … I had breast cancer.

The business side of me immediately went into creating my strategy and initiatives to "manage" this disease. The daughter side of me just wanted my mom and dad to make it all better. The mother side of me wanted to be sure my husband could put Catherine's hair in ponytails and knew how to give butterfly kisses and the wife side of me felt very sad that I wouldn't get to grow old with my true partner in life, my husband Jeff. Once I pulled myself together, I learned several important lessons about life *with* and *after* breast cancer. Here are five things I learned along the journey:

LESSON #1:
Focus on surviving … not dying

I read voraciously about breast cancer once diagnosed. Facts and figures … depending upon your outlook on life … were encouraging. Almost 75% of men and women survive breast cancer, diagnosis and death rates are on the decline, new and improved drugs are extending lives and with strong support and faith, I was going to make it! My doctor knew it too – she told me that the next year was going to stink, but I was going to survive breast cancer!

LESSON #2:
Take the time to build a great support team

I decided to invest the time to get multiple opinions once diagnosed. I had to select an oncologist, surgical oncologist, and plastic surgeon. The best selections for me were doctors with a combination of credentials, aggressive approaches, good bedside manner, and geographic location. I lined up my chemo team – one support person who could go with me to each chemo treatment and others who could take care of my daughter and husband, cook for my family and keep my house in order the weeks I had chemo. I had to get past asking for help and realize that people *wanted* to do something so I should let them.

LESSON #3:
Go aggressive

One thing I never wanted to regret was that I didn't "go for it" to eradicate my breast cancer. My oncologist, Dr. Janice Galleshaw with Georgia Cancer Specialists educated me in our first visit that cancer is a cellular disease. Even though my lumps would disappear after several rounds of chemo, I never forgot that it lived at the cellular level. I always opted for the most aggressive treatment. I never wanted to look back and wish I could have, should have, would have.

LESSON #4:
Acknowledge my breasts were not perfect to begin with ... but they could be better

The night before my double mastectomy I looked at my breasts for a long period of time and finally called my husband in to continue the critique. The left was larger than the right, one sagged more than the other after six months of breast feeding my daughter, one nipple faced slightly toward the right and so on and so on. After reconstruction my breasts actually look better ... youthful, more symmetrical and not to mention larger ... thanks to Dr. Randall Rudderman.

LESSON #5:
There is life after breast cancer ... and it is great!

I now have a 10-year-old daughter and a husband of 15 years who make me thankful every day that I survived this disease. I started a business where I spend time each day with a team of people I truly enjoy and respect, and I do business with the best clients in Atlanta. I love spending time with my parents and brothers and sisters and try to leave very few things unsaid. I suck the life out of each and every day and focus on what I *can* control to make a difference in my world.

Six months of chemo, a radical double mastectomy, seven surgeries and five years of hormonal therapy later I am elated to say that I reached my seventh year as a survivor. My deep faith became a great source of strength and my best hiding place during that difficult time. In the words attributed to Oprah Winfrey … I believe that "every single event in life happens as an opportunity to choose love over fear."

Today, I would encourage every woman diagnosed with breast cancer to choose love and draw strength by standing on the shoulders of friends, family and faith!

Blessed Time and Time Again

by Josette Fleszar

President/CEO
Jigsaw Meeting

GAINESVILLE, GEORGIA

Blessed Time and Time Again

LIFE IS SHORT. I know this because I have two great parents that I get the pleasure of having them live with us. They are both in their eighties, and when I ask them about how aging feels and what they have seen and accomplished in their lives, they both say it is hard to believe the age they are and how fast the time has past.

Every day I learn more about the world in which they grew up and can relate better to the one in which is being developed for the future generation. My parents' lessons and wisdom are priceless. There is so much to learn about growing and achieving from the past generation. I would like to share some amazing moments about my life, the blessings that I count every day, and some of the lessons that I have learned thus far.

I come from a rich family, but not the kind you might think. We did not have money, but Mom and Dad somehow always made ends meet. We were rich in these ways: we had love, respect, honor, hugs and kisses, trust, values, morals, play time, and each other. We were a solid family with a lot of diversity. Family time and being together was not an option, it was required! This time was relished. Every night we came together as a family for dinner. No one went their own way at dinnertime – you didn't eat what or when you wanted either. From this practice I learned a critical life lesson: make time for each other and provide an opportunity for each person to discuss their day and challenges faced. As a family we learned to love and understand who we really were. Now I understand how this practice made us stronger as a family. This simple ritual still exists in our home and reflects the foundation of riches with which we were raised. Here I am blessed.

I started my career when I was only fourteen years old. Remember, we were not a family with money and since I wanted a Porsche by the time I was sixteen, working seemed necessary. I had the opportunity to start working after school as a file clerk for a healthcare company. The president of the company was my mentor. She was also my catechism teacher. She saw that I had a desire and drive to succeed. I wanted to be more than just a kid who could not afford to get a new pair of jeans. I worked hard. I soaked up everything that I could from my mentor and anyone else around me who could teach me something I did not know. I learned. I listened. I made mistakes. Through it all I was always grateful for the people who shared knowledge with me, provided opportunities to me, and invested their trust in me. These people started my career by simply believing in me! Here I am blessed.

Over the summers and by the age of sixteen, my mentor taught me the skills of meeting with people and negotiating deals. With my very own money I had purchased a 1968 VW. The Porsche did not materialize, but I was happy. My job provided me with the opportunity to travel across the US to meet with CFOs and to review project results. These experiences were amazing and life altering. I knew I needed to be the best in whatever I did. I tried everything I could, listened consistently and of course I made mistakes! I had wonderful opportunities to learn.

My work gave me the opportunity to travel. Of course I had previously traveled with my family. Ever year we would pack up the car and drive straight through from Florida to New York to visit family. But imagine being able to get on a plane, stay at a hotel, rent a car and drive to locations you had never even heard! It was the most exciting gift a teenage girl could hope to receive. This opportunity made me independent, stronger, and confident. I am grateful for such a rare experience. Here I am blessed.

Like my family, I was educated in a public school. I took some college classes at a local Community College, but had experienced the taste of business, travel, people and a paycheck all of which seemed much more exciting than going to college did. My education was hands on in the real world. My education became learning lessons from experienced people who were willing to teach me and who were able to instill in me exceptional business values. Here I am blessed.

I continued traveling with this company until I was twenty-one. My visions for greater things began to take shape. I loved my work, my friends, and who I was becoming, but I wanted more. I wanted to change the world! I wanted to make the business bigger and better. I wanted to be the best!

As luck would have it, my dream of bigger, better and being the best came my way. While in New Orleans at Mardi Gras, (which is a whole other article) I received a call from a large company. Someone had told them that I was the answer they were looking for. They wanted to meet with me right away.

Hearing my mother's always encouraging words of "Go Do It", I jumped at the chance. I was afraid of what might happen; afraid of leaving the people who had taught me so much and who I loved. But I was ready and I wanted more! So, yes, "they made me an offer I couldn't refuse" which was probably about $35K at that time. I was so happy and knew I was climbing the ladder that most people with my background would not get the chance to climb. I felt so lucky and fortunate that this was happening to me. I know now that hard work, dedication, a strong foundation, and driving desire were huge contributors to my success. Here I am blessed.

There were important lessons along the way. I remember an important nugget that my Father once gave me when I was heading out to do a presentation to the Government. I was going to be meeting with Colonels and Majors of the Armed Forces and I was nervous about the meeting. At the Sunday family dinner table, my Father said to me, "just remember: we are all the same. We each get up in the morning and put our pants on the same way. We brush our teeth the same way. None are better than the other. We are all equal." I remember those words quite a lot as I face certain meetings or obstacles. We are all in this together. Working together there are no limits to what we can do. By the way, we won the deal! Here I am blessed.

I made a lot of money for that company and many others along the way. I continued to grow in knowledge, as well growing financially and emotionally. I started to encounter really smart people who seemed threatened by me. It seemed like some people were trying to keep me down. Some of these new bosses, who had education certificates hanging on their wall, began to dilute my efforts and minimize the impacts of my work and results. They reminded me that I did not have a college degree. This troubled me, but I was uncertain what to do. Over the course of my career, I had gained a wealth of knowledge, love, teachings, and life experiences that were much more than a certificate. I didn't understand why some people were trying to squash my dreams of making a difference? I discovered that not all people can appreciate each other and others did not have the foundation of family, love, and integrity to rely on. Therefore, their mode of operation was to disrespect others. They were threatened by the good that came from someone like me. This was a powerful lesson that took me longer to realize than I would have liked. I am glad I did. Here I am blessed.

So there I was – I had learned so much, had so much more to give and I was unstoppable! I kept coming back to that desire to follow my feelings and make my dreams happen! I put all the chips on the table: I knew my business, I knew my constituencies, I knew what it took to care for a customer, and I knew a great team of people who I had come to know over the years. This team was the core of making things happen. We were like a family with shared values and, more importantly, we respected and trusted one another implicitly. With all of this in mind, I jumped right in to starting my own business.

Together we started RPM, Receivable Process Management. Tempting as it might have been, we did not go out to our former customers for business. With a foundation of integrity we believed that if they wanted to find us, then they would. We wanted to make our mark on our own terms, through hard work, believing in each other and doing what was right. In four short years, we were awarded the *Atlanta Journal & Constitution's* Pacesetter's Award for 5th Fastest Growing Company and 2nd Fastest Growing Women Owned Business. The winning formula was a great team, knowing people make the difference, and doing the right things by our customers. I sold that company and it eventually became a part of United Healthcare. The dream lives on. Here I am blessed.

Ironically, the travel, which had been quite exciting in my younger years, was becoming more of a burden than a pleasure. Over the course of years, I recognized that being away from my loved ones had reduced my quality of life. At the ripe old age of forty-four, I decided it was time to do something different: start a new business! Jigsaw Meeting is an interactive platform designed with the hopes of bringing a higher quality of life to others. The opportunity to build this exciting new application and connect with people worldwide has been a great experience. Here I am blessed.

In closing, I never did get that Porsche. I could have purchased it, but much more important things always took precedence. I have been incredibly blessed to have loved and been loved. I have traveled to many places around the world; worked with some amazing people; partied like it was 1999; cried through devastating occurrences; and lost cherished people along the way. I have shared with you some tidbits, which I believe one should never take for granted. Your family is a priceless entity. Cherish and love them like it is your last day. Find your spiritual happiness. Remember to thank God for the good in your life. Make a difference in other people's lives, it will come back to you tenfold and is one of the most rewarding feelings you will ever experience. Face the things that make you scared the most, you will find confidence and courage that is invaluable. Make mistakes and learn from them, look at the positive. Work hard and follow your dreams. Believe in yourself and know that you have what it takes to be the person you want to be. Make it happen for you and you can help others along the way.

Find in your soul that true thing which you desire and go for it! Life is short. Hold no regrets. Love life and one another.

JOSETTE FLESZAR has over 28 years of hand-on and managerial experience in the healthcare industry. In 2000, she brought her experience, drive and enthusiasm to the marketplace by becoming the founder, President and CEO of RPM Receivable Process Management, LLC. In August 2004, RPM merged with Third Millennium Healthcare Systems, Inc and by 2005 became CareMedic Systems. By December 2009, CareMedic sold its company and the original RPM to United Healthcare. Ms. Fleszar has received numerous awards including being recognized as one of Atlanta's Top 50 Entrepreneur's in 2004 by *Catalyst Magazine*. The *Atlanta Business Chronicle* recognized her original company, RPM as Atlanta's 5th fastest growing private company in 2004, the Pacesetter's award, as well as being awarded The 2nd Fastest Women Owned Business.

Recently, Josette has channeled her passion for communication and bringing people together and has created a new company Jigsaw Meeting. This latest technology is being utilized locally and globally to connect people together on a daily basis. The application has a specific focus for education, corporate training and the healthcare market.

JIGSAW MEETING is an online corporate training and education delivery platform that works with online learning curriculums and learning management systems. JSM is the bridge between asynchronous education and live interaction between student and instructor.

Respect

by Vicki Gamble

Sourcing, Vendor & Contract Management
Information Technology
Southern Company

ATLANTA, GEORGIA

Respect

QUITE EARLY IN MY CAREER (approximately four years into it if you don't count my co-op time), I was in a meeting and behaved in a way that I can frown upon now being the seasoned career woman I am today. Here was the setting: three others, and me all three much older, more experienced and at much higher levels. The presenter of the information (female, by the way) didn't have all the facts, didn't really bring strong conclusions, and wasn't super polished. I made sure she knew what I thought … during the meeting … with her superiors present. Either my misbehavior was unnoticed by the other two participants (men, by the way – and these gender distinctions become important later) or acceptable because I not only didn't receive any parental-type "looks," I got nods of agreement from the men for every barb I threw. The meeting ends, participants start filing out, I'm feeling pretty good about being so much cleverer than the presenter, and she holds me back.

"Would you mind meeting with me for a few minutes?"

Of course, I mind you idiot. I've got things to do. "Sure."

My "sure" came with an eye roll, which I hid, from her and a sigh I didn't. She proceeded to let me know that she didn't appreciate how I had treated her during the meeting. She understood the temptation to come across as bright and on top of things with the "big guys" in the room. She was disappointed in me. She thought I was smart enough to know that succeeding didn't have to be at the expense of another. She told me, "You don't *have* to respect me. You *do* have to show respect."

Don't misunderstand me. I wasn't a horrible, unfeeling wretch. I fretted over my mistakes, apologized when necessary. The thing was, I wouldn't have given the meeting incident a second thought if I had not been lectured to. I'm just not as sensitive as some. Not a bad thing because it works both ways. While I can be harsh, I don't get my feelings hurt easily.

Truth be told, I didn't get a lot from that sermon – at least not immediately. Sure, I felt bad but I have to process things awhile. After some time – years – I decided she was gracious, diplomatic, and might have even been concerned for me and my future and not just making sure I wasn't a witch to her again.

It's now been over 16 years since I received this gift (yes, that's really how I see it now). I have applied that lesson, to my own behavior, the behaviors of others and as a coaching tool, more than any other single lesson.

"You don't *have* to respect me. You *do* have to show respect."

When I catch myself about to say something disrespectful, I hear it. When I see someone else behave that way (to me or anybody else), I say it. (And it's best to do this in private; it loses something if you call someone out with an audience.) When an employee, a peer, or anyone else for that matter comes to me about how to handle some difficult person, I tell them. The beauty of this learning is how simple it is. It's just a notch above common courtesy, but so much more effective. It makes you a better person. It makes you a person whom others will respect.

Now let me tell you about some collateral wisdom from this incident – and here's where the gender distinctions come into play. I don't know for sure, but I'm almost positive "the presenter" would not have approached me if I had been a man. In our culture, at least back then, she might have been deemed a "demanding woman who destroys men's confidence" (there's a much shorter term for this, by the way) if she had lectured a male, and even more so if that male was not in her chain of command. As for the men in the meeting, if they had found me out of line, then I suspect they more than likely wouldn't have done anything about it – unless another man had been my target. Things have certainly improved for the better – dramatically improved – but in our not too distant past, it truly was a good old boy network. Consider also that there was not a good old girl network. In fact, women were often one another's worst enemies. I don't know – it seemed like there was some unwritten limit to the number of women who could be successful and so everyone was out for herself.

Depending upon where you work, the industry, the part of the country, your current position, etc. there are many factors that influence this whole male/female environment. I contend that it doesn't matter. Demonstrate gender-agnostic respect. As for the network, it should be gender-agnostic too. And if you do have a bias, have a female one! At a minimum don't work against the females in your world.

"You don't *have* to respect me. You *do* have to show respect."

VICKI GAMBLE – Since beginning her career at Southern Company in 1984 as a cooperative education student in Georgia Power's capital budgeting department, Vicki has developed broad leadership and management skills in various positions and business units. The majority of her career has been in IT, but she also held positions in HR and Georgia Power's customer service organization. Vicki has been in management roles for the past 10 years.

Vicki holds a Bachelor of Science degree in industrial engineering from Georgia Tech. She lives in downtown Atlanta with her husband, Richard Hooker, and son, Jordan.

SOUTHERN COMPANY (NYSE: SO) is a super-regional energy company with 4.3 million customers and more than 42,000 megawatts of electric generating capacity in the Southeast. It is one of the largest producers of electricity in the U.S. Southern Company is the parent firm of Alabama Power, Georgia Power, Gulf Power, Mississippi Power, Southern Power, Southern Nuclear, SouthernLINC Wireless, and Southern Telecom. Southern Company brands are synonymous with excellent customer service, high reliability, and prices that are 15 percent below the national average.

Reflections on Being a Woman in the Technology Industry

by Kelly Gay

CEO
Omnilink

ATLANTA, GEORGIA

Reflections on Being a Woman in the Technology Industry

THERE I WAS, A POOR KID FROM ALBUQUERQUE, NM, having just graduated from Tulane University with a degree in Economics. IBM had come to campus, and ultimately, had offered me a job in the Dallas branch as a marketing representative. At the time, I didn't even understand what a marketing rep was, but I had a great offer from a great company, and hence began my career in the technology industry. I had no idea how lucky I was.

Technology is an industry in which focused, capable, smart women (and I'm sure men) can excel. Technology is about making the world a better place for all of us. It is an optimistic industry. It is at the forefront of leading-edge behavior. Technology looks to the future. But the reason the industry is good for women, and has served me well, is that it is an egalitarian industry. It's all about the best person, most creative idea, and highest contribution. We all know women do well against those bars.

What has worked for me that might be helpful?

Attitude is a critically important differentiator: At the very start of my career, I didn't know much at all about the technology industry or IBM, but I could tell immediately that I took a more positive and optimistic attitude about my ability to contribute to sales than others did. Selling was my job, despite the title of marketing representative. I remember my first manager saying to me, "I love watching you come back from a customer call because you always have good news." It wasn't always good news, believe me. Usually it was no news – just another step in the process of selling something. A person had to fight for success in the market in the '80s.

But my attitude was always positive, upbeat, and one of pulling people up with me. My manager didn't have to spend her limited time trying to convince me to go out there and do my job, which was to win in the market. And she didn't have to talk me into taking on difficult customers or tasks. If I was given a responsibility, then I went after it with the full expectation that I would win. Because of that, I was given disproportionate responsibility. It was easier to give it to me than cajole or convince someone else to take it, and then convince them that they could succeed.

I was in and out of training and direct sales in less than three years, and on to an IBM sales management position. My differentiation early in my career was simply an optimistic, positive, get-the-job-done-no-matter-what attitude. I did get great results, but I'm pretty sure I got the results because I had the attitude, not the other way around.

Figure out what you are good at, something that capitalizes on your personality and strengths, and then focus on contributing in a disproportionately positive way. In sales, and probably most jobs, the last thing a manager wants to have to deal with is someone who doesn't believe in themselves or their company, and drags others down. I consider it weak, taking the easy road, to be a pessimist. And even worse, to be a cynic.

How hard is it to think you are going to fail? How hard is it to fail? Both thinking you are going to fail and failing take no effort whatsoever. Inherent in a pessimistic attitude is the assumption that all those other people in an organization are the ones that can be counted on to get the job done, because the pessimist sure doesn't intend to. How can a career advance with that as its foundation?

It's all about the end result: When I first became the Chairman, CEO and President of KnowledgeStorm, it was a role I had never been in before, and therefore, had no experience base to pull from. I had friends who had experience as Presidents or CEOs, and I sought their advice constantly. But I myself had not walked the road of a CEO of a venture-backed company, needing to raise money, grow aggressively, and ultimately succeed with a favorable exit for the venture investors through the sale of the company to an acquirer.

It is an absolute luxury to know what an end result needs to be with such certainty. And I'm sure it is no surprise that I fully expected to succeed, despite the fact that I had never done it before. I did know how to manage outcomes, or at least attempt to manage outcomes. It takes purposeful, well-thought out actions, played out over a period of time, step-by-step. It could be a thousand-step journey, which just means you have to have a plan to take a thousand steps, starting with the first step.

Yes, it's time-consuming. But if it is worth doing, then it is worth doing with the intention of winning. Why would you do something that will ultimately be a waste of your time? Play to win all the way to the moment that you either win or lose. If you win, great, you got the outcome you expected all along, and your image as a go-to person with a magical ability to succeed is substantiated yet again. If you lose, it can be crushing, debilitating, but it is a moment in time to learn from, instead of a long period of mediocrity brought about by not believing and not planning.

Control the outcome you seek. Do it through preparation and thought. Don't leave an outcome to chance. Play each situation out in your head to the very end. If you can't see getting the result you seek, start over and come up with an approach that will get you that outcome. Do the research; role play conversations with smart people; prepare presentation materials well in advance; and test your approach with someone who can add valuable input. Be over-prepared. Get as much information and data as possible ahead of time, anticipate objections and questions, and be ready with answers. It takes time, but it is worth it. It makes you more credible and helps build a stellar reputation. More importantly, when you are the most prepared person in the room, you will get the result you seek because people will be looking to you for what's next.

What leadership truths have I learned?

There are many different styles of leadership, all of which can be effective. A leader can be authoritative, strategic and inspiring, analytical and data-driven, or empowering and inclusive, to name a few. No matter what the style, a great leader has a genuineness and believability that is undeniable. They are true to who they are, which is important because people can see right through a fraud. Regardless of the approach to leadership, some things need to stand above the style.

Ethics outweigh everything else: As a leader, ethics outweigh everything else. An ethical breach travels more quickly through an organization than almost anything else because people just expect ethical leadership. It's just an unspoken right that employees have. That doesn't mean they always get it, which is why it is such an affront when there is a breach. There is absolutely nothing worth jeopardizing a reputation over. There is no way back from that mistake. Do what is right for the business first and foremost.

Speed is more important than perfection: "Anything worth doing is worth doing poorly, until you can do it well." This expression is sometimes attributed to Zig Ziglar, the motivational speaker, and sometimes to Dave Packard of Hewlett Packard fame. Regardless, it's true. Quick and imperfect trumps slow and perfect every time. Organizations become frozen with no or slow decisions. Morass sets in. There are multiple ways to solve a problem or achieve a goal. Just pick an approach and do it. Correct as you go.

Try to get out of the critical path if you find that processes and actions are being held up at your desk. An organization will only move as fast as you, if you are the bottleneck. While it is often difficult to cede decisions and control to others, the speed of action will be hindered if everyone is waiting on you.

Leadership is a burden, not a privilege: There are two schools of thought regarding the role of leadership. One is that a person has worked hard and done well to earn a leadership position, and they deserve to rest on their accolades and manage from on high. It is a privilege to have earned a leadership position, with all of the ancillary benefits, special rights and advantages that the role has to offer. This is not the camp I sit in. I couldn't find this camp if I was standing right next to it.

The other school of thought is that a person has been asked to step into a leadership position to help pull others up and lead by example. It is about the team, not about the leader. It is a difficult role with lots of responsibility to the team. It is a burden to ensure that the team has been afforded every opportunity to succeed, and has the leadership to help them do so. People deserve the effort that leadership requires. I spend most of my time thinking about or acting upon what I need to do to help others do their job well. Your team derives their strength and desire to succeed from you. You are never done. It is never-ending. It is a burden to be enjoyed.

Change takes work: Very few people welcome or thrive on change. Change does not honor hierarchy. People don't quickly or easily incorporate change because they are told to by someone above them, but because they understand fully the importance and impact of not doing it. And those who have been the most successful in the past have the hardest time embracing change, which can be expected. They were succeeding with the past approach. Of course they will resist a new way of doing things.

There are five stages to accepting change, and the first four are stages of defiance. Be prepared to have to beat the drum multiple times before everyone in an organization has accepted a change and is ready to act upon it. People can't even hear what you are saying the first few times you say it because they are developing a context in which to think about it. Don't let it frustrate you that it takes time. View change as an organizational challenge to be conquered.

There is no such thing as over-communication: You can't over-communicate. There is no such thing. Keeping an organization focused demands communication, and the communication has to come from the leadership. As frustrating as it is to many executives, not everyone hears what they are told the first, second or third time. They get around to it eventually if you get around to communicating it enough times. Who knows why, and it doesn't really matter. Say the same thing via email, in conversations, in meetings, etc. until people start repeating it back to you. You'll know you are done when you quit hearing, "We all just need to get on the same page. I don't think everyone is aligned strategically," or something like that. What that can mean is that the person saying that to you has not yet gotten the message, but everyone else has. So try one more time.

Practice consistency: Consistency is king, especially in interacting with others. Healthy interaction between people takes a lot of time, and is a large part of a leader's job. Interpersonal dynamics are a spectator sport to people in the company. What you do is more interesting to others than you can possibly imagine, and they will watch your every move, comment, and action. Don't give them anything to talk about. A leader's mood should not play a role in whether people can be effective at their job. It shouldn't be a guessing game as to what kind of day people are going to have based upon what kind of mood their boss is in. Comport yourself in the same way, regardless of the situation. You set the tone on behavior, leadership, and interaction.

KELLY GAY is the CEO and President of Omnilink, a top-ranked services company providing advanced location-based solutions for both enterprise and consumer applications. Kelly joined Omnilink in April 2010, and is responsible for the overall strategic direction, growth and management of Omnilink.

Kelly is the past Chairman, CEO and President of KnowledgeStorm, an online media company providing search, lead generation, and marketing services to global technology organizations. Kelly led KnowledgeStorm from start-up to annual sales of $20 million in less than seven years, and from a significant operating loss to profitability. This success earned the company prestigious rankings and awards, including the Inc. 500, the Deloitte Technology Fast 500 and Georgia Fast 50, *BtoB's* Media Power 50 on the Internet, and *Software Magazine's* Software 500. TechTarget, a public media company serving the technology industry, recently acquired KnowledgeStorm.

Prior to joining KnowledgeStorm, Kelly led IBM in the entertainment, publishing, printing, advertising, broadcast, cable and sports markets as Vice President of IBM's North American Media and Entertainment division. Under her leadership, the IBM business unit grew to $1.2 billion in sales, with 18% annual growth over a three-year period.

Kelly serves on the boards of directors of the Bank of Atlanta, 1105 Media, ReachForce, Ashworth College, the Board of Directors Network, and the Georgia Department of Driver Services (DDS). Kelly was appointed by Governor Barnes as the first and founding Chairman of the Board of the Georgia Department of Motor Vehicle Services, and was subsequently re-appointed by Governor Purdue as Chairman of the same organization, now known as DDS. She is a past Chairman of the Technology Association of Georgia (TAG) and a past President of the Board of Directors Network.

She serves the Atlanta technology community through initiatives like the Advanced Technology Development Center CapVenture program. She has previously been appointed to the Governor's Trade Delegation to Israel and the Metro Atlanta Chamber of Commerce's Industries of the Mind Initiative. She has mentored promising female executives for Pathbuilders, and is a member of the Atlanta High Tech CEO Council.

Kelly was recognized by Pathbuilders as a 2009 Inspiria Award winner. In 2007, she was named to the *BtoB Media Business* Who's Who 100 in Business Publishing and *Catalyst's* Top 25 Atlanta Entrepreneurs. Prior to this, Kelly was chosen by *Catalyst* as one of Atlanta's Top 50 Entrepreneurs in 2002, 2003, 2004, and 2005. She was spotlighted in *Atlanta Woman* as a Leader to Watch and

Business to Business as an Atlanta Diva. She was also recognized by the *Atlanta Business Chronicle* in the annual Who's Who in Technology for four consecutive years, and was honored with the Atlanta Women's Foundation Shining Star award for her leadership in the industry and commitment to mentoring women in technology.

Kelly has addressed both industry and client-sponsored events, including Jupiter Media's Online Advertising Forum, the Entrepreneurship Institute's Presidents' Forum, Ad:tech, InfoCommerce, Emory University, Telco-Cable Conference, American Business Media events, MediaOne Convergence Conference, the Georgia Technology Forum, SIIA events, and the MIT Enterprise Forum. Kelly has also been a guest on CNN's *Lou Dobbs Tonight* and the *Georgia Business Report*.

Kelly is a magna cum laude graduate of Newcomb College of Tulane University with a Bachelor of Arts degree in economics.

OMNILINK SYSTEMS is a leading provider of end-to-end LBS (location-based services) for any tracking solution. Pairing its award-winning FocalPoint™ software with hardware, services and networks, Omnilink offers the most accurate, reliable and cost effective platform for powering location-aware mobile devices and applications. Working with tier-one carriers, Fortune 100 companies, leading nonprofits and hundreds of government agencies through its Platform-as-a-Service (PaaS) model, Omnilink helps ensure the safety, security and productivity of people and valuable assets

My Journey with Early WIT

by Shawn Grover

ALPHARETTA, GEORGIA

My Journey with Early WIT

THOUGH I CHOSE TO FOCUS ON OTHER ASPECTS of my life and left the technology community many years ago, my experience with WIT was a time of tremendous growth, both personally and professionally.

I worked for over 15 years in the Atlanta technology community with major computer and telecommunications firms, dealing with many aspects of the explosion of computers, primarily from a technical aspect – computer programming, systems analysis, project management, etc. However, I traveled extensively and so actually spent little time in Atlanta. As a result, networking and community service were just not on my agenda.

In 1992, I was accepted into the Executive MBA Program at Emory University. There were about eight women in my class of 52 students. At the time, I had a career, a husband, and a young son of one and a half years. Managing my time was a top priority! Through this educational experience, I began to take a more systems oriented and broad based approach to both technology businesses and careers.

WIT was in its very early infancy at the time I became involved with the organization. I had been invited to join the board by founder and president, Janet Wyche. Jane was aware of some events based fundraising experience I had obtained along the way and knew I could contribute my skills and experience. WIT was just starting out and at the time, the Business and Technology Alliance (BETA) and the Southeastern Software Association (SSA) were the flourishing professional organizations, filled with many men and few women, and somewhat intimidating (to me at least).

In contrast to those other organizations, the WIT organization was composed of busy women who were juggling careers, family, and community activities. We were all engaged in thinking long and hard on how to improve our careers, help other women improve their careers, *and* bring more balance to our lives. With these needs in mind, we oriented WIT to provide education, professional connectivity, and social action simultaneously – WIT as one-stop-shopping!

The programs began to grow and were fantastic. The WIT Connect event became a major vehicle for connectivity and community service. Our intent was that all profits from WIT Connect would go to charity. Today WIT Connect has raised hundreds of thousands of dollars for the WIT Foundation. Though the efforts during these early days were intense at times, our board meetings and retreats were a blast. In the midst of all the laughter and hard work, creativity soared and relationships were deepened.

In the meantime, my child grew, as did my career, primarily due to the contacts and experience I gained in helping a wonderful group of women make an impact in the community. We grew our organization and our brand. During the time I served as WIT president, WIT became one of the three key organizations to form the Technology Association of Georgia. It was an exhilarating ride and I am so proud of the work that the women of WIT accomplished and continue to deliver.

My own career came full circle, as I once again began to travel, leaving Atlanta frequently. My involvement with the Atlanta technology community dwindled, and new generations of very energetic and creative women took WIT to greater and greater levels. In the end, it is always the execution that counts, not the ideas, but I will always be grateful to have been a part of that phenomenal group of women who early in the game had the ideas.

If I have any words of wisdom for future generations, I think the greatest thing that I learned in my own career path and life is that one's perception is *not* reality – truer reality comes from a shared consensus of backgrounds, experiences, viewpoints, and respect. We have to *listen* to each other, face to face, eye to eye, no interruptions – all cell phones and devices off. Science is in fact proving that multitasking does not work, for anybody, our technically savvy generation of teenagers included. Focus matters!

I *was* the parent at football practice engrossed in the laptop, and I *was* the parent who missed a hockey goal because I was on the cell phone, and I *was* the wife who missed a wedding anniversary due to problems with a client, and I *was* the colleague who missed commitments and deadlines due to technical difficulties, over scheduling, traffic, or even God forbid, just plain old forgetfulness. Believe me, I can go on and on with regrets. But we can only ask forgiveness, and perhaps try to make it up, and forgive in return. We are all just human beings hopefully trying to seek higher levels of consciousness, listen and learn from each other, and do the best we can. And, you know, that is OK. In truth, that is totally perfect.

SHAWN GROVER – In a career that spanned 25 years, Shawn Grover held a variety of positions in the technology industry, retiring in 2003 to focus on non-professional aspects of life. Positions included President of BrainWorks Ventures Labs (BVL), a small public company founded by renowned economist Don Ratajczak; VP for Business Development and founding team member for Fountainhead Inc, an e-learning company focused on development of fast growth entrepreneurs; and Regional VP, Business Development for American InterContinental University, a public technology education company. Previous to these engagements, she served on the senior staff of the Advanced Technology Development Center (ATDC) at Georgia Tech and held technical and management positions with a variety of Fortune companies including Control Data Corporation, NEC Information Systems, and GTE as well as academic institutes including Emory University and the Georgia Tech Research Institute.

Grover was one of the architects and a founding member of the Technology Association of Georgia (TAG), and served on the board of directors. She joined WIT in 1995, serving on both their board of directors and advisory board, and as the 1998 president. Grover also served on the board of the Business and Technology Alliance and the Executive Committee for the Digital Ball – a major fundraiser in the Atlanta technology community. Grover had been named a Who's Who in Technology by the *Atlanta Business Chronicle*, and listed as one of the top 40 people in Atlanta entrepreneurs would most want to know when starting a technology or Internet business (one of three women named). She holds an Executive MBA from Emory University, and a Bachelors of Business Administration from Georgia State University.

Never Let Someone Else Dictate Your Destiny

by Vicki Hamilton

SVP, Enterprise Digital Operations & Performance
Turner Broadcasting System, Inc.

ATLANTA, GEORGIA

Never Let Someone Else Dictate Your Destiny

I ATTENDED THE SAME UNIVERSITY where my father taught. He was a professor in the business school and right down the hall from my MIS (Management Information Systems) chairman's office. You can imagine the stress and pressure on me to succeed. On one winter day, I had a major test. I was a hard worker and studied all the time. But this time it just wasn't enough. I failed the exam. My professor decided to pay my father a visit to tell him, "Vic, Vicki flunked her exam today. I just don't think she is cut out to make it. You should really talk to her about changing her major." My father came home and told me what he said. Not only was I devastated, but also I was hurt that my father just accepted his word. Yes, it caused me to think twice but I decided to stay focused and show him that I could and would be successful.

Not only did I graduate with a 3.6 GPA, I started my career with a great, well-paying job. Within eight years, I was making double my professor's salary. I decided to show him what being unsuccessful looked like. So, I mailed him a copy of my paycheck with a sweet note: "Hi Professor Dunn, I know it has been a while since we have spoken. I just wanted you to know that things are going very well for me. In fact, this is what being unsuccessful in MIS looks like – $75,000!!" I must say the satisfaction was monumental. But, more important was the lesson: Never let someone else dictate your destiny. You can do anything that you put your mind to.

Know the impact of your choices

Much earlier in my career and at a different company, I had a full-time job and was a single mother with a young son. I was responsible for a 24-hour technical operation, 365 days a year. We were preparing for a major launch of a major system within the plant.

When we launched a new system, it required working around the clock. We had to get the systems up and provide support/training upon installation.

On the day of the launch, my phone rang. It was my son's day-care. He was ill and I had to go and pick him up. I also knew that I had to be at work. So, I called a friend to see if she could meet me at the doctor's office and take him home after he was checked out. She agreed. First, I had to go and tell my boss. I knew that he was not going to be happy. I walked in his office and told him my son was sick. I said that I would go pick him up, take him to the doctor and leave him with a friend. Then I would come back and stay as long as needed.

Of course, I was hoping and praying that nothing was seriously wrong with my son. My boss turned around and said, "What do you mean? I don't pay you to take care of your son! I pay you to get the job done and get results at this plant!" I was stunned and almost in shock. I stopped and thought for a moment about the impact of my choice. I then turned to him and said, "Do whatever you have to do, but I have to get my son to the doctor. I will be back." I got in my car, cried and prayed all the way to get my son. I got him to the doctor and thank goodness it was not major. My friend took him home, so he could rest.

I returned to work and gave it all that I had. I was there until four o'clock in the morning. My boss left at about ten o'clock and said, "You know, this could limit your opportunities for promotion." I didn't say anything, but knew that I did what I had to do and accepted the consequences. We work for a company to provide results, but we all have a choice as to the culture and environment in which we work. Six months later, I received another opportunity, a promotion, at another company.

The importance of reading the tea leaves

In August 1997, my husband was transferred to Atlanta. We were very excited, as we had always wanted to live there. I moved to the new city unemployed. Thank goodness, it only took two weeks before I started work. I had always wanted to work for an international company and travel abroad. I got my wish.

The company was headquartered in the United Kingdom and I enjoyed many trips abroad. My responsibilities ranged from assisting sales to working directly with our customers on customized software solutions. I had a great staff of about 25 employees and managed the entire Atlanta office. It was a lot of fun, until about two years later.

The weekly staff calls began to slow down; there were fewer visits from the executives abroad and almost complete silence. Our office was extremely busy and working very hard! I began to feel in my gut that something was different and changing. So I started listening, watching everything around me. Several people in the UK office were leaving and taking new jobs. They were key individuals to the business. I know that individuals want to grow and develop, but it just seemed like too many at one time. I learned from a co-worker that we might be sold. I knew that we were a perfect takeover target, but I wasn't sure how real a threat takeover was.

Then I received a phone call from my boss – the call that the business wanted to move all functions back to the UK and close the Atlanta office. I wondered, "How can I help my staff?" After lots of thinking, I put my networking to work. I had a great recruiter friend. I sent all of my staff's resumes to him and asked him to look out for opportunities.

One by one, each employee walked in and said, "I got this great opportunity, but I don't want to leave you." Although flattered, I told them, "Go for it. This is about your growth and development. I would never stop you from moving ahead."

On a Monday afternoon, I was informed I had to let everyone go on Tuesday. Wednesday was my day. It was hard because there was not a severance package, only received unused vacation time. My boss asked me to come to work on Thursday and Friday to help pack up the office. I did it. You might ask why. I did it to close that chapter. Severance is a gift. No one owes you anything.

Here's what I learned: When the decisions are made, it is not personal. It is for the survival of the company. Networking business is important, even when it is time to help other people. Learn to read the tea leaves, and be prepared for change.

VICKI HAMILTON is senior vice president of enterprise digital operations and performance within Turner Broadcasting System, Inc. She is charged with providing leadership and strategic insight in support of TBS, Inc. business activity on emerging consumer platforms. She partners with business unit heads to identify and implement operating efficiencies, and facilitates project and resource management for large-scale cross-company technology initiatives.

Based in Atlanta, Hamilton is a Leadership Atlanta Alumni and currently serves as a board member for WIT, Global EXEC Women; the National Urban League's Black Executive Exchange Program (BEEP) and is also a member of several cable industry organizations, i.e. NAMIC, WICT and SCTE.

TURNER BROADCASTING SYSTEM, INC., a Time Warner company, creates and programs branded news, entertainment, animation and young adult media environments on television and other platforms for consumers around the world.

Fearless!

by Mary Lou Heastings

CEO
Executive Alliance, Inc.

MARIETTA, GEORGIA

Fearless!

I HAD TO BE FEARLESS IN BELIEVING that I could take my business and technology experience and make that leap of faith required to build a brand new company. I left a company, where I had developed twenty-plus years of experience, in order to launch the business in 2003. The vision was to serve a brand new market by showcasing leaders who were driving technology and by building programs to bring executives together from across the country and providing them a platform to share their successes. Frankly, I never doubted for a minute that the business would succeed. My background in technology had given me the self-confidence needed. For me, success was the only option.

After earning my MBA, I jumped at the opportunity to join the IT department at Delta Air Lines It changed my life. I found myself in an environment of high energy and exceptional creativity where decisions were made that impacted hundreds of thousands of travelers across the globe. We worked around the clock developing every conceivable function we imagined our passengers wanted as part of Delta's new loyalty programs. Days went by where we barely left the office. Design meetings were held; code was written, and then testing conducted for weeks and even months before going live into the reservation system. Your knees were knocking as your software program went into production at two o'clock in the morning. You knew that if it didn't work right, then travel agents and airlines across the globe could be impacted.

And not everything always went as designed. Often, you would have hundreds of programming staff in the office in the middle of the night during a major load of new programs into the reservation system. One single program error could wreak havoc – like a code error where databases were being written over. Not a good thing! Under intense pressure, you learned very quickly that you had to know the right questions to be asking: who is being impacted, how big is the impact, and which is the right team to help solve the problem? Every minute the system was down resulted in significant losses to the airlines. The pressure was huge and the pace was brutal.

I love it when the adrenalin is flowing and there is energy in the air. A little bit of chaos suits my temperament. In technology, it is the experimentation, the figuring out how things work, being able to visualize how things should flow, taking things apart and asking questions that makes this environment exciting. Emerging from this chaos provides a sense of accomplishment that builds confidence that you can be innovative and can bring a new product or a service to life.

As my technology career progressed, I ran corporate applications for Travelport, formerly Worldspan, a company that was created by Delta and several other airlines. The timing was perfect for the innovation required: the web was fast becoming the center of the universe where you could deploy self-service, drive down costs, leverage business intelligence, and find new revenue opportunities. Delta was moving at this time to self-service via the web for booking flights and passenger check-in. Word on the street was that this process wouldn't fly (no pun intended). Why would anyone want self-service when they could just call their travel agent to book their flights? The use of technology completely transformed the business. It was a bold decision that changed everything and I was working for a company that was at the heart of many of the new innovations going to market in the industry.

Whether it is a major corporation like Delta or an individual, leadership demands developing a new mindset. There is a driving sense of urgency: to serve the business, to serve your customers. This mindset requires confidence and self-reliance. Leadership requires boldness – making decisions that may be different from the norm. It also requires persistence to get it right and willingness to be fearless in the face of the unknown. You make a decision; you believe in it; and you go for it. My experiences over the years in technology built a great foundation for me to move into a leadership position. I loved the aspect of learning more about customers, the markets served, competitors, and how technology could change the business. I'm still taking things apart, seeing how they work, asking questions, testing ideas, and creating something where there was nothing before.

As CEO of a company bringing technology people together and providing great programs for them, I must stay focused on growing the business and bringing new programs to market. Our success today is the result of the team's hard work, dedication, and belief in their own abilities. Many of the staff are former airline employees who also took the leap of faith to join the new company many years ago and never looked back. They are fearless.

My experience in leadership has shown me that it takes more than education, technology, and business skills to be a success. It also requires character traits that can't be taught. As a business owner, an entrepreneur, and a closet technologist, my successes are the result, in no small part, of being fearless: standing up for what I believe in and uncompromising in treating people right.

Believing in myself and 'going for it' has changed my life. I now work in an environment surrounded by technologists and business leaders who are interesting, creative, and bold. These are the types of people to invest your time. They will help you grow as an employee or as an entrepreneur. Take the leap of faith. Be fearless!

MARY LOU HEASTINGS – As CEO of Executive Alliance, Mary Lou Heastings has responsibility for guiding the continued expansion of the company's portfolio of technology related executive summits, forums, and custom programs across the country. Ms. Heastings launched the publishing arm of Executive Alliance to promote the successes of executives in different industries and released three books in 2010 with a focus on information security and data center leadership. Ms. Heastings has significant experience in management, information technology, finance and operations.

Previous to Executive Alliance, Ms. Heastings had over 20

years of software experience in e-business and global reservations systems for the travel industry with responsibility for developing strategies and deploying enabling technologies in the business information environment. She directed a staff of 150+ technical professionals with responsibilities for implementing corporate business applications in the United States and 28 countries around the globe.

Ms. Heastings is a past president of Women in Technology and was co-recipient of the ATHENA Award for women business leaders having an impact on the workplace. She has been recognized in "Who's Who in Technology;" in the *Atlanta Business Chronicle*, on the cover of *Georgia Trend Magazine* as an executive leading change, and featured in the *Atlanta Journal and Constitution* for her leadership role in developing e-business strategies. An avid boater, Ms. Heastings received her U.S. Coast Guard Captain's license in 2004.

EXECUTIVE ALLIANCE is the premier provider of a national network of technology leadership forums. Through our summits, roundtables, and custom programs, these forums facilitate the building of deep relationships within a network of peers, provide visibility for executives and their companies, and offer access and insight into the people leading these industries. Since 2003, over 6000 executives have benefited from Executive Alliance events putting them in the right place at the right time with some of the smartest people in the world.

Wear Sunscreen

by Joan Herbig

CEO
ControlScan

ATLANTA, GEORGIA

Wear Sunscreen

Recently I was asked to speak to a group of executives and to share the top ten lessons I've learned throughout my career. Although the presentation was geared toward leadership of start-ups and early stage companies, I can see that these hard earned lessons might easily represent my own journey.

#10 *Get the right people on the bus:* Jim Collins brought this concept to light in *Good to Great*, one of my favorite business books. Great leaders know that you must surround yourself with people who are better than you. You must check your insecurities (and your ego) at the door. When you get the right people on the bus, treat them well and learn to trust your gut – it is usually right!

#9 *Listen more than you talk:* Work tirelessly to hone your listening skills (with customers, investors, colleagues, competitors and peers). Learn how to play the "listening game." It wasn't easy for me, but I also had to learn how to get comfortable with silence. Focus on using "we" more than "I". Good communication skills are critical and considering the other person's "story" usually provides a strong foundation for understanding.

#8 *Stay outside your comfort zone:* Frankly, being uncomfortable is part of start-up life – get comfortable with it! When you get too comfortable, you don't make the tough calls because you don't make many, if any, calls. Make a decision! It's far better to make the wrong call than to make no call at all. Celebrate fast failures as yet another opportunity to learn.

#7 *Live below your means:* For startups, raising money is hard (and not a rational process!) and I've found that it's best to raise as little money as required to capitalize on the opportunity available to the company. The goal is to get to breakeven as quickly as possible – paying attention to the evolution of the business model and knowing which dials to watch and which levers to pull. What is true in business is also often true in your personal life. Living below your means allows you to take more risks personally and professionally.

#6 *It's the market stupid!:* At the end of the day, the key to success in a start-up is the market opportunity. You can execute brilliantly in a bad market and not succeed. You can execute less brilliantly in a great market and succeed wildly. Get in the game; if the market is ripe, then the market will tell you how to improve your products and services (how to price the product, how to sell it, etc.). If you've mastered the "listening game," you'll learn quickly enough how to read a good market versus one that is doesn't value your product.

#5 *Make new friends, and keep your old ones:* As you are starting out, focus on forming strategic partnerships early. In your career, the same applies. A great mentor or someone who has your back is a treasure. Build a company for greatness, develop friendships that can help you succeed in your market, and have an exit in mind; but always keep your existing relationships alive.

#4 *Start, STOP, Keep*: At the beginning of each year, we ask our employees to nominate one activity that (as a company) we should "start" doing; one thing that we "stop" doing; and one that we should "keep" doing.... Every employee is encouraged to participate and this simple exercise always uncovers ways to continuously improve the organization. Consider implementing this simple, yet eye-opening exercise, each year.

#3 *Ask for help:* Seek counsel from trusted advisors. It is especially important to look to those advisors outside the organization, as they will probably have a unique perspective. Make a point of regularly asking new people for help and, of course, look for ways that you can help to others as well. Don't be afraid to ask stupid questions. Just remember to play that "listening game" again and again. It helps to be a Curious George ("Hmmm, really? How did you do it?"). You'll find that you learn a lot by just asking a few questions and listening to the answers.

#2 *Obsess on the customer:* If you listen to your customers, they will tell you where to go with your business. You might establish a customer council or a customer advisory board – whatever it takes to ensure your customer is part of the culture. Your employees are the face of your company to your customers; so make sure they are empowered with the authority and responsibility to deliver results.

#1 *Wear sunscreen!* I love the commentary attributed to Mary Schmich of the Chicago Tribune. When she was asked to give one tip for the future, she reportedly suggested, "wearing sunscreen." It's a proven scientific fact that wearing sunscreen has long-term benefits. The rest of what I've shared here is entirely my opinion based on personal experience. Take it for that. But whatever you do, work hard and have fun. You can't take yourself too seriously.

JOAN HERBIG has over 20 years experience in the high-tech world. She has served in many roles throughout her career and has managed her teams to consistently successful outcomes. Named CEO of ControlScan in September 2007, Joan is responsible for business operations and is focused on growing the company's revenues and expanding its position as a leading PCI compliance and security provider focused on small- to medium-sized merchants.

From January of 2005 until its acquisition by nCircle Network Security in May of 2007, Joan was CEO of Cambia Security, Inc., a leader in the configuration auditing space. Prior to Cambia, Joan was CEO of XcelleNet, Inc., an industry leader in wireless systems management, which was acquired by Sybase in May 2004. Before joining XcelleNet, Joan was with Digital Communications Associates (DCA) from 1987 to 1995, where she served as Senior Product Line Manager responsible for marketing and product management of DCA's software product lines.

Joan is also active in the PCI security and payments communities and serves on the Electronic Transaction Association's Risk and Fraud committee. In addition to her by-lined articles featured in *Transaction Trends* and *The Green Sheet* publications and her blog www.esecuritydiva.com, Joan is a sought after speaker on topics related to the challenges and solutions associated with small merchant PCI compliance. As a long-standing contributor to the Georgia technology community, Joan serves on the Board of Directors for the Technology Association of Georgia (TAG), and served as its Chairman in 2008. She was also named 2001 Woman of the Year in Technology by TAG. Joan earned a B.A. in French from the University of Louisville and a M.S. in Computer Science from the University of Kentucky. Joan and her husband, Joe, have been married for 31 years and have two daughters.

HEADQUARTERED IN ATLANTA, GEORGIA, CONTROLSCAN provides Payment Card Industry (PCI) compliance solutions that fit the specific needs of small- to medium-sized merchants (defined by Visa as 'Level 4'). The company helps simplify PCI compliance and reduce risk for banks by achieving high PCI compliance rates for their merchants. As a market leader in PCI compliance, ControlScan offers its acquirer partners the unique benefits of an exclusive focus on servicing Level 4 merchants, programs that work based on the needs of each acquirer and a track record of success in achieving high PCI compliance rates.

Take Advantage of Luck and Good Timing

by Bonnie Herron

Chief Financial Officer
Intelligent Systems Corporation

NORCROSS, GEORGIA

Take Advantage of Luck and Good Timing

FOR SOMEONE WHO LIKES TO PLAN and never embarks on a big initiative without a well-thought out project plan, my career has been spectacularly unplanned. I had no ambition whatsoever to achieve a certain position or financial status – indeed when I started my business career, I didn't even know there was such a position as Chief Financial Officer, the technology industry was in its infancy, and the concept of entrepreneurship, small business startups and business incubation was not on my radar. Unlike many young professional women today, I was unaware of my personal "brand" and would have found the idea of self-promotion a bit embarrassing! What success I've achieved was a matter of taking advantage of luck and good timing (which I believe is true for many careers and businesses) combined with an interest in and facility for doing good work with interesting and supportive people.

I started out as a high school Physical Education and English teacher in Ontario, Canada, and by age 28 I was the equivalent of Athletic Director at a high school in the Toronto suburbs, with responsibility for both men's and women's curricular and extracurricular programs. Combined with a full-time teaching load and coaching gymnastics and track, it was a demanding schedule but one that provided me with tremendous responsibility at an early age. Upon moving to Atlanta in 1979, I quickly realized that I would take a 50 percent pay cut to continue teaching and the idea of a young woman as Athletic Director with the high school football coach reporting to her was just not going to happen any time soon! The difference between Toronto and the deep South at that time was reinforced when I was not allowed to open a bank account without my husband's signature – never mind that I had been the primary breadwinner for the past two years while he earned an MBA and stayed home with our first son. "Welcome to the South, dearie," was how the banker put it.

Thus began my transition from "balance beam to balance sheet."

An MBA seemed like the best way to transition to a different career, although a law degree would probably have been my first choice had there been any opportunity to attend law school part-time in the early '80s. My husband and I reversed roles, with him working fulltime while I earned my MBA and had our second child between semesters. I had barely put together a resume when Leland Strange, one of my professors in marketing and entrepreneurial ventures, offered positions to me and three of my classmates at his technology startup, Quadram. The offer was quintessential Leland. "I don't know exactly what you'll be doing and I can't pay you market rates, but you'll learn a lot, have fun and you won't be bored." Almost thirty years later, he's kept his promise.

In 1982, Apple microcomputers had just hit the market, IBM launched its first PC and VisiCalc introduced the concept of spreadsheets to the business world. Quadram revenue was doubling almost every month, as the demand grew for its enhancement products (memory, graphics and multifunction boards, I/O interfaces, hard drives and such that actually made the early PCs usable). After Quadram merged with publicly traded, Intelligent Systems, we rapidly expanded through acquisitions and internal startup ventures. I did whatever needed to be done, whether that was writing the company's business plan, creating investor presentations (using slides in a carousel!), managing special promotions, conducting due diligence, negotiating acquisitions and divestitures, managing contracts, strategic planning, budgeting, producing the Annual Report or running our laptop computer subsidiary. There was never a written job description and, in the early years, I just picked whatever title made sense for what I was doing at the time.

An outsider looking at my career in technology would say I'd spent almost thirty years at the same, relatively small company. But, the insider perspective is quite different. Intelligent Systems has owned or been an investor in over 50 technology companies – all very entrepreneurial – and I have been involved with many, many of them on a regular basis, including Board of Director, executive, management and support roles. For the past twenty years, I have also run our company's technology business incubator, Gwinnett Innovation Park, one of the longest running, privately sponsored incubators in the county. I have worked with around 60 entrepreneurs through this program, sometimes as a mentor and advisor, or just providing the infrastructure to allow an entrepreneur to concentrate on growing the business quickly. As Chief Financial Officer of ISC since 1999, my finance, legal and SEC reporting duties have increased, but day-to-day involvement with lots of different subsidiary, portfolio and incubator companies provides a rich experience and opportunity to learn.

The advantages of working for smaller, high growth companies are many and I have no regrets about not taking the corporate route or jumping from company to company to get ahead. That said, there is often less exposure to different management and leadership styles and fewer formal training programs than in the corporate world. To offset this disadvantage, my advice is to take on leadership roles in different types of organizations, learn from situations that expand your horizons and challenge your way of doing things, and boost your self-confidence through recognition and experiences outside of your usual work place. My time as a board member and chair of the National Business Incubation Association has been a highlight of my career and very rewarding to engage with so many enthusiastic, capable women and men of all ages making a real difference in their communities.

In my case, the old, "politically incorrect" adage that "behind every successful man is a good woman" could be turned around to say that behind my success are two very good men: Terry, my husband of 42 years (and counting) and Leland Strange, CEO of Intelligent Systems. Without their support and encouragement, there is no doubt in my mind that my career would have been very different.

Terry and I met in grade ten, did the high school football captain – head cheerleader bit, married before our senior year of college, waited ten years before having our two boys and alternated working, grad school and staying home with the babies while in school. I don't know whether it was because we married so young and didn't know any better (I was only 20), because we grew up in Canada with its less conservative, traditional gender roles, or because we lived apart off and on for three years while Terry was in the Navy and I finished my teacher accreditation, but we always assumed we would both work and contribute equally to our family. Neither of us wanted sole responsibility for being the "breadwinner" and we both wanted to be very involved in our kids' lives. At home, we've never had defined roles – we both do everything, whether it's working in the yard, doing the budget, driving to soccer games, or doing laundry. Terry has passed up job opportunities because he felt my career and our family life were more important.

I've learned that people with very different personalities and approaches to problem solving can work together and be successful, if they have respect for each other and the same core values – a lesson that carries over into the workplace. His confidence in me often exceeds my own. I am in awe of women who can juggle career and family without having a partner to share the load with but, for me, there is no doubt that I owe much of my happiness and achievement to knowing that Terry is behind me, pushing me forward or propping me up, but he always "has my back".

Like many successful entrepreneurs, Leland Strange sees opportunities rather than problems, is unafraid of (maybe even thrives on) change and firmly believes there is no one tried and true formula for building successful companies. Leland throws lots of balls in the air and it's been my job to try to keep them from crashing to the ground. Our leadership styles and skill set are very different but complementary – he's the broad strategist and visionary, I'm more the detail person. As promised many years ago, I've learned a lot, had fun and never been bored.

Following are just a few of the lessons learned from working at Intelligent Systems with Leland.

Stay humble and recognize that luck and timing (combined

with the willingness to take advantage of opportunities) play a significant role in success – if you take all the credit for your successes, then you also need to take all the blame when things don't go so well. Because something works once doesn't mean that you can just repeat it and expect the same outcome – often the circumstances are different so carefully analyze your facts and assumptions rather than relying on a "formula". Be honest, a "straight shooter" and don't burn bridges, whether it's with employees, vendors, customers, business contacts, whomever; inevitably how you treat others will come back to you. You can set high expectations without the need to come down hard on the inevitable mistakes or berating anyone. Own your mistakes, fix them, learn from them and move on – it's hard to move forward looking back!

Being named one of WIT's *Women of the Year in Technology* award recipients was such a surprise and an honor. I hope other women will be encouraged to know that you don't need a grand plan, you don't need to be a technologist and you don't have to climb the corporate ladder to have a rewarding career in the technology industry. Just doing good work with good people is all it takes.

BONNIE L. HERRON is Chief Financial Officer, Corporate Secretary and Vice President of Intelligent Systems Corporation, a 37 year-old public company with operations and investments primarily in technology companies. Ms. Herron is responsible for investment due diligence, investor and corporate matters, strategic planning, budgeting, financial and SEC reporting, contract negotiations and legal matters. She also directs all operations, mentoring and entrepreneurial support programs for the Gwinnett Innovation Park, a technology incubator.

In 2005, Ms. Herron was named recipient of *Women of the Year in Technology* for businesses under $500 million by the Woman in Technology Association in Georgia in recognition of her many years of leadership in and contribution to the technology industry and its entrepreneurs.

Ms. Herron is past Chair and a two-term board member of the National Business Incubation Association. She is on the board of directors of the Atlanta Venture Forum and several of ISC's portfolio companies. She has previously served on the boards of the Technology Association of Georgia and Gwinnett Technology Forum, the Advisory Council of Georgia's Intellectual Capital Partnership Program, the Southeast Software Association and the AEA Southeastern Chapter.

Ms. Herron's prior positions include General Manager of Datavue Corporation, Director of Planning at Quadram Corporation and ISC, and Director of Athletics at a high school in Ontario, Canada. Ms. Herron received an M.B.A. from Mercer University, Atlanta and B.A. and B.P.H.E. degrees from the University of Toronto.

FOR OVER THIRTY-FIVE YEARS, INTELLIGENT SYSTEMS CORPORATION [NYSE AMEX: INS], www.intelsys.com, has identified, created, operated and grown early stage companies. Presently, the company has operations and investments in the information technology and industrial products industries, including its principal subsidiaries, CoreCard Software, Inc., a provider of software and services for prepaid and credit card processing, and ChemFree Corporation, a leader in bioremediating parts washer equipment and supplies. ISC also sponsors the Gwinnett Innovation Park, one of the longest-running, privately supported incubator programs in the country.

Reflections: Lessons from My Life & Career

by Susan B. Hitchcock

VP Client Services & Executive Director Women's Initiatives
Turknett Leadership Group

ATLANTA, GEORGIA

Reflections: Lessons from My Life & Career

My story is that of a small town Kentucky-born girl who learned early in life about overcoming challenges – i.e., I lost my mother to cancer when I was four and my father to heart disease when I was 15. Due to these and other family circumstances, my two brothers and I were separated during most of our adolescent years. Fortunately though, we had two sets of grandparents in KY and GA who helped to raise us and I was able to finish high school in KY under the guidance of my maternal grandparents.

Looking back, I realize that I learned some invaluable life lessons from those growing up experiences. Those lessons are the foundation of my belief system that has guided the rest of my life and career. They are: 1) faith in a higher power; 2) confidence in myself to overcome obstacles and to be resilient; 3) a positive attitude about the future; 4) gratitude for what I have, not complaining about what I don't; 5) a commitment to excellence – to do and be the best that I can be in everything I undertake; and 6) to live by the golden rule.

I began the "adult chapter" of my life by coming to the big city of Atlanta to attend Agnes Scott College, a small liberal arts college for women known for its high academic standards. I chose ASC for two reasons: I had two scholarships to help pay my way through college (very important) and … both my brothers lived in Atlanta and we could finally get back together as siblings. Four of the best-years-of-my-life later, I graduated with honor from ASC with a B.A. in Psychology and a minor in math. I believe that the leadership lessons, enlightened perspective, and knowledge / love of learning I gained there prepared me well for the professional and personal journey that lay ahead.

As luck or providence would have it, that journey began immediately. I got married one week after graduating from Agnes Scott, and the next week I started my career in the corporate world (with Southern Bell, later to become BellSouth Corporation.) To compress my 25-year telecom career into a few "lessons learned" is a daunting task, but here goes.

- I learned to be proud of my accomplishments – being among the first group of women to advance in the management ranks (starting in the '60s and '70s). (Note: When I started there were no women in senior leadership roles and only a few in middle management. When I left in December 1991, there were several female officers and a number of us were in the succession planning process for future officer positions.)
- I learned that I was most effective when I developed and led according to my own style (being authentic), not trying to emulate all the males who surrounded me – or even other women whose style differed from mine.
- I also learned that I could be a highly effective leader in a technology organization even though I wasn't a technologist. As a psych major, I could have been intimidated in Network Operations where I spent most of my career and where most of my supervisors, peers, and direct reports were engineers or IT "gurus." But my leadership, teambuilding, results orientation, and interpersonal skills gave me the confidence to take on increasingly tough assignments … and to succeed.
- Lastly, I learned that hard work, long hours, being flexible, building relationships up, down, and across the organization, selecting and developing good team players, being willing to take calculated risks, and having good mentors along the way made a significant difference in my career.

Of course, along my professional journey, there were personal ups and downs. I learned that being a working wife and mother is a challenge. I tried to be *Superwoman* – all things to all people, the best at everything every day (didn't work!). Sadly, I went through a divorce, but happily, I remarried and continued my life journey with my now husband of 38 years (plus two grown daughters – mine and his – and our four wonderful grandchildren.)

As I reflect on this aspect of my life, one critical lesson emerges. Work/life balance is important, but – there's no one definition. For me, it means, "being present" and focusing when you're at work and doing the same when you're at home. It's also assessing your priorities *each* day. Overall, I believe that women who are "Achievaholics" have to make sacrifices to get to the top of our professions. I couldn't (and you can't) do it all alone. Having it all *is* possible, but probably not all at the same time.

It's now been almost 18 years since my professional journey took a sharp turn, and I made a major transition from the corporate world to the consulting world (in a small company). What a shift – but what a joy! I've had the opportunity to develop my skills in marketing and sales, business development /"rainmaking," and in customer service.

But what I truly love is the opportunity to work with many different companies and organizations, helping them select, develop, promote and retain the best managers and leaders possible. Working with Dr. Robert (Bob) and Lyn Turknett, principals of Turknett Leadership Group, has been a blessing and an invaluable learning experience for me. They are the creators of the Leadership Character Model – a model that is based on Integrity and is balanced by Respect (the relationship side of leadership) and Responsibility (the results or bottom-line side of leadership). The Turknett's also authored a book about this model, *Decent People Decent Company: How to Lead with Character at Work and in Life*. I am honored to be included in the book in the dedication and in the chapter on Accountability.

My story would not be complete up to this point without mentioning my passion for women's leadership. I started Turknett's

Women in Leadership seminar series over seven years ago and have hosted 86 monthly programs. I also started a project called "The Age of SHEroes" which is a series of profiles written about women of achievement in fields from A to Z – about trailblazers and role models to inspire us all. Perhaps the most important lesson I've learned through these initiatives – and in my entire career – is that business is better when women join men at the leadership table. In fact, the world is better with women leaders.

SUSAN HITCHCOCK is a native of Franklin, KY, a cum laude graduate of Agnes Scott College and Boston University's Leadership Institute. Before joining Turknett Leadership Group in 1992, Susan had a very successful corporate career with BellSouth (now AT&T) where she held key positions in Network Services and in the Management Assessment and Training organization.

As a community volunteer, she has been a literacy tutor, a crisis counselor, and a teen mentor. Currently, Susan is on the board of the Literacy Volunteers of Atlanta, the Georgia Women's Institute, and the Agnes Scott Alumnae Association. In 2009 she was elected vice president of the Atlanta chapter of CEO Netweavers, a national organization founded on the principles of servant leadership.

Past board service includes the Atlanta Women's Network, the Georgia Executive Women's Network, and the Possible Woman Foundation International. As an advocate for women, Susan received GEWN's Founders' Award for Leadership, was profiled in *Atlanta Magazine*, and has served as a judge for Women in Technology's *Women of the Year in Technology Awards* and as a mentor with Pathbuilders. Susan is also a writer and speaker on women's leadership and has interviewed over 50 women in fields from A to Z. Read their inspirational profiles at http://www.turknett.com/sectionR/women.

Turknett Leadership Group is a full service talent management firm with over 25 years of experience working with diverse corporate and entrepreneurial enterprise. We are known for our Leadership Character Model and our expertise in succession planning, executive development, human performance consulting, and organization effectiveness.

The Charm Bracelet

by Sandra Hofmann

CIO-in-Residence
Advanced Technology Development Center

ATLANTA, GEORGIA

The Charm Bracelet

My story starts with what is perhaps one of the questions I most frequently hear: how can women have it all – career, family, community, and impact – the dreaded work/life balance question. All this to-do about work/life balance – I just don't get it. For me, the real question is how can any of us live an integrated life? It isn't about a balance of work with life. After all, isn't life balanced only with death? Frankly, unless science finds another way, the only thing that you can do about death is to avoid it for as long as possible! You can take care of your physical health and financial security. You can prepare for death by making a will and exploring your spirituality. The physical death is rarely debated.

Life on the other side of the scales – it's all about living across all the roles you play: spouse, daughter, sister, friend, leader, gardener, reader, and community member – all of the many positions we each have. Living is about your character and your values as you work, play, experience the world around you, and as you build relationships. We are struggling every day to balance all the multitude of efforts in life and keep focus on the priorities. Herein lies the real challenge – making the right choices in our life. No one has wrapped tinfoil around my head and beams decisions in. I make the choice to feel good or feel bad. I believe that every day we are making the choices that create our legacy.

I am fortunate to have parents who ensured that I understood the value of integrity. They provided me with a solid foundation to build upon. I didn't always realize that life was about choices, but in 1993 I had an experience that forever changed me. I stood by the graveside of my husband of fourteen years and heard those soft words of his legacy and the sobs of loss. My husband Bern took his own life with a gun and I lost my best friend, my lover, my confidant, and my guide.

I was destroyed. I saw no reason to go on living myself and I struggled at the edge of dark abbess that I saw no escape from. Indeed, I longed to fall into that darkness and end my pain. My entire world was immediately thrown into turmoil unlike any I have ever known. I'd faced life challenges before and thought I was strong – I had experienced rape at 18 and a marriage ending in divorce – but neither event prepared me for the devastation of Bern's suicide and the senselessness of his choice. I felt like his choice had dictated an end to my life as well.

Between the grief I experienced over losing Bern and having to suddenly deal with the business of life without my partner (to say nothing of the complexities of a funeral, probating a will and taking over management of our home), then there was the unexpected tragedy of a violent suicide and coping with that horror – well, I was a basket case!

Unlike a more natural death, grief following a suicide has so many extraordinary challenges for the family and friends who survive. Even in this enlightened era, social and cultural mores make it difficult to know how to behave. I had lost grandparents and other relatives, but this was a new experience and I was seriously adrift.

On top of all that drama, I was in the midst of a very challenging assignment integrating a recently acquired business into our company. I had to travel back and forth from Atlanta, Georgia to Montreal, Canada for about nine months. People were depending on me to take care of customers and employees when I was struggling to just survive. My company offered incredible support for me during this time and the compassion shown to me could never be forgotten. I am grateful for their confidence in me and appreciate that I didn't always make it easy for them to maintain that confidence. Their expectations kept me going. Having a purpose gave me a reason to keep going.

I did in fact survive – proof for me that what doesn't kill you makes you stronger. In that survival journey I discovered a number of significant gifts that have enriched my life – personally and professionally.

In the days following the loss of Bern, I had to get locked in on a vision of getting through each day. Each day I'd envision my destination and the path there. Those days became weeks. My destinations were both serious ones – releasing an important update for the software product I was responsible for – and more trivial as well. For example: I created a vision of finishing a charm bracelet that Bern had started for me. Each month I added a charm. I was doing a fair bit of international travel and picking up the perfect charm occupied lonely moments and also didn't add to my baggage! Months became years. Today my charm bracelet is a necklace! It is loaded with special memories and reminds me of my journey of survival. I don't wear it often because it is so heavy. Life is like that necklace: I've added charms of experiences and choices, and most treasured, the people I've come to know who are like sparkling jewels.

I developed a vision of my life without Bern, one where I had to rediscover me and recognize the choices before me personally and professionally. I found that in my work, it became important to create similar visions for where I needed to take my team. I drew on leadership readings of two academic writers, Kouzes and Posner, authors of *The Leadership Challenge*. I also incorporated into my vision my days as a '70s flower child. I envisioned my team all loaded up on a wildly painted old school bus, a Merry Prankster's creation, traveling down a highway toward a rainbow destination. This silly bus became my way of thinking about the journeys I would make with others.

I've continued to ride that day-glow bus! Sometimes I am a passenger and sometimes I'm driving or navigating for another. There are potholes along the way, side trips, and rest stops as well. I know that the journey is where there is learning and the destination marks only a new point of departure.

My sister Betty Coffey Amodeo shared with me another perspective on this journey. Her husband "Grandmaster" Michael Amodeo, who we lost to cancer in 2008, used this story with his martial arts' students to relate life to the study of this discipline.

Betty models the way in her own journey. She is an inspiration to me. Here's Michael's story:

A young boy traveled across Korea to the school of a famous martial artist. When he arrived at the Do Jang he was given audience by the Master. "What do you wish from me?" the Master asked. "I wish to be your student and become the finest martial artist in the land," the boy replied. "How long must I study?" "Ten years at least" the Master answered. "Ten years is a long time," said the boy. "What if I studied twice as hard as all your other students?" "Twenty years," replied the Master. "Twenty years! What if I practice day and night with all my effort?" "Thirty years," was the Master's reply. "How is it that each time I say I will work harder, you tell me that it will take longer?" the boy asked. "The answer is clear. When one eye is fixed upon the destination, there is only one eye left with which to find the way."

We don't know how long we will have with the people who are in our lives, so I actively look for ways to recognize the value of those around me, to keep my eyes open to life, and my ears open to the stories of others. I work hard to integrate all aspects of my life and balance the priorities against a bigger picture of achievement.

At the end of my life I want to hear that I made a difference. I want to hear that I gave respect; that I had uncompromising integrity; that I was fair; that I had executed with values and commitment and that I was a caring person. I want to hear that being on the bus with me was a trip filled with learning and with fun, and that I had celebrated the journey.

To paraphrase the words of Ralph Waldo Emerson, 'success is to laugh often, win respect of intelligent people, earn appreciation of honest critics, find the best in others, and leave the world a better place.' I hope to achieve this.

SANDRA HOFMANN is a *gadfly* – serving as a constructively provocative stimulus to build the technology community in Georgia. An innovative and inspiring executive who understands and drives the value of alignment across the enterprise, Sandy has successfully provided leadership to technology and manufacturing professionals for over 25 years. Sandy's broad management experience, including 14 years with IBM, has enabled her to effectively guide teams to realize goals and deliver desired results. Particularly adept at addressing issues associated with acquired and merged businesses, Sandy has frequently been recruited to address the most difficult and challenging environments.

Sandy has repeatedly demonstrated her exceptional strength of character and leadership, as well as her ability to serve as a change agent. She led the transition activities for one of the first application spin-offs from IBM. As Vice President of Technical Services, she faced the unique challenge of breaking the gender barrier at Simplex, while concurrently transforming the way service was delivered. She joined MAPICS, their first woman to be a member of the executive team, as the Vice President and General Manager for a newly acquired business unit and was then a lead participant in the company's re-engineering as a functional organization. She then stepped into the unique dual role of CIO and Chief People Officer and established the company's organizational model for the "virtual office" which provided extraordinary results in enterprise efficiency and expense benefits. Her introduction of information liberation, a project management office and portfolio management allowed the company to rapidly assimilate acquisitions (doubling in size) and then obtain full integration in less than six months.

Currently Sandy is serving as "CIO-in-Residence" with the Advanced Technology Development Center. Headquartered at Georgia Tech, ATDC is a nationally recognized science and technology incubator that helps Georgia entrepreneurs launch and build successful companies. Most recently she was Chief Operating Officer at Closets and More, the Southeast's largest custom closet design, installation, and manufacturer. Prior to that, Sandy served as Executive Vice President and Chief Operating Officer for Turknett Leadership Group. Turknett Leadership Group is a character-based management and consulting firm that focuses on aligning strategy, leadership and culture.

Sandy's management philosophy, leadership characteristics and business results have been acknowledged by numerous industry recognitions: Georgia CIO Leadership Association (GCLA) selected Sandy as the Georgia CIO of the Year which honors individuals who have demonstrated outstanding technology leadership in Georgia and excellence in managing their organization's enterprise wide information systems. In 2003 she was selected as one of five finalists for *Women of the Year in Technology* and again in 2004 she was one of seven finalists. PathBuilders selected Sandy as Mentor of the Year. Articles highlighting Sandy's results have been published in CIO and CFO *Magazine*, CIO *Insight*, CIO *Quarterly*, *Workforce Management*, *Human Resource Executive*, and PINK *Magazine*. Able to present and discuss information and strategies in a way that establishes rapport, persuades others, and gains commitment, Sandy is an often-requested speaker, moderator, and panelist for technology and community events.

Sandy's influence reaches beyond her professional undertakings and she is very engaged in her community with the promotion of technology and ethical leadership. She currently serves as President and Board Director for Women in Technology, and as a member of the TechBridge and the Technology Association of Georgia Board of Directors. Previously Sandy served on the Board of Directors for AAA Auto Club South, as chairman for the Board of Directors for Society for Human Resource Management-Atlanta, and Compensation Committee Chair for AkroMetrix Board of Directors. Sandy currently participates on numerous advisory boards including AAA Auto Club Georgia, Virima, Turknett Leadership Group and The University of Georgia Terry College of Business Atlanta Leadership Symposium. She serves as Honorary Chair of TechExecs. Twice a year she hosts over 300 people for charity benefit events at her home.

Sandy graduated from Georgia State University with a bachelor of science in education, has completed an intensive program for executive management at Stanford University and received Corporate Directors certification from University of Georgia Terry College of Business. A former exhibiting artist and self-proclaimed "biblioholic", Sandy has an extensive personal library, enjoys herb gardening, loom weaving, entertaining, target pistol shooting, and her Yorkshire Terriers, Nicky and Gracie.

THE ADVANCED TECHNOLOGY DEVELOPMENT CENTER (ATDC) is a start-up accelerator that helps Georgia technology entrepreneurs launch and build successful companies. Founded in 1980, ATDC has helped create millions of dollars in tax revenues by graduating more than 120 companies, which together have raised more than a billion dollars in outside financing. ATDC has provided business incubation and acceleration services to thousands of Georgians.

The Power of Connections

by Patricia S. Hughes

Director, Southeast
KnowledgeAdvisors

CHICAGO, ILLINOIS

The Power of Connections

I CLEARLY REMEMBER RECOGNIZING my ability to sell at about 12 years of age. I was part of a team of four girls, working with the U.N. Youth Council to sell fruitcakes to pay our way to a mini U.N. seminar in New York. About 10:00 AM we set up tables at a shopping center in Charlottesville, VA. We made many trips to the car to unload all the large boxes that held the individually packaged fruitcakes. The boxes were stacked high and lined the wall beside the Rexall Drug Store. Our mothers planned to come back around 2:00 PM to pick us up. We were excited to get started and proud to know that we were going to contribute to the funds raised for the trip.

When it was almost 2:00 there were still two boxes of 12 fruitcakes left to sell. Twenty-four more sales to make in just a few minutes. The other girls were getting restless and it was starting to rain. About that time I saw a group of men in uniform approaching the sidewalk. Looking back I don't know if they were from the military base or ROTC guys from the local school. Suddenly I had an idea. I bravely walked up to the group and recommended that they buy a whole box – 12 fruitcakes! They could take them back and share fruitcakes or give them as gifts. They did it! In one sale I'd sold twelve fruitcakes!

The other girls had stood carefully behind the table, but for some reason, it didn't bother me to walk up to people and persuade them of the importance of spending their money with me. I realized I enjoyed doing something that other people did not – I was a good sales person.

Whether it was cookies for Girl Scouts, candy for the church choir or airplane wash and wax that we did for the local civil air patrol, I was always the one who sold the most. My group leaders and peers always knew I would sell my share and if they couldn't sell the required number, I was the one to call.

I went to college majoring in business management and economics, knowing that I wanted to work in sales. During my senior year of college, my parent's encouraged me to take advantage of the placement center interviews and I was rewarded with several job offers. I accepted one of the management trainee jobs offered by a large financial services company. After only one week of sitting at a desk in their office in Atlanta, I knew I did not want that life. The office seemed dark, the halls were narrow and it was very quiet. I decided one thing for sure – if it required sitting behind a desk, I was not going to do that for a living. At the end of the week, I thanked the manager for the opportunity and moved on. That decision turned out to be a good one for me.

I began looking for a job in sales and even ended up selling cars for a short time. I'd always loved cars and began to notice that a lot of people who drove expensive cars worked in technology companies. I figured they must have been making a lot of money. I applied for a job with one of the new mainframe computer companies thinking that I could learn the technology and work my way into sales. The guy interviewing me said, "I don't hire women but I know a guy who does." He referred me to that guy in another company and I got hired. I loved people and enjoyed making the connections that are necessary in sales. I gained the experience and knowledge required to excel in technology sales but more importantly, I learned to nurture relationships with my co-workers, superiors and most importantly my clients. Recruited to move to new technologies, I gained confidence in my ability to position solutions and negotiate agreements in the best interests of my company and my clients. I began to move up and worked for several companies along the way.

Eventually I went to work with a division of GE. After assignments in the federal division, which became Prime Computer, and opening a regional office in the mid-Atlantic I was working as the National Account Manager for the U.S. Army account. It was there that I met a handsome Army Captain who captured my heart. We were married a short time later.

With the arrival of our first child, we decided that he should take a promotion winning assignment in Germany. Moving meant that I would give up my career and leave the business world. Not only were we in a foreign country, the military life was foreign to me as well. I'd never been without a job and although being an officer's wife and a mother is a job in itself, it was new territory for me. Soon I was taking on Red Cross and Army Wives Club fund raising responsibilities. Here I was able to leverage my skills and continue to use my sales abilities and build my network of contacts.

With my husband's promotion secured in 1996, we returned to Atlanta and his pre-retirement assignment at Fort McPherson. There was never a question in my mind that I would return to work now that we were back in the States despite having been out of work for four years. Even before we unpacked, I was using my carefully saved address books to reconnect with former colleagues, clients and friends. I soon accepted an opportunity in a business development role for a consulting company and went to work adding to my network. This was before LinkedIn and social media but we were engaging in important networking activities like meeting with people and attending networking events.

One day a former West Point classmate of my husband's, an executive at Lockheed, suggested that I talk to a woman who worked with him. This new connection and friend encouraged me to help her with a new women's organization – Women in Technology. They were in the middle of planning for the second Executive Auction where attendees could bid for one-on-one meetings with high-ranking executives. I was fascinated with the idea that women like me would have the opportunity to gain access to decision makers we needed to meet. This organization of women was interesting. I'd always worked in mostly male environments and didn't know a lot of professional women. Of course getting involved in the organization and helping to secure event sponsorships was a natural fit for me. In both 1998 and 1999, I won bids in the Executive Auction to meet and engage with executives I wanted to know. Both of these men became game-changing clients for me. One helped me to get my foot in the door of his company for a consulting project; the other led to a big company-training project.

'Networking' was a term that was just becoming popular in business. Women in Technology gave a voice to the activity I'd been doing all along and gave specific action to the activity. Their approach to networking crystallized my confidence in building relationships with and looking for the support of other women. Working on that early executive auction, we had no idea how important Women in Technology would become. In 2000, my global sales responsibilities absorbed my time after that third executive auction and I couldn't be as active but I continue to hold onto the connections I have made.

After many years of handling international accounts and reaching top sales status, making President's Club and receiving sales awards I was ready for a new challenge. In 2008, I left the corporate world to join the founding team of a startup company. This gave me the opportunity to use everything I had learned over the years on a daily basis. As a seasoned, experienced professional who can craft solutions, deliver results and mentor and coach a team; they needed what I had to offer. Being able to leverage things I had learned over the years and improve or adjust as I worked was exciting and rewarding. Infusion of venture capital allowed the new technology to find its best 'home' and let me take advantage of all I had learned and the network I'd built.

Today with new technologies such as LinkedIn, FaceBook and Twitter it is easier to network. People seem to be focused on how many connections or "friends" they can collect. As someone who has networked and nurtured relationships throughout my entire career I know that it's not about how many business cards or social media connections you can accumulate. It's about who will take your call. Having a name on your list of connections is meaningless if they wouldn't recognize your name and couldn't pick you out of a lineup. The connection is only solid if you can call on them when you need to. How do you make this type connection? That's where relationship building comes in. It's important to remember and be remembered. Your reputation is invaluable! Understanding what motivates the other person and helping them without expectation solidifies relationships. It takes an altruistic approach to networking. Looking back over my career I know that my success came through building and nurturing relationships.

PATRICIA S. HUGHES is an experienced sales and marketing professional. Her strengths include delivering enterprise level value propositions and managing go-to-market partnerships to increase revenue. Most recently, she was a part of the founding team for a marketing analytics company, VueLogic. She had overall business development responsibility, coordinating marketing and sales. Prior to joining the founding team at VueLogic, Patricia held a Global Business Development role with SkillSoft Corporation, managing key Fortune 500 international accounts, including AT&T, Northrop Grumman, General Dynamics, McKesson and GlaxoSmithKline.

Her prior experience includes business development for Cap Gemini's Telecommunications practice where she was responsible for selling and directing consulting activities to meet client requirements. Patricia enjoys working with emerging technologies and early stage companies and has held senior sales and market development positions for D2K, Concentra, now and a division of Oracle and General Electric's Calma Division.

Patricia lives in Marietta, an Atlanta suburb with her husband, Eric and son, Taylor. She is an active volunteer in community and professional organizations. She was a founding member of the Women's Leadership Exchange, Atlanta LEXCI Circle and currently holds a board position with the Association of Strategic Alliance Professionals.

KNOWLEDGEADVISORS is a Chicago based, global provider of learning and talent measurement solutions. Leading organizations access our measurement expertise and on-demand software to ensure a high-performing workforce. As the thought leader in Human Capital Analytics, KnowledgeAdvisors provides the most comprehensive analytics solutions available.

The Whole Story

by Shannon A. Johnston

Chief Technology Officer
Points of Light Institute

ATLANTA, GEORGIA

The Whole Story

My bio is misleading. It's not because there are any factual inaccuracies, but instead it is misleading because it fails to tell the whole story of my career 'success.' Reading my bio, it seems fairly 'flowers and roses,' including a quick rise to the "C-Suite" before turning 40. But it's the information that isn't in my bio – the information between the lines – that tells the real story of how I got where I am today. It wasn't always smooth. At various points over my 16+ year career, I have:

- Taken any job I could get to be working
- Stalled in positions
- Been hired badly
- Been laid off twice
- Gotten myself in over my head and spent months of 70 hour work weeks digging myself out
- Failed to tone down my personality enough
- Toned it down too much

In summary, it has been a good, bad, great, terrible, frightening, exhilarating ride – and I am only halfway there! But I'm getting ahead of myself. First, a bit of background:

When I was a little girl, I wanted to be a ballerina. Not a pink, frilly, tutu kind, but a real ballerina, and I chased that dream. I auditioned for the Royal Danish Ballet at 12, and at 15, my ballet teacher tried to get me to audition for the Boston Ballet (we moved around a lot). When it was time to go to college, I picked my school because of the dance program.

I was in dance class in college one day when I suddenly realized that I was going to end up working as a dance teacher. I realized I wasn't good enough to become a professional, and regardless, at 19, that ship had probably already sailed, since 19 in the ballet world is senior citizen territory. It had just never occurred to me to think about what I would do when I graduated. I knew I didn't want to be a dance teacher because, as silly as it sounds, I didn't want to wear tights to work and bang my stick to classical music while counting out the beat. It was time to find another calling.

After a winding road through a few different majors and a couple of schools, I ended up with a liberal arts degree from a little school in Savannah and was just happy to graduate. It was 1994 and the job market wasn't pretty. I took the only job I was offered. I think my annual salary was about $9,000 and I had no benefits.

What a wake-up call. My job was in sales. I had a great boss that told me, "Just do the basics. It's all about blocking and tackling. Make 100 calls to get 10 appointments to get 1 sale." It sounded so simple that it seemed like anyone, degree or not, could do it. But not everyone was doing it. Most folks tried to get around the basics with shortcuts, and they weren't successful. I quickly learned that "buddy" referrals are the easiest sale to make, so I immediately set out to build a network. I learned that providing amazing customer service made meeting my monthly goals easier because happy customers are your best sales force. Within two years, I quadrupled my annual salary, got benefits and was managing a staff of 50. I was 24 years old.

My next job resulted from a client taking notice of my performance at my then current job, which is when I learned that there are many benefits of performing your current job at a high level, including creating future career opportunities! They set up an interview for me with a company in a new industry, a technology company with significant room for growth. I took it, even though it was a 30% pay cut, because there was so much opportunity for growth and I felt strongly that the industry was where I wanted to be. I probably wasn't completely qualified for the job, but I effectively translated each "how would you" question in the interview to relevant examples in my current job with confidence – I believed I could be successful and wanted them to believe I could as well.

And that was my entry into technology. I worked for a company whose main product was mainframe processing. I jumped in with both feet. I was interested, really interested, in how stuff worked. I spent six years there in relationship management. I was fortunate to have a boss who was also a sponsor. Most importantly, he was honest with me. He gave me my first really good pieces of advice about being a woman in business. In the days of *Melrose Place* on TV, he cared enough about my success to explain that wearing miniskirts caused my interactions to be about what I was wearing, instead of what I was saying. He found a way to explain to a girl full of spirit, who refused to conform, how to turn the dial down, not off.

Eventually, he left the organization, and I lost my sponsor. You need a sponsor and I floundered for a few years without one. I got stuck. I realized after a year or two that I would always be "Sunshine" (that inexperienced, happy go lucky girl), and that I could either spend many months reworking my reputation or I could move to an organization that would give me a fresh start as the now "Optimistic Experienced" veteran that I felt I was. It was a tough decision, but I started interviewing. After quite a bit of searching, I found what I thought was the right job for me and I moved.

I was a bad hire at my new company. The company had both internal needs and client needs. They hired me based on internal needs and I spent the next year trying to counteract the missing skills which the client was looking for. I was in the travel rewards industry and was still struggling to fill the client need gap when the 9/11 tragedy hit. After 9/11, no one traveled, and I went from being busy to having way too much capacity. I was laid off – but to be totally honest, I had already started looking because I knew I wouldn't make it in my current position. I networked. I called old clients, as well as people I had met when I had interviewed for positions prior to accepting my current one. I was really happy I hadn't burned any bridges. One of my previous clients got me an interview. The position wasn't a good fit, but that interviewer referred me to another open position in the company. I got the job.

It was a good move. I found an organization that was young and growing. They hired me with a general idea of what they needed, but I didn't have much of a job description. I didn't know exactly what I was supposed to be doing, so I made it up as I went along. To my surprise, it worked. I realize now that I created three new roles for myself in eight years by just being willing to tackle odd jobs. My willingness to identify the needs of the organization and take on different roles – the "I'll do that" approach – is absolutely what has put me where I am today.

So as you can see, I learned some important lessons. The most important one is that it isn't about me. I have never achieved success in any position without amazing teams and individuals who went out of their way to support me, and most of the time, I just was lucky to be in the vicinity when they were successful.

But there are a few things that I have done consistently that, right or wrong, I plan to continue doing, because I believe they are responsible for my success. Simply, they have provided the consistent foundation I've relied on to persevere through a wild ride in this working world. Here they are:

Work hard. Nothing replaces hard work. Put your head down and do the job you are given with all the effort and care you can give it. I am completely convinced that talent is a factor far outweighed by sheer effort. I believe that how good you are at something is just a measure of how hard you are willing to work at it. Nothing is so distracting as worrying about 'what is next.' Be cautious about doing that since worrying can prevent you from doing your current job well and may actually harm your career more than it helps. Remember that your career is a marathon, not a sprint. An extra six months, a year, or even two years in a position over a 30-plus year career is not a long time.

Like what you do. Passion overcomes a lot of obstacles. When you share a common passion for work, the focus is on that, not on all the other distractions that get in the way.

Be self aware. Figure out how others view you. If you don't like or agree with it, recognize that your reputation wasn't built in a day, and it will take a good long stint of changed behavior to change your reputation and how you are seen. Then, once you've fixed it, add yourself back in. There's no reason to lose your personality – just don't make it a distraction.

Be honest. That may not sound like work advice, but it is. Nothing is worse than avoiding the conflict that happens when someone needs to hear the truth. Avoid something today and it grows and becomes a cancer. Nip it in the bud and it takes on only the importance that it should. When you mess up, admit it, fix it, and then move on.

Be grateful. I am still amazed that someone pays me to learn. I get to do amazing and fun things each day – and I try to focus on those, not the un-fun things that sometimes sneak into our days. My husband and I had a company move us into a new home recently, and it was one of the movers' birthday. When I mentioned that moving heavy furniture was a tough way to spend a birthday, he replied, "I woke up this morning breathing, I can take care of my kids, life is good."

SHANNON JOHNSTON is CTO at Points of Light Institute. She leads the technology organization and is responsible for Web, salesforce.com, and Infrastructure design and delivery, and affiliate and partner support for Points of Light's technology products. From 2001 to 2009 Shannon held various senior positions at CompuCredit, a financial services company, most recently Vice President, Global Infrastructure Services, responsible for worldwide IT Operations. She relocated to the UK for a year in 2007 to build and deliver the UK IT strategy and plan for CompuCredit's entrance into the EEU financial markets and prior to that built an eBusiness organization to bring the company to the internet for their corporate and customer service needs.

Prior to joining CompuCredit, Shannon held senior positions in relationship management in the financial services industry, both for TSYS (www.tsys.com) and Enhancement Services (www.es-cloyalty.com). Shannon is a member TAG (Technology Association of Georgia) and the MentorNet community. She is an active volunteer in TAG's societies, WIT (Women in Technology) and is on the board of directors for TAG's Diversity Society. She is the recipient of WIT's 2009 *Women of the Year in Technology* award for medium sized business. She currently resides in Atlanta with her husband, Alex.

POINTS OF LIGHT INSTITUTE inspires, equips and mobilizes people to take action that changes the world. The Institute has a global focus to redefine volunteerism and civic engagement for the 21st century, putting people at the center of community problem solving. Points of Light Institute operates three dynamic business units that share the mission: HandsOn Network, MissionFish and the Civic Incubator, which includes generationOn and AmeriCorps Alums. HandsOn Network is the volunteer-focused arm of Points of Light Institute with more than 250 Action Centers in 16 countries.

Be Courageous

by Gwen Jolley

Vice President
Gwen Jolley & Associates

ATLANTA, GEORGIA

Be Courageous

As women, sometimes we are more reticent than we should be about seeking out negative criticism. If someone is feeling negative toward our work product or performance, not hearing the message is not going to help us correct the situation. You might compare this situation to not stepping on the scales even though in our heart of hearts we know that we have gained ten pounds in the last (you name the time period). After all, the zipper on our favorite pair of jeans does not lie.

We can save ourselves a great deal of pain, heartache, some long nights at the office, if we ask the tough question: Just how am I really doing? Ask, and then just sit quietly and wait for the answer. Remain silent even if you think that you are going to pop; just hear the news.

There are times, of course, that the negative criticism catches us completely unaware. My story involved my new assignment as the CIO of Europe for Bovis Lend Lease. I was feeling somewhat proud of my accomplishments, my second back-to-back international assignment with a major global company. The call from my boss, the Global CIO, came on a day when I was feeling particularly good about what I was accomplishing in this new, strange environment, London.

It seems that my boss, Al, had been speaking with Peter, the global CEO for Bovis, who was just being relocated from Sydney to London. Peter shared with Al his impression that I was slow off the mark and after three to four months, still trying to feel my way.

To say that I was blindsided would have been an understatement. In my mind, I immediately began to rationalize about all of the things that I had done and all of the obstacles that I had overcome. Fortunately, thanks to some wonderful mentors that I had in the past, I did not stay in that rationalization mode very long. I began to look for ways to change the situation. I looked for actions that I could take.

That is a secret to success: take action, and take courageous action. My next call was to Peter's executive assistant to see if I could get fifteen minutes on his calendar for the following day. She, in her imitable, gatekeeper style, began to tell me why all of the times that I proposed would not work and how back-to-back Peter's calendar was full for the next fortnight. There was no hope of getting me on his calendar before the end of the month. We exchanged a few more pleasantries about London, my housing (always a subject for comment), the weather and finally I got to the question that I wanted to ask, "What time does Peter usually arrive at the office?"

Once again, when faced with a difficult situation take courageous action. When Peter walked into his building, a plush office complex in the Knightsbridge area of London on that next morning at 7:20 AM, I was wearing my very best suit and had been sitting in his lobby for almost an hour. He glanced in my direction. I took that as my cue. I walked up to him and introduced myself, not that an introduction was actually needed. I immediately reassured him that I knew that I did not have an appointment and I was very much aware of his crowded business calendar; however, I was prepared to wait throughout the day until he had ten minutes to speak with me.

Surprise can be your ally. Sometimes if someone underestimates you, it can give you a tremendous advantage, even if it is somewhat temporary in nature. When that happens, seize the moment. Peter replied that he would not pretend that he did not know what had prompted my visit, and then invited me up to wait in his suite on the fifth floor.

When my time came to have my ten minutes with Peter (I only had to wait two hours), I felt that the suspense of the situation was killing him, as much as me. I started out with a cultural explanation. I explained to Peter, as if he could not tell from my accent, that I was from the South, as I would say, the Deep South. In my world of gentility and manners, one does not allow someone to "mean mouth" them without either "sicing" on them the dogs or one's Papa (if the situation warrants that) or addressing the situation right away to put matters "right" (at least a two to three syllable word where I am from).

I proceeded to explain that I had no problem with him reaching out to my boss on an issue *if* we had first tried to resolve it and *if* I had not provided satisfaction (not the *Rolling Stone* variety, of course). We continued our conversation and it stretched to thirty minutes. It included a discussion of the illustrious small-town country lawyer involved with prosecuting the Watergate case, another Southern that he understood to be maybe more than they had originally appeared to be. We parted on very collegial terns and remained so for the length of that assignment.

I do not mean to say that one's courage will always be rewarded, that a surprise attack will always win. However, what do you have to lose?

GWEN JOLLEY is the former CIO for ChoicePoint, a LexisNexis company where she was responsible for the development and implementation of the custom applications to the insurance industry.

Gwen is formerly a member of the Deloitte & Touche CIO Services Consulting Practice and the Real Estate Services Practice. In that role, she provided advice and guidance to senior IT executives and, on occasion, filled the role of interim CIO for clients.

Her expertise covers both the public and the private sector in Information Technology, not only domestically, but also internationally, serving in the role of International CIO on three continents, UK, ASIA Pacific and the US. Gwen's specialty has been in aligning and realigning IT organizations to support their business missions, often following mergers and acquisitions.

GWEN JOLLEY & ASSOCIATES is a consulting company with fifteen plus years of experience, supplying expert technical resources for businesses having both software development and senior management consulting needs.

David and Goliath: It Only Takes a Village

by Margot King

Vice President Recruiting Solutions
ZeroChaos

ATLANTA, GEORGIA

David and Goliath: It Only Takes a Village

BEING AN ENTREPRENEUR REQUIRES persuasion and negotiation skills in the highest extreme. Many times you are growing things out of thin air, so you must be able to visualize the outcome you desire to achieve your dreams. It helps to channel back to your childhood when you played 'pretend' because your desired reality is only a figment of your imagination until you make it happen.

The art of negotiation is something that you start early in life; perhaps, when you need to talk your parents into letting you go to your first spend the night party or go on your first date. It takes on new dimensions as you progress in the business world – requiring a dash of confidence, a large dose of authenticity, and the ability to articulate your vision to your audience.

One of my earlier experiences of turning a dream into reality seemed preposterous at the time. I owned a boutique company of about 65 employees that designed and developed recruiting programs for corporations anywhere in the country. We had achieved significant success with a few blue chip companies and recognition in the automotive industry by helping our clients find design engineers capable of innovating new car designs. This was particularly ironic because most of our consultants were women who did not know a drive train from a chassis!

We learned that *the* Fortune #1 automotive company would be spinning off one of its largest business divisions into its own stand-alone company. Creating a workforce plan where position vacancies could readily be replaced with above average talent was key to the success of the spin-off company. Knowing about this opportunity, we began a very ambitious and arduous selling process against all the odds. Yes, we had a little automotive experience, but nothing on the scale of this project.

A warm introduction from the CEO of another automotive client to the Fortune #1 executive leadership kicked off our campaign.

While learning about the anticipated challenges a spinoff would cause, we developed a proposed strategy and delivery solution for discussion. One meeting led to many others including presentations to more than a dozen VPS. The proposal meetings involved extensive team travel to Detroit, Michigan over the course of six months. Every visit felt like a success for my sales team and I, but no definitive deals were inked. Then, the Detroit car company went radio silent. After all the meetings and the courting – nothing, not even a return phone call to say "No thanks." I was ready to file this endeavor, this dream, in the 'wasted a lot of time' basket.

Then, after months of silence, which felt like unofficial rejection, I got a phone call from someone whom I had never met in Detroit's Purchasing Division, "Ms. King, could you come to a meeting tomorrow morning so we can determine if we want to do business with your firm?" I responded that I was available but since I was in Atlanta, it would have to be later that next morning. He added, "And, bring your financial statements."

Yikes, no time to set up an entourage, no time to prepare an additional presentation. On top of that, toting along our financial statements, which sadly did not have near enough the number of commas or zeros with which I suspected the Fortune #1 was used to dealing.

I arrived the next morning (along with my petite financials) armed only with the confidence we could tackle this project and be successful. But, how to explain that such a tiny dot of a company could do business with a giant was causing butterflies in my stomach. A gentleman, without a speck of a smile on his face, ushered me into a grandiose conference room and seated me on one side of an imposing conference table. A few minutes later five other people entered the room and positioned themselves on the other side. No smiles, no pleasantry … just intimidating "suits". I felt as though I was presenting a case to the Supreme Court in a sundress waiting for the gavel to drop. Was I out of my league?

Their opening argument asserted that our pricing was too high and questioned what was going to be done about it. I stood my ground by responding that it *was* a fair price and that the work entailed many factors that could not be estimated in advance because this was new territory for us all. Again, there were no smiles or any indication of acceptance. But, they moved on to their next issue: the Fortune #1 *never* pays invoices before 90 days and would that cash flow be problematic. I replied, "No, we are well funded to cover the start-up costs and can wait until the gas gets out of the line, but that is another reason that we can't negotiate our pricing." Although he had never laid eyes on the details of my pocket-sized financials, the VP of Purchasing asked me why the Fortune #1 should work with a vendor that is so small. I felt as if he could see the reports and spreadsheets through the bound manila folders sitting on the table next to me. Clearly, the horse-trading that goes on when you negotiate to buy a car trickles down from the boardroom!

My head was swirling and my heart was about to burst as I struggled to give an answer that would satisfy. Then it came to me, as if I was playing 'pretend,' being Hillary Clinton in 'it only takes a village'. I pulled out my most confident voice and replied, "Gentlemen, I appreciate your consideration of our company as a vendor to such a venerable organization, but you must understand how intimidating it is to come in to a meeting at corporate headquarters of the Fortune #1 and to bring my pint-sized financial statement. If it is size that matters, we aren't the firm for you. If it is quality you seek, then we may be. The way I see it is, if one of our consultants can influence just one person in your company that has upside impact on a department that triggers gains on the division's bottom line, *and* we can repeat those results, then we are the right firm for you." Then I shut up.

Surely, I was about to be escorted off the premises by a security guard. But, the lead VP's face lit up with a grin and he chuckled. "You know, we like to take small companies and make them real big! How would you like that?" It took me a second or two to believe my ears were transmitting the words accurately. My ears couldn't believe what I was hearing!

Everyone began shaking my hand, congratulating me, and they asked me to join them for lunch. But first I had to get to an alone place, I was shaking so hard, my heart was racing, I felt I could faint. I escaped to the restroom where I nearly collapsed. In tears, I called my husband and my office manager to let them know that we had won the Detroit account! "If I die before I get back home, please be sure to put on my epitaph, that I sold *the* Fortune One!"

MARGOT KING currently serves as President of the WIT Foundation, the philanthropic arm of Women in Technology. Prior to her current role on the board of WITF, Margot has served as Vice President (2009), Secretary (2008), and as Co-Chair of WIT Connect (2006) in presenting the premier networking and fund-raising event in Atlanta's technology community.

As President of WIT Foundation, Margot is involved with bringing awareness of Science, Technology, Engineering and Math (STEM) studies and future career pathways to middle and high school young women. "It is our mission to attract young women to explore and enroll in STEM related college programs that will increase a future female workforce population." This year the WIT Foundation signature program Girls Get IT will touch over 200 young women offering corporate hosted events where they can see behind the scenes how technology drives all aspects of the business world. "It is truly gratifying to see girls get excited about how everyday lives are impacted by science and technology, and helps them visualize themselves being a future innovator."

Margot King is the Founder and Vice President of OnSite Resource Solutions, a ZeroChaos Company that specialize in global workforce solutions by optimizing talent acquisition processes. Margot has had 25 years experience in the human resource consulting business and is a nationally recognized pioneer in the concept of on-site recruitment and retention solutions. She is the co-author of *Perfect Phrases for Perfect Hiring*, a McGraw-Hill publication (2007). She has been the creator, producer and host of Job Talk, a nationally syndicated radio talk show about career empowerment. She is the recipient of the NAWBo 2009 WE Award recognized for entrepreneurial leadership.

Margot and her husband, Jerry Watkins have been residents of Atlanta, Georgia for over twenty-five years, and have a daughter who is a practicing attorney in Nashville, Tennessee.

HEADQUARTERED IN ORLANDO, FLORIDA, ZEROCHAOS is a ground-breaking workforce management company. ZeroChaos helps visionary companies achieve greater management and financial control of their workforce and talent supply chains through innovative private-label solutions and full-disclosure pricing. ZeroChaos is one of the largest and fastest growing firms in the country.

Riding the Career Rollercoaster

by Barbara Kunkel

Chief Information Officer
Troutman Sanders LLP

ATLANTA, GEORGIA

Riding the Career Rollercoaster

When sharing stories from my own experiences, I find it almost comical how I somehow managed to stay focused on a career in the field of technology in the midst of so many challenges. In high school, I knew that a career in the new field of computers was in the cards for me. I had an affinity for math, and computer programming seemed to be a logical fit with my interests. Solving problems in an organized, step-by-step fashion is a key strength of mine. Also, it is how software programs are written and business problems are approached. The stark reality of affording a college education, at a time when money was so scarce in my family, was but the first of many rollercoaster rides throughout my life.

CAREER LESSON #1:
Never fear technology, leverage it for opportunity.

In 1977, my high school guidance counselor, Mr. Lissow, secretly led me into the room where the school had recently bought a computer to assist in conducting college searches. Students were not allowed on the computer because it required a certain level of expertise to operate. I had never operated a computer before and this one required some understanding of computer BASIC programming. However, I had just completed a newly offered course in programming with Mr. Alampi, my math teacher. Mr. Lissow was confident I would have no problem figuring out how to operate the equipment. After hooking up the phone to the rubber sockets on an acoustic coupler modem and dialing into the college search database, I was able to write some computer code to narrow my college search. This high school experience was the spark that ignited my interest and passion in the field of technology.

In the years that followed, I experienced many incredibly rewarding moments working in IT, as well as some embarrassing situations. Each humiliating experience was a temporary low point in my career (e.g., bringing down a Fortune 100 company's computer system because of an infinite loop in my computer program or speaking for the first time in front of C-level executives and spewing out more techno-speak then anyone cared to hear). It was those low points in my techy life, combined with a positive, no-fear attitude that fueled my ability to turn things around by leveraging IT to create valuable opportunities.

I still smile when I think of Mr. Lissow and Mr. Alampi. Did they conspire to influence my future in the field of technology? If so, thank you gentlemen! My college choice was perfect. The college I wanted to attend offered both computer science and accounting courses. And after living 17 years at home with seven brothers and two sisters, I was quite motivated to escape the daily chaos at home to face the new challenges of academic life. Yet, the affordability of my dream was in serious doubt.

CAREER LESSON #2:
Think creatively and work the angles.

My parents were my role models for having given all of us kids an exceptional work ethic. To that end, I was able to figure out a way to afford, at a minimum, my first year of college. I decided after that I would come up with Plan B for the next three years. At that time, I was working at K-mart 12 hours a week in the fashion accessories department and saving every penny for college. It wasn't going to be enough and the reality was that balancing school, my sport activities, and volunteer work, did not leave time to work additional hours at K-mart. Something had to give.

It was time for a different plan of attack. I decided to convince each of my high school teachers to allow me to take their course through an independent study program. After agreeing to each of their concessions, I was able to work an additional 20 hours a week at K-mart. This experience really tested my time management skills, taught me a lesson about the value of creative thinking; and, showed me the importance of effective negotiations.

Thinking creatively (or embracing innovation) has been a maxim throughout my career. I have repeatedly heard the cliché from my bosses and respected colleagues to do more with less. The creative application of technology to real business problems has been the key to my success. For instance, facilitating a meeting with a team of technologists and business leaders, we identified areas within the organization where we may have extra capacity with our people, within the processes, or with our technology. We then brainstormed ideas of how we might utilize this extra capacity through process redesign. Over a three year period, we successfully implemented many of the ideas. This type of creative thinking and the practical application of technology had generated significant bottom-line savings for the organization.

CAREER LESSON #3:
Embrace diversity.

College was my first experience with gender diversity. In the late '70s, computer science classes were populated predominately with male students. Thankfully, my seven brothers taught me not to be intimidated by male dominated situations. It was challenging at first to find common ground with my male counterparts when working on team assignments. For me, I saw tremendous value in this experience because it forced me to work harder to prove that I was totally capable. In turn, my teammates came to appreciate a woman's prospective and a creative problem solving approach to class assignments.

Although my college experiences had opened my eyes to the value of diversity, my worldview was truly rocked when 15 years later I stepped into my first director level position in a professional services firm. My department included members with varied experience and educational backgrounds and different personality styles.

It was difficult to bring this organization together because many had become accustomed to maintaining the status quo. Moreover, my IT department had the lowest internal customer service ratings among the administrative organizations.

Over the next several months, I reached out to my boss, colleagues, and the internal customers to learn more about the firm culture and the perceptions of my department. I concluded that this was not a situation where the baby needed to be thrown out with the bath water. I had decided to restructure the organization and change some key leadership positions. I then assembled my new leadership team for their first among many leadership team meetings – which later came to be known as the "cabin in the woods" meetings.

One of my colleagues in the Human Resources department had agreed to facilitate my first leadership team meeting. We spent several hours preparing and planning for the meeting. Utilizing an "outsider" to facilitate the first meeting was an approach designed to help break down the walls between sub-groups within the organization, without fear of career repercussions. Having an outsider to encourage the freedom of thought and the exchange of ideas also helped bring different values and perspectives to the leadership development and decision-making process.

Future cabin in the woods meetings were held and led by me. Over time, the leadership team gelled and maintaining the status quo was no longer the norm. The internal customer satisfaction survey rose by more than two percentage points and our technology platform had become much more robust. Embracing the principles of diversity really made a difference. The cabin in the woods meetings (yes, we actually went to a cabin in the woods for our meetings) brought us all back to opening our eyes to the rewarding possibilities within our work environment.

CAREER LESSON #4:
Stick with a Balanced Scorecard – at work and at home.

Everyone on my leadership team is encouraged to have a personal leadership plan. My plan incorporates elements that are in balance with the customer, the shareholders, and the employees. A balanced scorecard is simply a model for bridging the gap between the corporate strategy and the work of your team. It includes a focus on five strategic areas: financial results, customer satisfaction, quality results, employee motivation and professional development.

The linkage between the corporate or firm vision and strategy and the employees while measuring their contributions using the balanced scorecard approach can be enormously successful. I have found that when your goals and objectives process are combined with effective leadership, it brings clarity to the employees, which in turn, results in increased profitability, productivity and employee moral.

I keep the process simple and consistent. For example, in my organization, the professional development strategy includes a measurable objective for each employee to complete 40 hours of training each year. In IT, keeping up with advances in technology requires a commitment to continuous learning. Otherwise, you run the risk of becoming outdated, or worse yet, obsolete with your tech skills. Development of a balanced scorecard and effectively leading efforts that will link this scorecard to the defined strategies will increase the overall performance of an organization. I have come to appreciate leaders who guide with both head (balanced scorecard) and heart (emotional intelligence) because the end result fosters environments that promote teamwork, collaboration, and success.

Balancing work and personal life can also be a challenge. Early on in my career, part of my job was to be on-call. I was a mother of two children under the age of five years old at that time. I enjoyed playing on company sponsored sport teams and found this to be an excellent source for career networking. I really enjoyed the exercise! But balancing everything took real focus and ingenuity.

Imagine being on the soccer field playing in the game, while your kids were on the sidelines under the watchful eye of the babysitter, and the pager hooked to your soccer shorts starts to buzz. You then wave over to the coach that it was time to take you out of the game. You jump in the car, drive to a nearby restaurant, and because of your connections with the restaurant owner and your pre-planning activities, the laptop is sitting on the kitchen counter ready to be remotely connected to work. You get real good at balancing everything when you plan your work, and work your plan!

CAREER LESSON #5:
Discover the authentic you.

On your road ahead, engaging in a self-assessment process provides invaluable learning. A personal self-assessment is an interlude of appreciating your strengths and accepting (and effectively managing) the limitations of your weaknesses. Discovering who you are, what inspires your passion, and how you can build yourself into a better person are my final words of advice to all aspiring leaders.

Accept constructive criticism throughout your career and realize that it will help to make you a better person. Most seasoned leaders discover that both personal and professional diversions can result in never taking the time to probe their inner self. I have found that self-discovery through a 360-degree feedback program, as well as through team collaboration, is an amazing and rewarding experience. My journey thus far has been a truly eyes wide-open experience. I have thoroughly enjoyed the ride.

BARBARA KUNKEL is CIO at Troutman Sanders LLP with over twenty-five years of IT leadership, including more than a decade in a premier law firm. She directs all aspects of information management including Information Technology, e-discovery Support,

Library & Research Services, Conflicts, and Records Management. She is responsible for the administrative management of these departments.

Prior to Troutman Sanders, Barb worked for Nixon Peabody for twelve years as CIO and for the Eastman Kodak Company for twelve years as a programmer, senior systems analyst, and software development manager. She also spent one year at the Rochester Telephone Company as an applications development supervisor for one of their subsidiary start-up companies.

Barb completed her Bachelor of Science degree at Bowling Green State University (in Bowling Green, Ohio), earned her M.B.A. degree at the University of Rochester's Simon School, and is currently working on her Doctorate in Business Administration (D.B.A.) at the University of Phoenix.

Barb is recipient of the 2005 Computerworld Premier 100 IT Leaders Award and 2001 Information Technology Women of the Year Award presented by the Women's Council of the Greater Rochester Metro Chamber-of-Commerce. Her talent for building successful teams in the business arena is extended to the soccer field. She has coached girls soccer at all levels for over twenty years. She is also devoted to developing young people who have a passion for technology and business management. In addition to serving as a mentor to the twenty-something generation, Barb is involved with organizations such as Women in Technology, Year Up, and TechBridge.

Barb and her life partner, Phil Headley, reside in Atlanta, Georgia. Her daughter is a practicing attorney in New York City and her son is an electrical engineer working in Silicon Valley.

TROUTMAN SANDERS LLP is an international law firm with more than 650 lawyers and 16 offices in North America, Europe and Asia. Founded in 1897, the firm's heritage of extensive experience, exceptional responsiveness and an unwavering commitment to service has garnered strong, long-standing relationships with clients across the globe. These clients range from multinational corporations to individual entrepreneurs, federal and state agencies to foreign governments, and non-profit organizations to businesses representing virtually every sector and industry. Troutman Sanders lawyers provide counsel and advice in practically every aspect of civil and commercial law related to the firm's core practice areas: Corporate, Finance, Litigation, Public Law and Real Estate. With more than 50 practice groups focused on specific aspects of these areas, the firm is defined by its considerable knowledge base and proactive approach to addressing legal and business challenges.

Quiet Reflections

by Kathleen Kurre

CEO
TechBridge

ATLANTA, GEORGIA

Quiet Reflections

I AM A WOMAN IN TECHNOLOGY. Upon reflection, this is a natural state of being for me. I suspect that it is true for you too. We, as women in technology, have the perfect match: technology tickles our brain and the people we work with; creating, implementing and using the technologies, tickle our hearts. This combination is the creative canvas for smart, intuitive and powerful women, which we all are.

There is more. We are daughters, sisters, friends, mothers, volunteers, and vital contributors in our companies and communities. And, we are our own, constant companion. As a result, a conversation about leadership propels us into a broader perspective – one that lives beyond our gender and profession.

At is essence, leadership is a paradox: It happens in the presence of others and at its root it is a solitary adventure. Said another way, it is a choice, a word, and an action we put into motion with others and it is propelled by the energy of our experience deep within our being. Little did I know when the concept of "leadership" entered my life, it would ask me to understand my relationship to others and myself. Nor, did I truly comprehend its calling to be curious and fearless; or that it would ask me to participate fully in the world, and to honor and love it all.

There are days when I feel the elation of being and working within this knowing. Invariably there are other days, well, simply stated, nothing works as planned. At times, I want to literally control life and have it go my way and in others, I discover the delight it didn't; that life had its own flow and wisdom. Are we leaders only when things go the way we thought? Or does true leadership ask us to tap into an unseen flow?

There have been many days when I feel confident and step easily into the unknown. And there are others when all the "what-ifs" seem scary and stop me abruptly in my tracks. Leadership treatises often lure us to believe that leaders moved confidently forward and step into the unknown, but what do we do with the dark moments and sleepless nights when the next step is shrouded in confusion?

It is interesting isn't it … the many questions that appear? They, in and of themselves, are a revolutionary discovery, particularly being a woman in technology, where answers are often considered to be a sign of competence. This discovery is the heart of the matter. As I thought about my life experiences, looking for conclusions and insights, I realized that in the midst of chaotic, inspiring, unclear, dangerous, or explosive situations, "leading" was not in my thinking vocabulary. How do I write about something that I didn't even know I was doing?

Upon further reflection on this last question, I discovered that as we live our lives fully in the moment – with all the activity around and within us – we naturally participate and contribute where and when we are needed. Afterwards, retrospectively, we decide to call it leadership, or not. It is the distance that allows us to categorize events, reconcile emotions, and create an understandable cause and effect dialogue. My invitation to you is to consider leadership as a call to awareness. Begin by asking a question. Continue by being attentive to your range of experiences and being comfortable with their diversity. In this awareness, our personal, sweet nectar of leadership emerges.

My life has been, and continues to be an adventure – full of stories: successes and failures, endings and new beginnings, relationships, friendships, marriages, jobs, travel, leisure and quiet. The weaving together of the stories has provided fertile ground for awareness. What have I learned?

Watch and listen; seek advice; listen to your heart.

From the time we are infants, we learn from those around us. This is very valuable, as we all know. And yet, the uniqueness of our knowing comes by filtering what we have learned through our own experience. Leadership happens when we blend our knowledge and our experience: we cannot lead like someone else; we can only lead as ourselves. The world needs you, as you, just like the forest needs every tree, every worm, and every blade of grass, animal and plant. The ecosystem thrives because of your unique knowing and contribution.

Relax, smile, and enjoy the ride.

Leadership is a serious subject. We talk about it, analyze it, and strategize our plans. At the end of the day, it is a happy, full, and fulfilled, life that makes our hearts sing. Lighten up and remember that there is always retail therapy. Call a friend and go shopping. You'll have a great time, see lots of different people and the choices of clothes, purses, shoes and colors will remind you that life is full of diversity and wonder. And, remember that after finding a suit you like in your size, you still try it on to see if you like it.

Clarity always follows uncertainty.

A dilemma is brewing, or perhaps has already exploded. You are in the midst of it. You might be the decision maker (positional leader) or you might be part of the team (quiet leader and influencer). Everyone in the dilemma has chosen their corner: they have their facts and opinions that function as conclusions and next steps. You are shrouded in the dark night of the unknown, confusion, and uncertainty as you think your way through the possible actions and outcomes.

What do you do next? Nothing, for a moment; then, breathe and try this exercise. Stand up where you are and notice what is in front of you. Now, take a quarter turn to your right. What do you see? Notice that this small movement creates a new perspective. Now, turn back to where you started. Breathe. Take a quarter turn to the left. Voilà, another new perspective. Take another quarter turn to the left, and the view changes yet again. One more time, take a quarter turn to the left. Stop and breathe. You have just turned to the left three times; you have seen different views in the room in which you stand – all of them presenting options. And, your third left turn is the same as your quarter turn to the right.

Silly exercise? Perhaps. Insightful? You decide. In my experience, when a dilemma arises (there have been plenty) and I feel caught in a box of dead-end options, I breathe and turn in these simple directions. Breathing and seeing the range of perspectives in the room open the space in my being to know that there are always possibilities when I am willing to change my perspective. Plus, the little voice inside chuckles "three lefts do make a right" and in my smile, I release the old belief that there is one right answer. What is the moral of the story? In your dilemma, breathe, and take the next available step. This next step is the action of clarity and leadership.

Begin at the beginning.

Have you had the experience with someone showing you how to do something, telling you how easy it is? Then, you try it; not only is it *not* easy, you may or may not be able to do it. There is a cadence to learning and it starts with where we are. Being a mom, I watched this first hand through the years as my daughter learned to speak, walk, master fractions and then calculus, and play softball.

Working at the leading edge of technology, implementing new technology and using existing technology in new ways, has been a similar teacher. Someone can show me how a new technology works, and yet, my interaction and understanding of it begins with what I know and the technology I have used before.

Leadership, being in relationship with others, and ourselves works within this framework: we begin where we are, whether we are asking ourselves or someone else to consider a new idea or to try something different. And yet, there is more: not only does each of us have our own starting point, we also have free will and the ability to choose our next step even when we don't like the choices.

In my experience, the patina of leadership deepens as I stop to consider that leadership is always an invitation to begin.

It is both an honor and a daunting task to write about leadership in a personal way. I have listened, read, and contemplated the paths that others have taken. It is inspiring. After it is all said and done, the adventure of leadership is personal and unique like our fingerprint. Each of us blossoms into our path as we listen to the wisdom within us, trust it, and share it with others.

The ancient Chinese philosopher, Lao-tzu, through Stephen Mitchell's translation in the Tao te Ching[1] beautifully describes this flow.

Knowing others is intelligence;

knowing yourself is true wisdom.

Mastering others is strength;

mastering yourself is true power.

KATHLEEN KURRE is CEO of TechBridge, a nonprofit that helps other nonprofits leverage technology to do more and reach more people. TechBridge has supported 300+ nonprofits and partners with 100+ technology companies to achieve community-wide impact.

Kathleen has over thirty years experience in the corporate technology sector and as an entrepreneur executive. She has developed and implemented new technologies, led interdisciplinary teams, and built innovative services and businesses. Her experience includes: financial services (PNC Bank, KPMG consulting and

1 Mitchell, Stephen, Tao TE Ching (Harper Collins, First HarperPerennial edition, 1992), 33.

Aegon), healthcare (Humana, Inc.), and technology/healthcare entrepreneur (Healthcare Recoveries and Intellego).

Prior to TechBridge, Kathleen was Lecturer, College of Management and Executive-in-Residence, Interdisciplinary Institute for Leadership and Entrepreneurship at Georgia Tech where she taught technology entrepreneurship and leadership at the graduate and undergraduate levels. She is the founder of Fusion Advisors, LLC that focused on integrating business concepts and processes with individuals' and organizations' capacity to change and expand.

Kathleen has a Bachelor of Science degree, magna cum laude, from Purdue University and a Masters of Divinity from the Beloved Community in Ashland, OR.

TECHBRIDGE is an Atlanta-based nonprofit organization with one mission – to help nonprofits use technology to increase capacity to serve our community. We focus on technology enabling nonprofits to focus on their mission so they can do more and reach more people. Each year, over 100 technology companies who donate dollars, technology, expertise and people support TechBridge. In 2010, TechBridge and the technology community celebrated the 10th annual Digital Ball, the premier Atlanta technology gala.

What is *Your* Story?

by Helene G. Lollis

President
Pathbuilders, Inc.

ATLANTA, GEORGIA

What is *Your* Story?

WHILE IT IS OVERLY SIMPLISTIC and perhaps too binary, I tend to believe that there are two types of people in the world – those for whom life just keeps getting better, with more growth, more awareness, and more anticipation of what is to come; and those who, for some reason, behave as if their best days are behind them – complacent or less interested in learning, reveling in great moments in their past, and caught up in the drudgery of each day. As I am a card-carrying member of Group 1, I actually find the exercise to share my own story challenging, because I feel that I am still creating my story. *And*, since my passion is helping professional women to reach their full potential, I can only take this exercise and combine the 'telling' of my story with the guide for you to develop your own.

The stories of our professional lives are comprised of those unique moments – opportunities, decision points, roles, choices, and experiences that change us, moments that alter the paths of our careers, and after they occur we are never the same. But how often do we take the time to consciously think about our own stories? You may believe that others already know your story, but others only know their own interpretations of the facts as they see them – they don't know how you see them or more importantly how those factual elements impacted you – your learning, your reactions, or how events prepared you for your future and all that is ahead of you. It is critical that you know and tell your story well, because in large part, it is your job to tell others what you want them to know, and no one should ever or will ever be as vested in your career success as you are.

So, let me share four of those key moments in my own career, and weave them into my story, but pay attention … you, too, will be tasked with completing this exercise on your own.

Four key events

I decided to pursue engineering as a field of study in college. After a high school career where I captained the debate team, was president of an Explorer post focused on Law, and fully convinced everyone around me that I would be an attorney, I rather drastically announced that I wanted to be a chemical engineer. Fortunately I took time to think about my real strengths and what felt natural, and chemistry and calculus were just like 'breathing' to me; I think like an engineer. I solve problems, I fix things that are broken, and I am always focused on finding simpler and easier ways to do things. With both my BS and MS in ChemE, I embarked on a very rewarding career in commodity plastics process development with a company called Amoco, and I had great success.

About six years into my career I was ready to make a change. While I was ready to move into product development and marketing, my leadership wanted me to stay where I was. I asked for a meeting with my boss' boss who literally told me that I was 'too valuable' to move and that I needed to remain in my position. (Please.) I was fortunate to have mentors around me who both encouraged me to pursue what I wanted but also helped me to think about the situation from the perspective of my boss' boss – thinking through what could constitute a 'win' for him. What a huge learning … because in business, any move requires risk, and given that I was performing well, minimizing risk was more important to this leader than my development. So, I found my own replacement, built a solid transition plan, and scheduled another meeting (this time with my replacement in tow) to lay out the plan. I began to understand corporate politics, the power of taking charge of your own career, the importance of mentors, and the criticality of creating win-wins for your management – I had to overcome *his* fears, not mine.

Ten years into my career I was placed in a role to draft our business unit's strategic plan. Our industry was on the verge of massive consolidation, there were too many competitors employing too many technologies, and not enough margin to support that dynamic. By now, we were a part of BP, and we needed a plan – who we wanted to buy or merge with, what capacity to take out of the system, etc. I remember being surprised that I was asked to lead the effort. I had not yet spent time in our strategic planning group; I had focused my time in manufacturing, R&D, product development, and marketing. It wasn't until I gave my first briefing for our executive team meeting that I realized why I had been asked to take this on. Because of the multi-functional background that I had in our business unit, there were few others who had the depth of understanding around what implementation of this strategy would really mean – to our people, to our technologies, and to our customers. I learned to understand the value of cross-functional experience, and how critical cross-functional thinking is for aligning strategy and execution, and also for positioning yourself as a senior leader.

After twelve years at Amoco and BP I decided to take my career in a new direction. Together with two other women, I purchased a small consulting firm focused on helping companies to develop their female talent. We have more than tripled the size of the firm, we have built meaningful programs and experiences, and we have changed women and their companies for the better. I found my passions – helping organizations to leverage their talent, developing professional women, leading an organization, managing a P&L, and being an entrepreneur. This new direction caused me to draw on all that I had learned, and while many saw it as a drastic career change, the way I see it, 'my story' if you will, is that it is a natural evolution, having been headed to just this point for years.

My story

So, just put the pieces together … I'm a problem-solver, I constantly want things to be better. I'm able to help professional people grow, because I understand corporate politics, I deeply value mentors and meaningful insights into how companies work, and I know that you have to take charge of your own career and create win-wins for yourself and the organization. I also know how critically important it is to build a multi-functional career path so that you can integrate all of your learning to grow into senior leadership. And, my good fortune is that I have found a way to marry all of that with my passions of helping companies and women, and leading an organization.

That's *my* story. No question there were bumps and missteps along the way, and no question these same experiences could be viewed differently, but this is the way I choose to tell it. I could take that same experience where I was told I couldn't move and focus on the negative aspects of my leader prioritizing risk management over my professional development, or highlight how our new strategy was critically needed because the insights of manufacturing and technology had long been left out of our strategic planning process. But as a member of Group 1 I did not, because that is not how those factual elements impacted me – my story tells you how they impacted me.

Ahh – but now it is your turn – you must map the transitions in your career to the learning's that they produced and then *choose* how you are going to describe them. This is even more important for the missteps – identifying the key learning's and how they impacted the direction of your career. Each of you has a story that describes your career, and your ability to succeed relies in part on how you tell that story.

Crafting your story

For every key decision or event or transition point, there are two critical things for you to consider: first, what is the impact that it had on you that is relevant today; and second, what is the story that describes that impact. I encourage you to grid this out on paper.

Take for example my finding 'Mary' to replace me when I wanted to move out of process development:

Key Decision / Transition Points	*Impact Today*	*The Story*
Finding Mary to replace me; building and presenting a transition plan	Learned lesson from mentor of how business works – you are less risky where you are performing	I began to understand corporate politics and the power of taking charge of your own career. Learned how to create win-win situations.

While this is a simple practice, I am hazarding a guess that few of you will have taken the time to do this, and I can attest from my own experience, how powerful this practice is. Carve out some time to do this exercise, and resist the urge to focus only on the positives – those experiences with negative outcomes are the most important to map through, because you should own the way that story is told.

As you grow in your career, it becomes more and more important to reflect on learning's, to integrate seemingly disparate ideas, and to bring all that you have experienced into your work. That is your personal power that allows you to do what others cannot, and it is all already inside of you, you just need to tell the rest of us.

HELENE LOLLIS is the President of Pathbuilders, Inc., an organization focused on helping companies shape the future with high-performing people. Since 1995, the organization has worked with over 300 organizations and has impacted the career success of thousands of individuals. Prior to being with Pathbuilders, Helene spent 12 years with Amoco and then BP Corporations in a wide range of responsibilities in the commodity plastics arena. An engineer by education, her work spanned the areas of process and product development, marketing, strategic planning, and mergers/acquisitions.

Helene is frequently invited to speak on the topics of mentoring, women in the workplace, and career planning. She has been published in HR *Magazine*, *Diversity Executive*, and *Talent Management*, and the work of Pathbuilders has been featured in *The Wall Street Journal*, the *Atlanta Business Chronicle*, and PINK *Magazine*. Helene serves on the Executive Committee for the Board of Directors of the Metro Atlanta Chamber of Commerce, where she chairs the Education Committee. She also serves on the Executive Committee for Junior Achievement of Georgia and the Board of the Society of Human Resources – Atlanta.

She is a graduate of the Leadership Atlanta Class of 2008. She was selected as a finalist for the Metro Atlanta Chamber's Small Business Person of the Year Award in 2005 and in 2007 was recognized by the Executive Women of Goizueta as the Guiding Star Award Winner.

PATHBUILDERS partners with Fortune-ranked companies to create gender-diverse senior leadership teams that directly contribute to the bottom-line. Pathbuilders combines executive education and peer exchange with structured mentoring to develop high-impact female leaders who move their companies forward. The company offers formal mentoring programs and customized solutions to develop high-potential female talent at each of the four distinct phases of women's careers.

Technology is Transactional, Relationships Should Not Be

by Sonia T. Lucas

Vice President of Sales
Payformance Corporation

JACKSONVILLE, FLORIDA

Technology is Transactional, Relationships Should Not Be

THE YEAR IS 1996 and being new in the Atlanta community, I found myself perusing through the *Atlanta Business Chronicle*. I read an informational segment about Women In Technology and noted the contact person was Luba Brock, WIT President. Making the call, I found myself speaking to Luba herself! Following her enthusiastic and welcoming words, I committed to attend the next monthly meeting. Very much like that first call, the meeting was highly energetic and proved to be a wonderful gathering of driven, supportive and ambitious women who shared a common intersection in technology.

What a great first impression these women left with me! To name a few of the women I met: Luba Brock, Gayle McMahon, Sue Miller (who ended up being my Vice President in 1999), Besty Cagle (a future WIT President), Marci McCarthy (a future WIT President), Shawn Grover (a future WIT President), Jan Spurlin (in 1998 we were co-chairs of WIT Connect) and the list goes on and on.

What an assortment of professional women attended the WIT meetings. I encountered managers from entry level to senior level; developers, analysts, project managers, attorneys, marketers, business developers, and entrepreneurs. There were middle-aged women and young bloods. The varied combination of women made me instantly feel like I could fit right in with my business development background in the technology sector.

What struck me the most about the membership was the ability of these women to break down typical barriers, define clear goals, define a reasonable, yet aggressive plan and successfully *execute* on a plan – quickly! It was amazing – we all know situations in companies or groups we've worked with were you see analysis paralysis or grandiose plans that never get executed. Not at WIT. WIT was (and still is) a group of women who wanted to make an impact helping other women and the community and through hard-work – and usually blood, sweat and tears effectively and efficiently eliminated obstacles and pushed through to accomplish the defined goals.

At WIT, the vision was clear and the women were motivated and empowered. WIT has a unique way of luring you in (as a volunteer – we were all volunteers), setting the hook, and reeling you in and then before you know it, you've bought it all in – hook, line and sinker! I believe the reason for this success is WIT's ability to create an environment where you can contribute and make a substantial impact, while providing a visible platform not usually afforded to women – much less women in technology. Almost immediately, I found the place where I could add value within WIT.

Being in sales management, my focus was to generate and nurture relationships for my employer, Computer Associates. By 1999, I was honored to be elected to the position of WIT President. The year proved to be a year of firsts. WIT, along with B&TA and SSA, joined together to form the Technology Association of Georgia (TAG). The founding of TAG had been the 1996 vision of WIT President Luba Brock, B&TA President Barbara Stafford, and SSA President Chris Coleman. Suddenly, I was not only in the leadership role at WIT, I also held the first WIT board seat at TAG in its inaugural year.

WIT wanted to elevate the executive relationships held with the Atlanta community, so the WIT Corporate Advisory Board was created. The Board was composed of executive management level women from some of the largest companies based in Atlanta. Overwhelmingly, we found executive women who were very interested in playing a part to facilitate success for other women in the technology community.

I am most proud of my accomplishments in leading people to connect and bring value to one another. Along the way, I learned the importance of meeting people where they are (and not where you want them to be) and I confirmed the importance of having a service mindset in relationships. All too often, people are very transactional in their approach to relationships. I believe having a more expansive view of a relationship – even a cradle to grave outlook – can really turn an acquaintance, meeting or situation into a value driven relationship and provide a journey capable of life lesson level impact.

Throughout my career, I've been blessed to experience many functions of the technology industry (consulting, product management and service management) and in multiple capacities (direct sales, executive sales management, marketing management, client implementations and services). I've worked for myself, for small boutique firms, and large organizations. I've focused on many industry verticals ranging from hospitality, financial services, transportation, retail, manufacturing and healthcare.

Sure, cool and exciting products, technology and service offerings are rampant in my career, but it's the people that I've been blessed to meet and work with that really have added the most value to my life – not just my work life but my total life. The advice I would share with anyone willing to listen is to never underestimate the importance of a relationship. People will always come and go throughout your career. The special relationships you nurture and take time for can have life lasting impact. True value can be exchanged over a very long time – way beyond the deal or opportunity you are working on. The key is being able to meet people where they are, to embrace differences, and to focus on serving the relationship and adding value. When this is done authentically and with the right motivation, the value-add becomes reciprocal and automatic.

WIT delivers value – real, meaningful value. I am very proud to be associated with such an organization and truly appreciate the lasting impact: the opportunities given to me and the many relationships developed over the course of my time with WIT.

SONIA T. LUCAS is a dynamic executive with proven ability to build and lead winning sales teams and effectively drive strategic business results. Ms. Lucas has over 20 years professional experience including strategic sales and client implementation services in the Fortune 500 market. Her career achievements have included eight-figure revenue growth, Fortune 500 market penetration, and the building and management of highly successful teams.

Ms. Lucas has proven effectiveness in the analysis of business and IT requirements, defining and implementing sales and customer service strategies, change and organizational management. She applies a results-oriented leadership approach, which has led to the success of various teams responsible for driving revenue. Ms. Lucas' broad industry experience includes healthcare, financial services, technology, and hospitality sectors.

As Vice President of Sales for Payformance Corporation, Ms. Lucas is responsible for driving revenue, developing and maintaining executive relationships for the organization. Payformance is dedicated to being the leader and trusted source for solutions to simplify and remove costs from the healthcare payment and settlement process.

Over the years, Ms. Lucas has held a number of executive sales management positions with such technology product and consulting services firms as Computer Associates, Novations Project Management, LDA Systems and CBM Technologies. In 2003, she successfully co-founded and funded LucQue Group, a business management consulting firm serving the financial services sector.

In 1999, Ms. Lucas effectively served as President of Women in Technology. Ms. Lucas led WIT along with the leadership of B&TA and SSA to become founding societies of Technology Association of Georgia (TAG). During the same year, Ms. Lucas served on the board for TAG.

Ms. Lucas has a passion for enriching women and their families. As a Board Member for Harvest Link, Ms. Lucas plays a key role in developing and implementing enrichment programs for individuals, families and business owners. Harvest Link is an interdenominational Christian outreach group focused on advancing the Kingdom of God here on Earth.

Second to her relationship with God, Ms. Lucas' top responsibility is her family. Ms. Lucas has been married for over 15 years to a loving and supportive husband, Sean, and is mother to a ten-year-old daughter, Chanel, and four–year-old twin girls, Alexis and Brianna. She is an avid tennis player and competes year round in the ALTA and USTA leagues.

FOCUSED SOLELY ON THE HEALTHCARE INDUSTRY, PAYFORMANCE brings passion to solving challenges related to healthcare claims settlement. With a reputation for innovation, Payformance develops solutions that enable healthcare payers and providers to settle claims electronically, with significant savings over historical methods and improving operations by increasing efficiency.

What Makes WIT Special?

by Tino Mantella

President
Technology Association of Georgia

ATLANTA, GEORGIA

What Makes WIT Special?

TAG's ANNUAL "STATE OF THE INDUSTRY REPORT" has historically highlighted that women are playing an ever-increasing role leading and owning Georgia companies. High-tech was the predominant field in respect to women owned/led businesses. Further, between 2000 and 2005, Georgia made the greatest gains (66% increase), compared to benchmark states, in the number of women graduating from Georgia universities with science and/or engineering degrees. Benchmark states include California, Florida, Massachusetts, North Carolina, and Texas. The point I am making is one I often make: Georgia boasts a strong and growing technology industry and women are playing an ever increasing role in our state's progress.

Since taking the helm of the Technology Association of Georgia six years ago, I have heard and read a multitude of theories around what it takes to build a tech-based economy. Having a nurturing environment for people and companies is one constant factor expressed by the theorists. WIT fits the bill when it comes to providing infrastructure, support, and motivation, for Georgia's women of technology. Over the course of my personal business journey, I have been fortunate to have led major non-profit institutions for more than 25 years. Non-profits are all about creating nurturing environments and from my vantage point, very few measure up to WIT in respect to impact.

So what makes WIT special? The essential factor is the people involved. Based on my six years as a key WIT partner, the words I would use to describe the culture are engaged, motivated, passionate, and strategic. Of these words, "strategic" is the driving force and the one I will focus on in the remainder of my observations.

Six years prior to my arrival on the job, TAG was being formed by three organizations that joined forces: Women in Technology, Business and Technology Alliance, and the Southeastern Software Association. They realized that they could derive an economy of scale by coming together as one. This was a merger of three independent not-for-profits. Those that have been in the non-profit ranks know how hard it is for organizations to leave their egos at the door for the greater good. This strategic move by WIT, as well as B&TA and SSA has paid off, as 12 years later each of these organizations are supporting their stakeholders. Additionally, they formed TAG, which as of this writing has 27 unique special interest groups under its umbrella and is serving nearly 11,000 members.

When I stepped into the TAG door in 2004, it was at a low point. Facing declining membership, a loss of key financial supporters, and a downward-spiraling economy, there were questions about its very survival. Dawn Patrick, a partner with Deloitte at the time, and leading women on the Georgia technology scene, was Chair of the Board at the time and hired me! She also had implemented many critical, strategic, and tough decisions prior to my arrival, to begin righting our limping organization. I have always credited Dawn, and the small leadership team that didn't abandon us in 2004, for saving TAG.

Even during our most challenging period WIT was a shining star. WIT, in 2004, had grown to become the most significant contributor to the TAG family. Along with their successful programs, they were running in the black. The combination of WIT's strength and desire to take their initiatives to the next level, and TAG's transition, led to another significant strategic decision on the part of WIT. The Board of Directors determined it was time to spread their wings and forge out on their own, by creating another separate organization. I was personally included in the discussions to help determine what would be best for WIT and TAG. Our collaborative approach resulted in a quality outcome that still stands today. WIT would charter independently yet stay as a society of TAG, as well as being apart of its membership program. Looking back on the decisions that were made then, I have concluded that it was the right thing to do. Both WIT and TAG have evolved and are contributing more to our respective communities than ever before.

Some organizations stagnate while others evolve. Some maintain their relevance while others become irrelevant. It's true in the for-profit and not-for-profit worlds. Because of people and strategy I give WIT high marks in respect to their ongoing evolution and their relevance. They, for example, have recently added an Executive Director position to provide day-to-day support operations and to create program continuity. Mentoring initiatives for women have hit a new level of excellence, and the WIT Connect event has become the envy of the Georgia non-profit fundraising community. The WIT Board and volunteers have always been the backbone of the institution. Their dedication to the cause has been exemplary and many staff-driven organizations can't match their outputs.

It's been a privilege to partner with WIT over these past six years. The leadership has been able to effectively change while sustaining enviable continuity in mission and strategic direction. There is no reason to anticipate anything but continued growth and impact from WIT and it's been a privilege to partner with such a great organization.

TINO MANTELLA joined TAG in September, 2004 as the organization's new President. Mantella, prior to joining TAG, had amassed over 20 years of related experience leading two of the nations more prestigious volunteer-driven organizations – National Arthritis Foundation and YMCA of Metropolitan Chicago. As President and CEO of two multifaceted and complex charities, he spearheaded agendas that led to the development of innovative new services, resulting in the facilitation of significant membership growth. In addition, Mantella's track record reflects impressive results in fund raising, advocacy, and economic development.

Since coming to TAG, Mantella has worked with a team of dedicated volunteers and staff to: build a prestigious board made up of 60 technology stakeholders; grow membership by more than 400%; and add a series of program and services that support TAG's vision of educating, informing and uniting the technology community, while driving technology based economic development for Georgia.

Mantella serves on the board of Catholic Charities of Atlanta, and on the Executive Committee of Technology Councils of North America (TECNA), and is a past member of the Kellogg Board of Advisors.

TAG is a leading technology industry association dedicated to the promotion and economic advancement of the state's technology industry. TAG provides leadership in driving initiatives in the areas of policy, capital, education and giving, and also brings the technology community together through events, initiative programs and networking opportunities. TAG serves as an umbrella organization for 27 special interest groups, or Societies, including Women in Technology (WIT). Additionally, TAG's charitable arm, the TAG Education Collaborative, is focused on helping science, technology, engineering, and math (STEM) education initiatives thrive.

New, New and New – A Time of "Firsts"

by Marci McCarthy

CEO & President
T.E.N. – Tech Exec Networks, Inc.

ATLANTA, GEORGIA

New, New and New – A Time of "Firsts"

DURING MY DAYS AS A MARKETING MAJOR at Babson College, technology was the furthest thing from my mind. Drawn to the creative side of business, I entertained visions of fashion design; but I couldn't sew well or sketch the models and designs fast enough. With fashion hopes dashed, upon graduation, I turned my attention to retail, only to discover the incredibly low salaries attached to the industry.

I began looking for better paying positions, and it was at that point that technology found me. I landed my dream job as a marketing coordinator with a small, family-owned, startup software company that developed information systems for human resources. The year was 1993 and it was my real first foray into the world of technology. I quickly discovered that while Babson provided an excellent education, it was slanted toward marketing and selling consumer brands and did little to prepare me for the business-to-business marketplace. Selling technology products and services was a new industry, and I had to adapt to transfer my retail knowledge and marketing skills to the business-to-business environment.

The first defining moment in my career came when, with one year of work experience, I decided to leave Boston. Blustery winters, long commutes and a high cost of living drove me to seek employment opportunities elsewhere. An offer from a firm called UserTech was my ticket to Atlanta – and to another set of "firsts." I joined Betsy Cagle as the second employee in the newly opened Atlanta office. Tasked with training responsibilities for ERP implementations, it was my first foray into the world of consulting.

WIT – the early days

Moving to Atlanta and meeting Betsy opened a new world of connections and experiences for me. While I didn't know it at the time, it was also setting the stage for a true business education. It was 1994 and Women in Technology (WIT) was just beginning to be formed. I was fortunate to be there from the beginning as Betsy Cagle, Jane Wyche, Shawn Grover, Valerie Crelia-Shaw, Luba Czura Brock, and others who were active in the Business & Technology Alliance (B&TA) and Southeaster Software Association (SSA) recognized an opportunity to create a new organization, focused their vision, drew on their experiences and created Women in Technology.

These inspiring women were the most amazing and energetic group of women that I have ever had the fortune to work and become acquainted with on a professional and personal level. Although I was ten to twenty years their junior, they treated me as an equal business professional. I vowed to learn from these women and, through their Southern charm, I was able to develop a business network and become involved in, and passionate about, a number of exciting fund-raising and recognition activities that have become an important part of the Atlanta technology community – and still are to this day.

The evolving WIT community provided a fertile, unlimited, empowering learning opportunity. My involvement in WIT gave me a chance to step out of my role as an end-user trainer and expand my skills, build my network and develop my business acumen and leadership abilities. It was a wonderful period of life and one had free reign to invent it at will. Soon I was chairing events and activities such as the Women of the Year in Technology Award (WOTY) program and the annual WIT Connect, an executive auction of Atlanta's top CIOs and IT executives. As my involvement in and passion for WIT grew, so did the membership's belief in me. After six short years, I was asked to take on the role of president of WIT. I assumed the presidency in 2001 and served as the youngest president of the organization at the age of 29.

Opened doors

In addition to providing me with the opportunity to hone my

business skills, WIT opened numerous doors for me, especially employment opportunities. It's fair to say that all of my positions after UserTech came to me because of the exposure afforded to me through WIT.

The second defining moment in my career occurred when, as chairperson for the Woman of the Year program, I met Joan Lyman, founder of SecureWorks. Joan invited me to interview for the director of product marketing position at her company. Although I knew little about networks or information security, I was offered the position because, by being involved in WIT, Joan was able to get to know more about me than what a paper resume could convey. It was 2001 and it was my first foray into information security, an emerging industry with a lot of sizzle and mystique.

Today, I am still aspiring and the most recent defining moment in my career is the decision to launch my own company, T.E.N. – Tech Exec Networks. This is a time of rebirth and renewal as I love bringing people together. Similar to the way in which WIT opened doors for me, I look to open doors for my customers. When I hear about how IT and information security executives have had their lives changed because of the doors that were opened for them through our channels, relationships and programs, such as the Information Security Executive™ (ISE™) of the Year Award Program Series, it gives me the passion and desire to continue every day. This is what inspires me on a day-to-day basis – to bring people together in such a special and unique way.

On being a leader

A leader, especially in a small company, is able to work with people who they like and respect. A level of friendship may have previously existed or may develop as they work together, but there are still boundaries of which one has to be cognizant. A leader can't always be friends with employees, can't always make them happy and can't always agree, which means that leadership can sometimes be a very lonely place.

All eyes are on the leader. The smallest thing said, done or purchased, while seemingly insignificant or a non-issue to the leader, can be perceived as unnecessary, extravagant or hold greater meaning by the employee than intended. Unbalanced perceptions can cause employees to begin questioning the leader, lead to dissatisfaction or strain working relationships. It's better to address issues as they arise than allow them to linger.

Thinking about all the challenges of running a business – Will people think I'm crazy? Are customers interested in buying our services? Will I be able to deliver? Will my team? Or will I be able make a payroll? – can cause many a sleepless night. The days when everything comes together are the best days that you have – and make it all worthwhile.

For those who aspire

As I reflect on my career, I found that regardless of which industry you are in – or your state in the industry – what matters above all are the relationships. Relationships are what bind us together and move us forward. Although most people have a primary mentor, I believe it is most important to cultivate relationships with a number of people in order to learn more than one leadership style. Aligning with a diverse, core group of people will bring something different to the table for each part of your goal.

If you set goals for yourself and surround yourself with people who have similar goals to which you aspire, you can be very successful because you can learn from their strengths and weaknesses, failures and success. Also, success is measured in many different ways and levels. One must define one's own meaning of success; just because one isn't a CEO doesn't mean that one isn't successful.

When starting a business, there will be difficult days and money will always be a factor; but if you have a dream and a solid idea that can bring something different to the marketplace, something that doesn't exist, and you can get other people to believe in you, you will be successful. A key element of success is to never accept "*no*" as a "*no*." Use the *no* as an opportunity to step back, review the situation and find another way to move forward.

WIT made a life-changing difference in my entire professional career and I will be forever grateful to the organization and to the women who were leading the organization when I was fully involved. Doors have been opened for me that I don't believe would have ever opened had I not been involved from the first day. Joining and becoming involved in a professional organization provides opportunity for development on many levels. It allows one to do something that one is good at, and try things that one is not so good at, without having to be concerned about failure or risk one's career. The experiences, relationships and open doors, which may never open in the course of one's job or profession, will open a world of opportunity.

MARCI MCCARTHY is currently the CEO and President of Tech Exec Networks (T.E.N.), a technology and information security executive networking and relationship-marketing firm. As founder of the organization, she is responsible for driving the strategic direction of this widely respected, privately held company, remaining deeply engaged with a vast network of IT and information security professionals and solution providers.

She has nearly 20 years of business management, networking and marketing experience, including the development in 2003 of T.E.N.'s flagship program, the Information Security Executive of the Year Program Series and Awards™ (ISE Program Series), considered by many to be "the premier recognition and networking program for security professionals." The ISE program recognizes the need for security professionals to be recognized by their peers and exchange information about best practices and current technology solutions. Under McCarthy's direction, it has expanded from a local level to a nationally acclaimed regional and national program series in major cities including Atlanta, Dallas, New York City, San Francisco, and Washington D.C.

Previously, McCarthy was the CEO and co-founder of Executive Alliance, an organization that hosts leadership-recognition forums to honor and recognize outstanding achievements of executives and their companies. Earlier in her career, she held management positions with Lancope, SecureWorks, Deloitte, and PricewaterhouseCoopers (PwC).

McCarthy currently serves on TechBridge's Board of Directors and their Executive Committee for its annual fundraiser, the Digital Ball. As president of Women in Technology (WIT) in 2001, McCarthy was responsible for the highly successful *Women of the Year in Technology Awards* (WOTY) program. In addition, she served on its Board of Directors for six years. Other non-profit boards that she has served on include the Technology Association of Georgia (TAG) and SciTrek's Advisory Board of Directors. She is the past Chairman of the American Diabetes Association Father's Day Council and its acclaimed Father of the Year Awards program.

She also has been recognized in "Who's Who in Georgia's Technology Community" by the *Atlanta Business Chronicle* and as a "Woman to Watch" by *Atlanta's BroadSheet*. A guest lecturer at George Washington University, McCarthy is a nationally sought-after speaker for panel discussions and executive roundtables on strategic technology and leadership topics.

A magna cum laude graduate of Babson College, McCarthy holds a B.S. in Marketing.

T.E.N. is a national technology and information security executive networking and relationship marketing organization, facilitates interaction with peers, industry visionaries and solutions providers. Executive programs include the Information Security Executive™ (ISE™) Program Series, roundtables, receptions, and marketing programs.

Thoughts on Leadership

by Myra McElhaney

Corporate Trainer/Speaker/Writer

ALPHARETTA, GEORGIA

Thoughts on Leadership

I WAS VERY EXCITED WHEN I first had an opportunity to manage people early in my career. I wanted so badly to be professional, to make a good impression and to be respected by my co-workers and the women I managed. I was in a new position overseeing a team of promotional sales people working in a group of department stores to promote our company's cosmetic products.

These were contract sales people who freelanced working on an as-needed basis with whichever cosmetic company was doing promotions or hiring at the time. Several had already worked in the same stores where we were scheduling them to promote our products. Although the sales people we hired were all experienced, I put together notebooks detailing the job description, product information and rules and regulations surrounding their duties. I met with each salesperson individually talking with them about the job, the days and hours they were scheduled and giving them the training manual and my business card.

As they began to do the scheduled hours I was surprised by how many questions I was asked that were covered in the manual. It didn't take me long to realize that most of them didn't read the manual but just did the job as they had when they'd had the same job with different companies. The beautiful manuals I'd worked hard to prepare probably ended up in the trunk of their cars or in the trash right away. It wasn't something they were accustomed to reading or referring to.

Later as I got to know the women better and settled into the job I became friendly with them. On day while having lunch with a couple of these women we were laughing and enjoying ourselves. One of the women, who no longer worked for my company said, "You're so much fun! When I first met you I thought you were such a cold stick-in-the-mud!" She went on to remind me of how I didn't smile, spoke concisely talking only of business and then gave her the training manual. I realized that in my eagerness to appear professional, knowledgeable and more experienced than I was, I overcompensated and came across as cold and unapproachable. This is a common mistake in new or insecure managers.

Unfortunately by the time I had this insight I had swung to the other end of the pendulum and had become too much of a friend to the people I supervised. They loved working with me and when we had a new product to launch or hired extra help for the holidays many good and experienced promotional sales people wanted to work with me. Why wouldn't they? I had a well-earned reputation for being easy to work with, nice and fun. What I didn't realize until later is that I was also way too soft. I did more of their jobs than I should have, went out of my way to make their jobs easy and avoided conflict or having them not like me by not giving constructive feedback when they weren't performing well, broke rules or asked for schedule changes. I had gone from unapproachable to pushover!

After I progressed through my career and transitioned into training which later involved leadership and management training I realized that I had committed not one but two of the most common mistakes that women and men who move into management positions make.

One was trying too hard to appear professional or "tough" and coming across as cold, unapproachable and distant. This doesn't get the best efforts from the people working for you as they don't have a personal connection to you. The other common mistake is being too much of a friend to the people you manage which makes it more difficult to give feedback and hold them to high expectations. This often results in a more lax attitude and not trying to do their best.

Here are some of the leadership lessons I've learned by studying and conducting leadership and management training and in taking on various leadership roles over the years.

There is a big difference between leading and managing. Managing and leading are often used interchangeably in business but there is a difference. Managing refers to being in charge of something like a department or project and making sure that it runs smoothly and effectively. Management is more about the skillful handling of processes and resources to accomplish tasks or meet criteria. Leadership refers more to the relationship with people. It's about being able to guide, influence and get results through inspiring people. The desired result may involve setting a new direction or breaking new ground rather than simply meeting requirements. I like to think of it this way – a manager oversees people where they are and a leader can take them to a new place. That new place may be a new way of doing things, a new level of achievement or a completely new direction. In my career I've worked for managers who were there to ensure that the processes and procedures were followed. I've also worked for leaders who inspire me to accomplish things I never thought possible.

People may be promoted into positions of management and can be successful managers without being viewed as leaders. But some managers do become real leaders. It's said that leaders are defined by people choosing to follow them. You often see unofficial leaders. This is someone that people gravitate to and follow even if the person has no official authority.

In my corporate training business I work with small and mid-size companies and even some large companies where I see that people are good at their jobs, whether it be selling, administrative work, customer service or whatever; then they are promoted to supervise others who do that job. Being good at your job doesn't necessarily mean you'll be good at managing projects or departments. Being good at managing doesn't mean you'll become a good leader. If you want to be a leader the first step is to realize that leadership is a skill and has techniques that can be learned.

Leadership is both a talent and a skill. People often ask whether someone can be a "born leader." One thing makes me answer, "yes". Look at kids on a playground. You'll see that in groups one child will quickly take charge and begin setting direction and the others will follow. What about bullies, gang leaders and the central figure in school cliques? These children haven't been taught leadership skills yet people choose to go along with their ideas and they are naturally able to influence others.

That being said, just as someone with natural musical ability can improve and become excellent with training and practice, a natural born leader can move to a much greater position of influence with training and practice. Just as someone without natural musical talent can learn to plan an instrument adequately, someone who isn't a natural born leader can learn skills and techniques that allow them to be effective leaders. Will they ever be as influential as someone with both talent and skill? Maybe not but with focus and practice they can still be successful leaders.

In addition to the ability to influence people, leaders have vision. They have the ability to see the big picture, to know where they want to go and how to get there. In working on a global women's conference I had the opportunity to work with a young executive who was a great example of a leader. Sarah had a great vision of what the overall conference should look like and could see how all the parts fit together to make that happen. Some people are great with big-picture views. Others are great with details.

What Sarah and other leaders I've observed have in common is the ability to see the big picture without ever losing sight of the details. I call this telescopic vision. Just as you could see a vast landscape with your eye then look through a telescope to see the details, these leaders have the ability to easily move between the big-picture and detail view. When committees or individuals working on this conference would sometimes get caught up in one aspect or part of the conference such as the program or logistics,

Sarah could always see the bigger picture and bring the discussion back to what needed to be done for the overall good of the conference. Yet she always had a handle on the details of each aspect, whether it is the budget, the specifics of what each committee was doing or logistical issues. Her vision not only gave us the direction in the beginning, it kept the various pieces of the project working together toward that end and kept details from being overlooked. All the while her ability to inspire people to get involved and motivate them to do exceptional work brought many talented people to the project.

The ability to lead is tremendously valuable in any business and in the community. There are many great books and resources on leadership. Whether you desire to be a leader in your company, your community or in a smaller group; whether you aspire to positions of leadership or want to be a person of influence in a more personal way I encourage you to consider the various characteristics of leadership that you encounter every day.

MYRA MCELHANEY is frequently quoted in publications such as *Investor's Business Daily*, *The Employment Review*, *Woman's World*, and the *Atlanta Journal and Constitution*. Her articles have appeared in various publications including *Atlanta Woman*, *Customer Relationship Management*, *Competitive Edge*, and *USIndustry Today*.

Myra currently serves on the board of The Possible Woman Foundation and the advisory board of the Professional Women's Information Network. She is a former board member of The International Alliance of Women, the Georgia Women's Institute, Georgia Executive Women's Network and the Georgia Chapter of the National Speaker's Association.

Her professional affiliations include membership in The National Association of Female Executives, the Board of Director's Network and the Atlanta Alliance for Women. Myra's research for various writing projects includes having interviewed over 100 women who were trailblazers in business, government and athletic endeavors.

Myra speaks for associations, corporate audiences and women's groups. Her goal is to inspire people to work with purpose, live with passion and make a difference.

What About Women in Technology?

by Ephraim R. McLean

Regents' Professor
George E. Smith Eminent Scholar's Chair in Information Systems
Chair, Computer Information Systems Department
Director, Center for Research in Information Systems
Robinson College of Business, Georgia State University

ATLANTA, GEORGIA

What About Women in Technology?

I AM A MAN. Why am I writing an essay for a book on *Women in Technology*? For one reason, I have been asked to; but more importantly, because I want to. Women have played a huge part in my personal and professional life and I believe that this influence has shaped my life in various important ways that I would like to share with the readers of this book.

Let me begin with some personal background. I have been married for 45 years to the same wonderful woman, Jane McLean. We have three daughters and one granddaughter. In helping our daughters grow up, we stressed to each of them to "Be the best you can. There is nothing that you cannot do, if you set your mind to it." To reinforce this, I would sit around the dining room table and help each of them, in turn, with their homework. But they would complain, "Daddy, you are not helping me! Just give me the answer to the problem. Don't make me reason it out." I responded that if I told them the answers, they would be ill prepared to figure out new problems that they had not yet encountered. It wasn't until many years later that they reluctantly admitted that I might have been right.

Our first daughter, Ann, went off to UCLA at 16 and is now married and teaches Honors chemistry at Culver City High School. She has her Bachelor's and Master's degrees. Our middle daughter, Janet, also married and with our first grandchild, has a degree in molecular biology, with a minor in French, from the University of Texas in Austin. She is a senior executive in a biotech firm in San Diego. Our youngest daughter, Susan, just graduated Phi Beta Kappa in art history from Mills College in Oakland, and is now job hunting! Each of them is so different from her sisters that it is sometimes hard to believe that they have the same parents. But, as our youngest daughter says: "You and Mom taught us all to be strong, independent women – and we are. Therefore, why are you so surprised that we're different?"

I think our raising them to be strong women was due, in addition to my wife, to the example of my mother. She was flapper in the '20s, with an undergraduate degree from Southern Cal – her sister, my aunt, dated Marion Morrison (John Wayne) there – and mother later did graduate work at the Sorbonne in Paris. One summer, she toured France in the company of Ted Geisel (Dr. Seuss). During World War II, she was an ambulance driver for the Red Cross. She was married to my father, a career naval officer, for 53 years until he passed away. She died shortly thereafter. She had smoked three packs of Camel unfiltered cigarettes a day since she was 15; so, when she was diagnosed with lung cancer 70 years later, I urged her to talk to my daughters about the terrible consequences of smoking. She said: "Look; I'm 85 years old. I love to smoke; have all my life. And you have to die of something. It might as well be something I love to do, like smoking." I told her just to forget about the lecture on the evils of smoking to her granddaughters.

When my father retired from the Navy, as a vice admiral, he pointed out at his retirement ceremony that, of his 39 years in the Navy, he had been at sea for 20 of those years. It is not surprising therefore that I was raised by my mother. There was no household chore or repair that she could not do, a skill that I believe that I have inherited from her. She was quite a gal.

But what about women in technology? After I graduated with my Bachelor's and a Master's degree in mechanical engineering – again, a product of my mother's influence – I went to work as a manufacturing manager at Procter & Gamble after my Army service. It was in the early '60s and P&G was just beginning to bring computers into its factories. I was tapped to be one of its first "end users," to leave the P&G plant in New York City, and to go to corporate headquarters in Cincinnati. In preparation for my move, I took my first course in assembler programming (SPS) in the fall of 1962 on the IBM 1401 – and my instructor was a woman. At the time, I was not surprised. Why shouldn't it have been a woman? Later, in Cincinnati, our entry computer class at

P&G had 15 people, six of whom were women. Again, why should I be surprised? It was only later, when I saw men, who were less qualified than some of these women, move ahead faster that I realized something was wrong. And this is an occurrence that I have seen repeated many times since.

In my undergraduate mechanical engineering program at Cornell, I had one female classmate out of a class of 110. Women weren't supposed to be engineers. Ten years later at M.I.T.'s Sloan School, we had three women in my Master's class of 100. Not much of an improvement. But when I joined the faculty of UCLA's School of Management in 1969, things began to improve. By the time I left UCLA in 1987 to come to Georgia State, the MBA program was almost half women! And they were, if anything, more qualified than the men.

These women MBA students formed a support group, WIM – Women in Management, with T-shirts emblazoned with "The Best Man for the Job … May Be a Woman!" They held monthly meetings, with high-level female executives from the Los Angeles business community as speakers. They graciously invited the faculty – who were overwhelming male – to attend, but few ever bothered to accept their invitation. When I decided to go to their next meeting, it proved to be a profound eye-opener for me. I walked into the large seminar room, filled with women students and guest executives, all extremely well dressed in their business attire. I was the only male in the room; and although it was my turf – after all, I was a member of the School faculty and had taught many of them – I was extremely ill at ease and uncomfortable in my minority role. And then it struck me; this is how women must feel when they walk into a room filled with men, "all extremely well dressed in their business attire." From that moment on, it changed how I viewed the workplace and the roles of men and women in it. The sole criteria should be talent and performance, not gender. I then had the realization that what I had practiced with my daughters, I was not practicing with my female colleagues; and I made a commitment, going forward, to change.

A few years ago, after coming here to Atlanta and Georgia State, I was talking to a senior woman executive at a major firm here in town. She shared with me that, although there were a number of IT-support organizations (including Women in Technology), there really wasn't anything aimed specifically at CIO-level women. In addition to all of the usual issues that women IT professionals face, such as glass ceilings, work-life balance, lack of mentoring, etc., there were other concerns of particular interest to senior women IT executives, such as relationships with other C-suite executives, line responsibilities for substantial portions of the corporate budget, challenges of women working for women, etc. I suggested that it might make sense to have an informal luncheon for women like her, where they could candidly talk about these issues and share their experiences. I also offered to provide the administrative support for the luncheons from my office at the university and to maintain the name and address master list. She agreed and urged me to go ahead with the idea. To my surprise, I was able to identify 31 women CIOs (or similar titles) in Atlanta and nearby communities. The first few luncheons were held at The Ashford Club and later at McKendrick's Steak House in Dunwoody. These luncheons continued for about two years and varied from as few as four or five women to twelve to fifteen at the luncheons. But, like many good things, it ran its course and the leaders got pulled away into other things (e.g., Georgia CIO Leadership Association, Women in Technology).

Well, where has this journey taken me? It has had, as I stated at the beginning, a profound, and beneficial, impact on my personal and professional life. I would also like to believe that it has had a positive effect on those around me, particular the women with whom I've worked. I leave this final assessment to the judgment of the reader and to my many women friends.

DR. EPHRAIM R. MCLEAN, or Eph McLean for short, is currently the Chair of the nationally-ranked CIS Department in Georgia State University's Robinson College of Business, where he has been on the faculty for 23 years. He came here from the Anderson School of Management at UCLA in 1987 to become the first Georgia Eminent Scholar at GSU and one of the first four in the state. In 2002, he was promoted to Regents' Professor, representing less than one percent of the faculty in the University System of Georgia. He was elected by the Association for Information Systems as an AIS Fellow in 1999 and was awarded the LEO Award for Lifetime Exceptional Achievement in Information Systems in 2007. He has worked in the computer field for 48 years, stating as a systems analyst for Procter & Gamble in 1962. He earned his Bachelor's and Master's degrees in mechanical engineering from Cornell University and his Master's and Ph.D. from M.I.T.'s Sloan School of Management.

THE COMPUTER INFORMATION SYSTEM DEPARTMENT IN THE ROBINSON COLLEGE OF BUSINESS AT GEORGIA STATE UNIVERSITY is one of the largest information systems departments in the country, with 19 full-time faculty and over 700 students, pursuing bachelors, masters, MBA, or doctoral degrees. For more than a decade, the Department has been ranked by *U.S. News & World Report* as number one in the southeast and in the top ten nationally.

In 2007, the journal, *CommAIS*, reported that CIS faculty were the most productive in the world in terms of published IS research, and second (only to M.I.T.) in the world in cited IS research. Six (out of 30) of the most productive IS scholars in the world are in Robinson's CIS Department. Beginning last year, the Department is now home to the Center for Research in Information Systems (CRIS, for short), an academic-professional organization designed to serve the Atlanta IT business community. It is also the home of the one-year Executive Master's degree in Managing Information Technology, now in its second year and housed in Robinson's new executive education building in Alpharetta.

Career Paths Aren't Usually Straight – Don't Be Afraid to Try New Things

by Sue Miller

Managing Consultant
MDI Group

ATLANTA, GEORGIA

Career Paths Aren't Usually Straight – Don't Be Afraid to Try New Things

I STARTED MY CAREER WORKING FOR C&S National Bank in Atlanta, Georgia. I had joined as a teller at the Howell Mill branch and within six months when the head teller left I was promoted to her position. I spent another 4½ years as the head teller at that same branch until I left the branch and customer side of the business to work in the Retail Loan Operations group. I spent one year in the operations group before moving to the Consumer Credit Services department. Among other responsibilities, this department was responsible for the program management (e.g. implementing new products, ensuring regulatory compliance, converting systems of purchased banks, etc.) for all the bank's retail lending applications, which included loans, collections, and loan loss applications. The department worked with various other departments such as Systems Development, Loan Operations and Production Support. I spent the next 10 years working in this department where I functioned as the business analyst, project manager, program manager, quality assurance tester, trainer, conversion specialist and production support simultaneously – learning while doing and trying things I had never done before.

In addition to all of the organizational and process skills that come with business analysis, project management and quality assurance work, I can also read database structures, do conversion mapping and many other technical things. I don't like to code nor can I program anything but I understand it well, which is critical in technology process. There's a lot of value in being able to think and execute on two levels – understanding the big picture but not forgetting the details. I gained an understanding of how technology enabled processes that made it possible for the business to provide new or improved products and increased services to the end customer while generating more revenue for the company. During my tenure with the Bank, I had grown from an individual contributor to a team lead to the department manager over a consolidated Consumer Credit Services and Systems Development team for all of the Retail Lending applications for three states with a promotion to Assistant Vice President along the way.

Through a series of mergers and acquisitions in the early '90s, we became NationsBank (a predecessor of The Bank of America). NationsBank had decided to move all of the corporate and back office functions, including the department I was working in, out of Georgia to North Carolina. I was asked to move to North Carolina, but I had already decided that after fifteen years of service I was ready for a move out of the banking industry. I wanted to work for a much smaller company where you were much closer to the decision makers and could make more of a direct impact on the people you were providing your services for.

In addition to working several different retail part-time jobs in the evenings, I had also been going to Georgia State University part-time to finish my undergrad degree. I did not know what type of degree I wanted to get but I had always been good at and enjoyed mathematics so I started on the path towards an accounting degree. When I took Cost Accounting, I decided "There is no way I want to do this the rest of my life." At work, I was exposed to a tremendous amount of technology working with the systems development group and I loved it! I thought "Maybe I'll go to the computer side" and changed my major to Computer Information Systems.

I updated my resume and started responding to want ads in late 1994. Six months and few responses later, I said "I've got to do something different. This is just not working! Maybe I can find a group of people to network with." Coincidentally, I saw ad in the same paper for an organization called Women InTechnology (WIT) and attended my first meeting in August of 1995. On the program agenda that morning was a call for volunteers for a new event the organization was creating for the fall of that year. A very professional looking woman took the stage to describe the volunteer needs, a young woman named Marci Baer[1]. I watched Marci, a petite firecracker, pitching the Re-Engineering Style[2] event and when she said she needed help on administration and organizational tasks, I thought to myself "I can do that job easily" so I walked up to her and said, "I'd love to help you." I jumped right in and I've never looked back. I did all the correspondence with auction candidates, invoicing for sponsorships and purchased auction candidates, and assisted Martha O'Brien, our current Finance Director at the time, with reservations and the check in/checkout table at the event.

WIT also led me to my next job in 1995. It was at a WIT committee meeting for the Re-Engineering Style event where I overheard a woman talking about her recent job interview. It was a technical role at a small custom development company and when I said it sounded interesting, she suggested that I send in my resume because they had additional positions open. I did and went to work as a business analyst on the company's largest project – developing a custom floor planning system from "scratch" for a financial client. I was in heaven! Business analysis work at a company where I was the 56th employee, the CEO and Owner of the company knew me by name and talked to me every day about the project and our client worked with us on site and I interacted with him daily. It was extremely hard work and we had the usual ridiculously tight deadlines that are normal with any development project but it was very gratifying to see your work have a direct impact on the client and the company. I was thriving and taking on more and more responsibility in the project team, the company and in WIT. There was a small, core group of women "running" WIT at the time and

---

1 Marci Baer is Marci McCarthy's maiden name. Marci McCarthy is the former 2001 WIT President.

2 The Re-Engineering Style event became known at WIT Connect in its 3rd year.

they had a passion for the work and each other that you could wrap yourself around and watch what it was doing for so many others. It was infectious.

The WIT Board of Directors was created in 1996 and I was part of that first board when the existing Finance Director chose to step down for personal reasons and nominated me to take her place and the rest of the board members with open arms welcomed me. Unfortunately, I missed the first Board of Directors retreat, which I heard was quite the experience! – but that is a story for another WIT book. Actually no, some things should remain untold. I digress. For four years, I happily completed my duties as Finance Director, ensured every single monthly meeting we had during that time was set up, brought the food and beverages, completed check in/checkout, ensured our newsletters got mailed, worked tirelessly with a host of other dedicated women to execute WIT Connect every year and a whole host of other activities. As a working board team, we gave over $100,000 to the Boys & Girls Clubs of Metro Atlanta's College Bound Scholarship program, sent several women to Harvard's Women Leading Business seminar, sent over two dozen WIT members to various technology-related courses and seminars at colleges and universities in GA and across the country. I made some incredible friendships along the way, met a lot of incredible men and women who remain some of WIT's biggest supporters and sponsors today and had a lot of fun doing it all. I enjoyed this supporting role as I'm more of the "doer" than the strategist. Someone else (or team of women) would be the visionary on what needed to be done, and I managed the tactical operations and processes. My actions sold me. The Board asked me to be President in 1999, but I said "I'm not ready, give me one more year." Sonia Lucas was our next President in 1999 and I was her VP. I had one more year to make sure I *was* ready to be President of WIT and my oh my, what a year of preparation it was! 1999 was the year that the Technology of Association (TAG) was created and as a founding organization of TAG, we had our hands full. It was quite an interesting year. Speaking of TAG, little known factoid is that the idea for TAG and its first beginnings came about due to three women Presidents of local organizations.[3]

At that point, I knew it was time for another job change. I had worked for a big bank, then a small software development company, and then I went to a four-person startup! What a change but I loved it and I found I really liked the entrepreneurial type of company. In 2000 when I was VP of Portal Operations for BuildNet, the Chief Operations Officer (COO), Todd Mann, pushed me in ways I hadn't thought I could achieve – he really stretched and challenged me. He was a huge proponent of working with the community and he knew about WIT. He encouraged me to be the best President I could be for WIT and was behind my efforts in that role 100%. I became the President of WIT in 2000, and was President of the WIT Foundation in 2007 and 2008. I was an active member of the WIT and/or WIT Foundation boards from 1996 through 2009.[4]

The beginnings of Girls Get IT

A large majority of our core WIT membership was made up of women who joined the Information Technology (IT) industry from other industries like banking, hospitality, or retail. Partnering with Matrix Resources Inc.[5] and other companies, I lead the effort to put events and programs in place to help women learn how to

3 In 1996, Luba Brock, President of WIT, Barbara Stafford, President of the Southeastern Software Association (SSA) and Chris Coleman, President of the Business & Technology Association (B&TA) created the concept of TAG when they began working together on a monthly basis to see how the three organizations could collaborate together.

4 Served on the WIT Board from 1996 through 2008, Served on the WIT Foundation Board from 2006–2009.

5 Matrix Resources Inc. was one of WIT's original sponsors and remains a sponsor and supporter of the organization today.

switch careers, mostly by making them aware of the different roles involved in the technology sector and understanding which skills they already had that could be used in IT roles. It was a great way to build WIT's reputation in the community while maintaining an education and community focus.

I saw the need for a program for girls as well. This had always been a passion of mine. I began a conversation with the Atlanta Girls' School in 2001. The school is "wired for sound" as they have a robust network, wireless intranet/internet and each girl gets her own laptop for her school work as they used the suite of Microsoft Office products in their class work in a lot of cases, etc. They had a tech group that was made up of a small group of girls who volunteered to be first line support for any girl who encountered any technology related issues (e.g. cannot connect to the network, cannot open a document, etc. This small group of girls took the load off of the single faculty member who was responsible for the technology infrastructure that the entire school used. The school was and continues to be very interested in technology and tech-related careers. We took that group of young women to a Lunch and Learn program at the XcelleNet offices. Working closely with the CEO, Joan Herbig at the time, her Administrative Assistant, Deborah Cox, and other women in the company, we took the girls on a tour of the company, described the operations, showed them various machines, and explained the development and testing areas. Then we sat down for lunch with the CEO herself. Joan Herbig came downstairs and spent the lunchtime with the girls, asking them questions and allowing them to ask her questions about what she does in her job as the CEO of the company. The girls were fascinated, learning about what a CEO does and how the company worked. It was clear that it had a huge impact on the girls. This Lunch and Learn event at XcelleNet was the inspiration for what was to become our Girls Get IT program. We knew we needed to reach more girls with more events, to not only tour tech-related companies, but also to shadow employees in technology roles.

Through many partnerships with the likes of Sherpani Partners and others and sponsorships, our girls' programs began to develop.

FIRST Robotics

One of these partnerships WIT developed was with Georgia FIRST (For Inspiration and Recognition of Science and Technology) program. Patty Crone, the Founding Head of School with the Atlanta Girls' School at the time, introduced me to Georgia's Executive Director, Pattie Cook, when they were kicking off the very first Peachtree Regional competition. Patty recognized that through this program, the girls could be engaged in a community mentor-based program that builds science, engineering and technology skills as well as fostering self-confidence, communication and leadership. Each team must not only build a robot to compete in the chosen game for the competition in a very short amount of time, but they must also find sponsors, create marketing materials, build a website, and even go out in to the community and raise awareness.

The more I talked with Pattie, the more I realized that if more girls were to get involved on a robotics team, they would gain so much more from the experience than a single new skill. That first year, WIT was unable to sponsor the Peachtree Regional or any of the teams but we did have a few of our members get involved as volunteers at the event. I spent the weekend in a "queuing" role and witnessed firsthand what an incredible program this was and that WIT just had to find a way to get involved.

How could we get teams encouraged to get more girls on board? How could we help the girls realize that math or engineering maybe isn't as hard as they think? Because the focus of the WIT Foundation was on educational initiatives for women and girls, in late 2006 the WIT Foundation was able to provide $50,000 to support the costs of the upcoming Peachtree Regional Competition. A stipulation of our donation was that 50% be set aside for teams to apply for a grant, if they could substantiate that 50% of design, build and drive sub-teams were comprised of girls.[6] That was the first year of WIT's involvement and we have been involved since.

I am an absolute believer in what the partnership between WIT and Georgia FIRST is trying to do. I have watched several young high school women – sophomores to seniors – go through the robotics program as well as several of the WIT Foundation's Girls Get IT programs and have watched them discover talents and interests they never knew they had.

I am even more of a proponent and change agent for Georgia FIRST itself. I now serve on the Georgia FIRST Executive Advisory Board and look forward to working with WIT and our community on achieving our long-range goals of having a robotics team in every high school in our state. The "WIT forever woman" in me, of course, wants that to be "to have a robotics team made up of 50% girls in every high school in our state!"

Words of wisdom to girls and young women

No matter what roles you play in life, it's all about the people that you meet and the things that you do. Our careers are paths that are not usually straight. You need to get exposure. Meet people. Try as many things out as you can, to figure out if it's right for you. If you keep trying new things, five years later, you'll be surprised at all you know and who you know. You'll be able to see what you can do and how you can contribute.

Technology and business skills are integral parts of being in the community. You may first get those skills in a grocery store or restaurant. Every job will give you skills or teach you business

6 The design, build and drive sub-teams make up the majority of the more technical functions of the robotics team. The other functions such as web design, marketing, PR, etc. make up other sub-teams.

processes that can be applied in multiple ways. You need to figure out how to leverage that when you leave that specific role. In doing that, we'll know that you get IT! Bringing those skills forward will be a win for yourself, a win for your job, and a win for your community.

SUE MILLER is an IT professional with over three decades experience in project management, business process and testing disciplines spanning dozens of industries while working for companies of varying sizes from start-up to Fortune 100. She is currently a Managing Consultant with MDI Group. She is also a member of the Georgia FIRST Executive Advisory Board and a past President of both WIT and its Foundation.

MDI GROUP is a premier IT Workforce Solutions provider with more than 20 years of success finding 'best-fit' IT talent for mid-sized to Fortune 500 clients nationwide. Offering IT Staffing Solutions and Contingent Workforce Management, MDI is headquartered in Atlanta, Georgia, and has been named one of Atlanta's 40 best places to work.

The Value of Enduring Relationships and Unwavering Faith

by Eleanor Morgan

CEO
MD&E Inc.

ATLANTA, GEORGIA

The Value of Enduring Relationships and Unwavering Faith

My key advice for someone just starting into business is always about the value of relationships and how important they are to your career. We hear a lot about networking, but relationships go much deeper as they are formed from a mutual agreement between two people to share with each other in knowledge, skills, work, and social areas. These relationships are so important to your professional and personal growth and development. If chosen properly, these relationships will bring both you and the other person an added satisfaction in your life. There is no greater feeling than having a person to depend upon for help when you run into a problem or opportunity that you are not equipped to handle.

For me, business success did not come overnight and was not a solo pursuit. The career path that has led me to be the founder and CEO of a technology business, has been populated by countless individuals – family, friends, clients, and employees – whose generosity of time, knowledge, and wisdom has helped me define and refine my business goals, while discovering my best strengths as a hard-working and focused business manager, leader, and entrepreneur. Without my constant interaction with these individuals, and the effort I've put forth – most willingly – to sustain these relationships over time, my progress in business would have been greatly inhibited. While business is a microcosm unto itself, it is still a microcosm of people whose collective efforts make things happen. No man, and certainly no woman, is an island in this regard. To be successful in business requires finding and nurturing those positive contacts and relationships that inspire, transform, and enhance your capabilities and qualities as a professional and as a person. It also requires collaboration in its truest sense, mutual respect, and a willingness to share ideas and talents.

When you are just starting out, one way to ease into building business relationships is to keep an open mind, listen and learn from those around you, make the effort to share your ideas and perspective (and the workload), and if mentoring is what you seek, ask for it. You'll be surprised how many people in the business world are willing to give of their time and talent to help. After all, an individual's true legacy in business, as in life, is the contributions they make to enrich others and the world around them. In my experience, the people who came forward to mentor me have been the ones who have had the greatest impact on my progress and success. Because I value what my many mentors and business relationships have taught me, I continually make the effort to keep these individuals in my life to acknowledge, appreciate, and to show my gratitude for what they've shown me.

A successful business is not about "me" and "what I did." It's about what we can accomplish together. Feeding the all-important "we," strengthening relationships, and building a team in the office on a day-to-day basis, for example, is so very important. When we first started our business, I knew that to succeed we would need a steady stream of innovative ideas and expertise. I asked for and often accepted new ideas from the relationships I developed in the early stages of MD&E. Training, nurturing, and providing direction and motivation to employees is the key to creating and managing a successful business team. No one can do it all alone. Relationships change lives and guide business; good relationships build happy lives and successful businesses.

Relationships also taught me the invaluable lesson of "letting go." Business owners are accustomed to being involved in every aspect of their company. Drawing back from the daily operation can be downright painful for both the owner and the employees who have grown accustomed to the owner's decisions and decision-making process. Turning loose a business – particularly one in which you've shared all-nighters, birthed ideas, celebrated victories, and mourned losses – is painful. However, that pain is a crucial step in the maturing of a company. Once my confidence in my staff was established, I was able to "turn loose" from the daily operation. What I quickly learned and felt was a long-suppressed freedom and a sense of satisfaction and accomplishment knowing that my talented staff would grow to the meet the company's needs through their own maturity, skills, and initiative. Further, turning loose and trusting those well-nurtured employee relationships also allowed me to grow in my role as my company's CEO and to focus on and plan the strategic direction of the company. Previously, I had found that I could not effectively move back and forth between strategic thinking and daily problem-solving without underperforming at each. As a full-time strategic leader, I was able to get the company certified as a woman-owned business. The certification process alone helped us grow by making me aware of gaps in our company structure. I wasted no time in closing those gaps to create a healthier company. If I had been stuck between my previous dual role of strategy and daily operations, I may have missed or delayed this opportunity longer than would have been healthy for the company.

Throughout my career, and indeed through all areas of my life, I have faith in God's direction for me. Business and personal relationships have supported my passions and dreams. While the main physical and mental energy has come from me, it was based on an internal voice that told me at many turns along the way that this was the right thing to do. I have achieved success through hard work, the grace of God, a loving husband, and the generous spirit of people I have encountered along the way – people who shared their knowledge and skills to help me develop my own. I have worked long and hard to help repay, in part, the gifts that I have received.

Relationships don't just happen. Even those most promising initial meetings cannot develop into a full-fledged relationship without a significant investment of time, energy, and sincerity on the parts of both people. A seed may be perfect and ripe with promise and potential, but without constant care and nourishment it will never grow and its potential will never be realized. Business relationships come in all shapes and sizes. They might be associations with colleagues, competitors, customers, vendors, suppliers, neighbors, co-workers, bosses, partners, and employees, to name the most obvious examples. There is no escaping these interactions, even for the most self-reliant or anti-social among us. By definition, no business can subsist on a single-person basis. Even a sole proprietor must have external affiliations to survive and to thrive. One excellent and much-appreciated method of establishing relationships is to pitch in and share the burden of heavy workloads with employees rather than standing back in a classic "I manage; you work" stance which only adds to the weight of a task. Working outside or beyond a typical 8-to-5 schedule provides some special opportunities to get to know employees better and build better relationships.

It is amazing how the relationships you experience throughout life can dovetail in so many unexpected – and unexpectedly rewarding – ways. In essence, good relationships make the difference between stagnation and opportunity, discontent and happiness, and frustration and success in your personal and professional life. An opportunity to form a meaningful relationship is a door to possibilities that can literally change your life. Be open to and enjoy where those opportunities take you in your life's journey.

ELEANOR MORGAN contributes her time and talent to speaking opportunities and to mentoring young professionals and entrepreneurial businesses just starting out. With a fervent commitment to fostering both personal and professional relationships, Eleanor regularly shares her valued perspective, executive leadership talent and vast networking resources, to help guide and motivate up and coming professionals. As an active Board member for Red Cross Blood Services and Dream House for Medically Fragile Children she gives back to the community. She is the owner and founder of several businesses, including MD&E, an IT services firm that she founded with her husband Charles. Eleanor is CEO of MD&E.

MD&E, INC., a Georgia based technology company, provides tactical solutions for businesses. Founded in 1992, the firm is a WBENC certified Woman Owned Business led by founder and CEO, Eleanor Morgan. As a privately-held company, MD&E provides business process and IT consulting to Fortune 500 companies. Clarity, a division of MD&E, provides data consulting services to facilitate business processes and to provide access to high-quality data for improved CRM, better reporting, better decision-making, focusing in the HealthCare and Government Marketplace. The People Network, an MD&E company, is an information services firm specializing in permanent and contract placement of IT professionals.

I Wish Someone Had Told Me....

by Marie Mouchet

Vice President and CIO, Southern Company Generation
CIO, Southern Nuclear
CIO, Southern Power Company

BIRMINGHAM, ALABAMA

I Wish Someone Had Told Me….

I HAVE WORKED FOR MANY YEARS in several professions and have been exposed to many leaders, managers and colleagues throughout my career. Through my observations I have captured what I see as common themes and building blocks for success that transcend many stages of our careers and across industries – I worked in retail as I was going to college; I was a teacher in high school and junior college; and I have worked for the largest electric utility for the majority of my work life. I would suggest it does not matter what profession you choose, there is a common theme for the foundations for success and *I wish someone had told me….*

One of the ways I have mentored employees and encouraged employee development, is to share my experiences over my career with a presentation entitled, "I wish someone had told me…." Below is an excerpt from that presentation that discusses how important it is for you to build your brand recognition, as if you were marketing yourself and your skills to others who may hire you or be in a position to support you in your quest for new opportunities as you build your career.

If you think about companies and their commercials, you realize they are marketing their brand with the goal for consumers to choose them. You begin to form opinions about companies through their branding efforts and how they deliver service or treat you as a customer or what they do within the community or through a variety of their actions. A brand helps you remember that company or is a differentiator between companies – it helps you recognize that company and guides you in how you think about that company. As we begin our careers, we are beginning to build our brand – what we will be known for and how others will remember us or think about us – which will help us get more opportunities.

As you begin to build your brand, I would propose these behaviors that are common themes across industries and ages that are foundational for success and strong brands: integrity, attitude &

image, performance, continuous learner, relationships & mentoring, and flexibility & adaptability.

Integrity – Integrity is the best indicator of your current and future potential. If you are viewed as a person of integrity, you will have the overwhelming support of your peers and management, your teammates and your coaches, your fellow students and your administrators and professors. Integrity does not mean you have to be perfect or that you cannot make mistakes. It does mean that you are known as a person who is honest, moral, and ethical. No matter how smart you are, your character will have a direct impact on how successful you can be and how far you will go. It also is a direct indicator if others will trust you and support you; even when you make mistakes.

Attitude & Image – People like to be around positive people. A positive can-do attitude can take you a long way with your teammates and your management. You are responsible for your attitude. Additionally, the image you portray is what people perceive you to be. People's perception of who we are and what we can do may not be fair, but perception is reality. It is important to remember first impressions are real – people observe your demeanor, mannerisms, body language, and even assess your grooming. And people draw conclusions based on your attitude and your image. It may not be what we like, but impressions are many times based on what people see – so to help yourself, think about the attitude you exhibit and the image you portray in all of your activities.

Performance – Next to integrity, your performance is crucial. As a student you begin to learn accountability for what you produce and that continues into the workplace. Your performance and your lessons learned will become your foundation for your professional future. And as you continue to build your career, it is built on the results you produce over time. You earn your credibility through your performance.

One of the challenges that can be a barrier to your performance is when all of your focus is on the next job and thereby you overlook your current assignment. I encourage you to put forth your best effort where you are – deliver quality results, be positive, practice teamwork, and don't be afraid to ask questions. Take advantage of each assignment and position to learn and grow and earn your credibility.

The quality of your results and your commitment to excellence in each of your assignments, no matter what stage you are in your career, establishes and reinforces your credibility as you move throughout your career. Your credibility is the platform that allows you more and greater opportunities.

Continuous Learner – When you graduate from college, you sometimes think you are through with school. But you quickly learn being a life long learner is a requirement no matter what you choose to do after you graduate. There are always new innovations, new technologies, changes in regulations, and other changes that will require you to stay current in whatever you choose to do. In all of my roles I had to learn; I had skills I could apply, but I had to learn how to use them.

Stay up to date within your respective discipline and with the industry you are in because all disciplines evolve and all companies change. Drivers of change include demographics in the work place, the growth of new competitors, changing regulations, and technologies. Change is the norm in today's world.

Stay current and up to date with technologies; because now more than ever information technologies are integrated in everything we do – how we communicate, how we keep in touch with others, how we research, how we manage our daily lives. The speed of change in information technology is so rapid it is critical for us to stay current to be effective in the work place and throughout our careers.

While you are a continuous learner within your discipline and with information technology, it is also important to be a continuous learner about yourself. What are your strengths; what are you good at doing; what are your areas that need more development.

Invest in yourself – your personal and professional development. Spend time on professional development – ensure you are growing and energized about what you are doing; strengthen your skills; and pay attention to those areas you need to work on that will help you move forward in your career. Knowing your strengths, skills and developmental needs will help you and others select opportunities where you will be successful.

Relationships & Mentoring – Relationships are crucial to your future. Treat everyone with respect – because it is the right thing to do. But also, in today's world and through technology, it is a small world. Facebook is proof of this. You never know who may be a friend or relative of someone you work with or of the person that may interview or hire you. Peer relationships are important to provide you a network of support as you tackle opportunities or struggle with assignments – these relationships can provide you a safety net even when you don't know you need one.

Relationships and mentoring go hand in hand. I never had a "formal" mentor but I do value many leaders and colleagues I have had in my life. I think of mentoring as "coaching" or a sounding board opportunity. I do not look at mentoring as a stepping stone to the next job but more about guidance as you move through your career.

I also encourage being a mentor. As you learn and grow, give back to others. And keep in mind, a mentoring relationship is not always someone older and higher up in a company than you. I would encourage peer mentoring relationships and upward mentoring relationships because of the value these can provide to more seasoned employees. I have observed the value the new generation in the workplace can provide through mentoring on technology because they have grown up with it. I would also suggest peer mentoring can provide more insight on teamwork and collaboration which will help the individual be a more effective team member on assignments and within the organization.

Relationships are very important in all walks of life and are the key to successful networks that help you maneuver within your industry, company, or provide support in your daily life.

Flexibility & Adaptability – Things change. It is important for you to be able to change too. Being flexible and adaptable along the way will ensure you are successful. It is important to have goals and it is important to stay focused but your goals may change throughout your career. And it is important to do your best. But as you see in sports, for teams to stay at the top of their game, they change their game plan, they change their defensive strategies, or they change their offensive strategies, or they change their players, or they change their coaches – but in most cases, the individuals that are adaptable and flexible as things change build on past success and sustain success.

No matter where you are in your career stage, focusing on these behaviors will help you with your brand. You don't have to be like everyone else; be yourself but you can learn best practices and tips and tricks that you can adopt to make you more effective as you.

If you are beginning your career, you don't have to have all of the answers now. You need to remain open minded and flexible.

Give your all in what you do. Take risks. Stay positive. Be a continuous learner. And be passionate about what you do. Live a little! Enjoy your life so that you don't look back and wonder what if!

MARIE MOUCHET is Vice President and Chief Information Officer for Southern Company Generation & CIO for Southern Nuclear and Southern Power. In this role, Mouchet leads the development and implementation of IT strategy and operations for Southern Company's regulated and non-regulated generation business units. Her role provides strategic and tactical planning and direction for information technology at fossil, hydro and nuclear generating plants, as well as fuel services, a real-time trading floor and the engineering and construction organization.

Throughout her career Mouchet has served in leadership positions across numerous Southern Company business lines including regulatory, financial services, public relations, marketing, sales, and generation. She is one of 14 women selected internationally for the 2003–2004 class of the prestigious Leadership Foundation Fellows Program of the International Women's Forum. In 2007, Mouchet was named recipient of *Women of the Year in Technology* for the Enterprise Division by WIT and Woman of Excellence by *Business to Business Magazine*. In 2009 was she was selected by *ComputerWorld* as one of the Premier 100 IT Professionals.

SOUTHERN COMPANY's generation business consists of 77 electric generating plants operated by Southern Company's four regulated regional electric utilities; Southern Power, a growing competitive generation business serving the wholesale market; and Southern Nuclear, operator of three nuclear plants.

When You Volunteer, You Often Gain More Than You Give

by Kasie Scott Palmer

Senior Principal, Corporate Business Development
CA Technologies

ATLANTA, GEORGIA

When You Volunteer, You Often Gain More Than You Give

I STILL RECALL THE QUESTIONS PEOPLE POSED OF ME my first few years in IT: "How did you go from developing restaurants and private clubs to selling IT staffing/services? It's quite a difference! How did you transition?" My reply then and now is: "I'm doing the same thing today as I did then. I find out what people need, what makes them successful, and if I cannot deliver help, I point them to someone who can."

My involvement with WIT ran from October 1998 until 2006, when I 'retired' from the Board of Directors as the first ever WIT Foundation Past President. And so much happened during my WIT Presidency in 2004–5! I hope that by sharing my experiences you will understand how WIT became, and still is, part of who I am today. Of all my successes in life, of all my accomplishments, WIT is up there with the ones that shine the brightest. It is an experience that, when I allow myself to look back, reminds me of the person I want to continue to be.

I met WIT in October 1998 at WIT Connect. What an event! As someone who created environments for people to exchange ideas, build friendships and business relationships, I could see that WIT Connect had it all! It was similar to the large events I had planned in my former career at the Roswell Founders Club – but better: the money raised went to charity, to helping others. I was hooked, and once I jumped in I never looked back. I started my WIT career a few weeks later. It was an easy decision. The more time I spent with these genuine and amazing women, the more I wanted to be part of this group, to give all I could give and know I was helping people help others.

WIT Connect 1999 needed an Auction Candidate Chair. This was right up my alley and I volunteered. I was tasked with shaking things up and making more money, which we did. That year we changed up the majority of executives 'auctioned off,' and also grew revenues beyond wildest expectations. I was involved in WIT Connect for two more years, each year changing the design – like adding in silent auctions – so more people could connect. Even in the worst economic times (post-".com"), the event still drew people wanting to help the IT community grow and give back to those less fortunate. This magic cannot be found anywhere else. Other groups have tried versions of WIT Connect, but there is only one; the community impact and spirit that we helped create still stands today.

My professional role at the time wholly supported this volunteer role. I was fully engaged in business development for CTG, a mid-market application maintenance outsourcer. What a perfect pairing of WIT and CTG! What better way to build personal relationships with the executives we sought as clients than by finding a way to help them give back to the technology community – and not just the IT community, but women *in* the technology community. Back in the late '90s, all we heard about was the Glass Ceiling: breaking it, cracking it, and how to/how not to play the "It's a man's world" game. WIT Connect was key in helping the predominantly-male Atlanta IT executive leadership engage with a growing cadre of female peers while giving of themselves to our worthwhile cause. An amazing byproduct of the whole WIT Connect experience was the public recognition of the growing talent pool of female executives in the IT community. In 2001, the ratio of women to men was considerably off balance, while today the number of women in senior executive technology leadership roles is more closely aligned with that of men.

I changed companies in May of 2000 but continued on with WIT. From 2000–2003, I spent three fantastic years growing my career at CA Technologies and with WIT. Interestingly, it is due to Sonia Lucas, another WIT President, that I owe my beginnings at CA Technologies. It was at her recommendation that I accepted the WIT Board position as the WIT Connect Chair. WIT was my second job. It was my love, the thing I did every day that made me smile and look beyond the paycheck and corporate machinations. I have been very fortunate that CA Technologies has been an amazing supporter of my commitment to WIT. I could not ask for a better company to back my personal volunteer goals and desires.

WIT gave me so much. It allowed me the opportunity to grow, to meet and experience life through the eyes of other executives, other women, and other roles, as each year I took on new responsibilities. We built the WIT Executive Coaching Program, sponsored by CA Technologies, from the ground up. Our first group of executives had titles running the gamut from Senior Director through VP, SVP, and CIO. Each participant was successful; however, the common thread was that none of them saw themselves as a "brand", nor did they fully understand how to market their special skills and strengths. The closing event was an evening of testimonials from women successful in everyone's eyes but their own. The program taught them how to recognize their value and to be proud of what they offered their companies and other professional relationships. Many of the women who attended that first class have experienced success and career advancement since then. Whether or not the program was directly responsible, all agreed they were changed for the better by participating in it.

All these experiences ensured I was ready to be President, to put my stamp on the history of WIT. WIT Presidency was my dream obtained. It was my honor to lead this exceptional group of women for one year. Who could have foreseen the changes that would occur during 2004–5? I for one could not have imagined the direction we would take: Survival. Commitment. Quality. Growth. All these elements drove our decision to become who WIT is today; a separate financial entity from TAG, the complete opposite of what we decided in 1999. Back then, WIT, B&TA and SSA joined to form TAG, The Technology Association of Georgia. It was a great decision for the growth of the technology community in Atlanta. In the first few years, TAG and WIT developed a strong and successful partnership. TAG helped brand the associations and provided execution support and sponsorship attainment. We used this partnership to enable us to focus on the content of our offerings, and it was a great time for all. WIT and TAG grew in membership, sponsorship, and funds raised/ distributed to the community.

Dawn Patrick was President in 2003 and I was her VP. By then, it became clear that WIT and TAG needed to re-assess the working relationship in order for WIT to grow to the next level. By 2004, believing fully in the need for a successful Georgia technology community, while recognizing the need to gain full control of the funds generated by WIT events and programs, the WIT Board of Directors voted unanimously to create the WIT Foundation and incorporate WIT.

Of all the things I did for WIT, it is the financial separation and regaining full control of our funds that I am most proud of. The creation of the WIT Foundation gave WIT a new lease on life and provided a venue for WIT and others to give directly to our philanthropic mission. Before TAG, WIT gave a check every year at WIT Connect to charities, scholarships and other programs. In 2004, we renewed that focus and have never looked back. In 2005, The WIT Foundation launched the first WIT On Track program. This partnership between WIT, GCAPP and AGL Resources spoke directly to a new audience we wanted to help. The leadership of Kristin Kirkconnel and Sue Miller, in concert with Jane Fonda's extraordinary group of leaders, allowed us the privilege of working with one very special young lady and awarding the first WIT On Track Scholarship of $5000 towards her higher education.

Throughout my years of involvement with WIT, my hope is that I gave back as much as I received. Never have I met such an organization: one that believes in pulling strengths from all its members to deliver life-changing opportunities for those who ask for them. During my tenure with WIT, I have experienced my own steady career advancement. I am currently still at CA Technologies, now working for the Mergers and Acquisitions group out of our corporate headquarters. And I love my job! WIT helped me to realize who I am as a professional and how to be the person I was for WIT all the time. I am a change agent. I bring about positive change and help people assimilate and be productive in the new state. My wish for every woman, regardless of the career phase she is currently in, would be to take advantage of WIT and what WIT offers. It is a relationship you won't regret. I promise.

KASIE SCOTT PALMER is a change agent experienced in launching new companies and developing new roles and organizations within Fortune 500 organizations. Her overarching strength is to ensure that the strategy aligns with an execution plan that is repeatable and measurable. Capable of developing business enhancing strategies and identifying immediate steps needed to achieve the goals, her expertise is best leveraged when organizations are reaching for the next level of growth. When assessing existing business processes & deliverables, her approach is to clearly define the organizations baseline, vision and goals, facilitate gap analysis, and then outline the tactical road map to achieve the desired objectives.

She offers over twenty years experience in the development and execution of profitable business initiatives and possesses a successful track record of business strategy development and implementing business change management/readiness programs, and is experienced with Six Sigma and DMAIC methodologies. Along the way she has also had the opportunity to have leadership roles in direct and channel marketing strategy and execution, consulting services sales, new business development, customer experience management, relationship management and operational management. Of the fourteen years Kasie has spent in the Information Technology industry, eight of those years have been with CA Technologies.

In October 2009, upon returning to the US after living in the UK helping CA Technologies implement SAP throughout their EMEA (Europe/Middle East) region, Kasie joined CA's Corporate

Business Development group in the mergers and acquisitions team. As a Senior Principal, she assumes the lead role in change management and communications for all acquisitions, mergers and divestitures, collaborating with corporate and regional business unit executives globally. In this new role, Kasie works with Public, Investor and Analyst relations' leaders when announcing CA's intent to purchase or divest. She also has developed a comprehensive communications change program to support the acquisition lifecycle, from inception through integration; and is currently focused on delivering programs to expedite the successful integration of acquisition employees into their new CA Technologies roles.

Kasie resides in Alpharetta, Georgia, with her husband Chris and their four-legged children; Grey and Rex.

CA TECHNOLOGIES is an IT management software and solutions company with expertise across all IT environments – from mainframe and physical to virtual and cloud. CA Technologies manages and secures IT environments, enabling our customers to deliver more flexible IT services. Its solutions help its customers gain a level of deep insight into and exceptional control over complex, mixed IT environments. It's that level of insight and control that enables IT organizations to power business agility.

Stepping Stone

by Dawn Patrick

Partner
Cherry, Bekaert & Holland, L.L.P.

ATLANTA, GEORGIA

Stepping Stone

I WAS PRIVILEGED TO LEAD Women in Technology (WIT) at a time when the organization was reexamining its priorities and expanding its goals and aspirations. We were truly positioning to be the strong independent organization that WIT is today. The year 2003 was not the best for a technology related organization as the tech boom was over and a different reality was setting in. However, the women of WIT continued to challenge each other to create value for the technology community and the women who were a part of it.

WIT, for me personally, was a stepping-stone to many other wonderful opportunities. I truly had never considered the possibility of being the president of WIT. I have Marci McCarthy to thank for believing that I would be a good leader for the organization. I can still remember the lunch where she asked me if I would consider serving as president. I guess I thought so highly of the women who led before me that I just didn't see myself as being at their level.

WIT was a unique experience for me since growing up in the world of accounting I had been exposed to primarily male leaders as role models. I found working with women to lead an organization to be highly rewarding and enlightening. The WIT board was full of high performing women who put their ego at the door to take on whatever role was needed to propel WIT forward.

My time at WIT was special and led Tripp Rackley, then Chair of the Technology Association of Georgia (TAG), to reach out to me to ask me to succeed him as the Chair of TAG in 2004. And little did I know the adventure and opportunities ahead. I was privileged to chair TAG in 2004 and 2005 and that experience allowed me to truly understand my own strengths as a leader.

Those were extremely challenging times for TAG and WIT. TAG was under extreme economic duress due to the fall off in sponsorships and membership as a result of the technology industry decline. With help from many exceptional people who stepped up financially and with their time and energy, we survived. Many wonderful things were achieved during that difficult time. We hired Tino Mantella, who has done a fantastic job as President of TAG. And WIT became financially independent of TAG during that timeframe, which was a significant achievement in the life of the organization. TAG and WIT are both thriving organizations today. I count my time leading both organizations as a period of my most profound growth and development.

DAWN PATRICK is a Certified Public Accountant with over 27 years of experience serving the tax planning and compliance needs of public and private companies, primarily in the financial services and technology sectors.

As a Tax Partner with CB&H and leader of the firm's Metro Atlanta Tax Practice, Dawn directs tax department operations, including financial management, quality control, and client and personnel management. She also serves on the leadership of CB&H's Technology & Life Sciences industry group.

Prior to joining CB&H, Dawn spent 22 years in the tax service practices of an international accounting firm, and almost three years in a large Atlanta local firm working with companies ranging from startups to large, multinational corporations. Dawn also previously served as a tax director with the multinational Intercontinental Hotels Group, where she managed the team responsible for corporate tax operations in the western hemisphere.

Dawn received her Bachelor of Science in Accounting from Auburn University. She is licensed as a Certified Public Accountant in Georgia, and is a member of the American Institute of Certified Public Accountants (AICPA) and the Georgia Society of Certified Public Accountants (GSCPA).

The recipient of the 2009 Pathbuilders' Inspiria Award for high-achieving women, Dawn currently serves on the board of the Technology Association of Georgia and is a past board chairman.

She served as President of Women in Technology and is a founding member of the Georgia CIO Leadership Association. She was nominated for *Women of the Year in Technology*, and named one of the *Atlanta Business Chronicle's* Who's Who in Technology in Atlanta.

AS THE SOUTHEAST'S ACCOUNTING AND CONSULTING FIRM OF CHOICE, CHERRY, BEKAERT & HOLLAND, L.L.P. (CB&H) is uniquely positioned to provide quality, cost-effective and value-added services to a diverse and successful client base. The Firm sets itself apart by delivering the extensive industry specialization, resource depth and service opportunities of a national firm, but with the accessibility, service continuity and level of personal relationship expected from a local business. Ranked among the nation's Top 30 CPA firms, CB&H's resource network stretches regionally across six states, and nationally and internationally through an alliance with Baker Tilly International.

How You Do Things is as Important as What You Do … (Confessions of Mistakes Made Along the Way)

by Sue Powers

CEO
Travelport Airline IT Solutions

ATLANTA, GEORGIA

How You Do Things is as Important as What You Do … (Confessions of Mistakes Made Along the Way)

TECHNOLOGY IS CALLING YOU! If you are reading this letter it is a sure bet that you are either interested in or already have embarked on a career in technology. Further, I am guessing that you not only want a career in technology but your goal is to be a technology leader. If I am right, please read on, these are lessons I learned the hard way!

For those of us in technology, if we are honest, we know that we didn't just pick technology as a field to pursue, but we had a technology calling. We excel in technology – it comes easily to us. We enjoy the challenge, rapid change, and problem solving that comes along with technology. Other things we like include the satisfaction of delivering a project, the order that goes with project management, creatively solving a business problem with our craft, the constant innovation in the field, and the ability to work with other bright, motivated people.

Most of us start as programmers – we are assigned a set of deliverables that fit into an overall system. We do much of our work on our own – interfacing with others in predefined ways. We progress along and across the several possible career paths – development, business requirements, operations, architecture, data base administration, project management. Along the way we get assignments of increasing scope and responsibility. One of the things we like about technology is that it is a meritocracy – good work is recognized and rewarded. Each promotion is a reflection of the good work we have done – reinforcing what we have learned in delivering our work product. The next logical step is to move into a leadership role.

Your best isn't good enough anymore: Hard work, commitment, technology know how, attention to detail, and doing whatever it takes to deliver are some of the key characteristics that are typically demonstrated by high performing technologists – the tools you use to define success. Strong delivery and performance in these areas are precisely why you were or will be promoted to a leadership role.

That was then and this is now, you should forget about all of that! Your role as a technology leader is not just about those characteristics – those things are table stakes. To succeed as an IT leader takes an entirely new skill set.

You need a balanced scorecard: Starting now, *how you do things is as important as what you do*. This is a difficult transition for those of us who are used to living in a world of tactical performance metrics like:

- Operational performance of "four nines" or 99.99% up-time
- Projects delivered on time and within budget
- Code Quality
- Productivity
- Service Level Agreement (SLA) performance
- Achieving business case results

You will still need to deliver the tactical performance metrics but now you need to think of your success measure as a balanced score card – you will need to consider the future state of your organization and perform on a strategic level. You will need to focus your energy in different ways to motivate your team and interact with your business partners. It is no longer about you working hard and personally delivering results – now you must lead. Your new success tools are communication, collaboration, talent management and innovation.

Communicate, communicate, communicate some more: I once read that adults learn most effectively when they know the big picture and then understand the steps to get there. For example, if you are giving driving directions, you need to explain where you are going and then describe the turn by turn details – put the trip into perspective. Your team will perform best when they know the big picture–the business benefits and how you define success. IT people are bright and motivated and want to work on important and beneficial projects. Taking the time to connect the dots will motivate your team and drive results.

In working with your business partners – keep the KISS (Keep it simple stupid) philosophy in mind. It is your job to make technology relevant and easy. Technology enables business benefits and you are there to help others to realize the benefit and demystify technology. Think of yourself as their personal tour guide – you are there to ensure the business realizes what technology can do – and make it happen. Speak their language not techno-speak.

Put everyone on the team: Collaboration is a key to success. Make everyone a part of your team – help your business partners understand how they can assist in driving success – everyone is motivated to achieve business success. Invite HR, Finance, and your internal customers to be part of your team and let them help solve problems – how to measure productivity; how to design compensation to drive results, how to define business benefits. Better understand their problems – go on sales calls for example – and partner with them to solve the root cause problem – don't be an order taker but partner in driving better business results. Have regular one-on-one sessions with your key stakeholders – not just project status meetings. Harness the power of the entire team to make you successful.

Collaborate with your team – they know the solution to the problems. Your first line managers set the culture of the organization – tap into them. Ask them what the top 2–3 areas for improvement are, and assign special projects to the managers to work with you to resolve those issues – involve your other business partners in the process.

Reach outside of your own organization. Join professional organizations and collaborate with others to get the best in class thinking and ideas. This includes organizations like TAG, WIT and the GCLA. Talk to other technology leaders – chances are you can learn from their mistakes, get good ideas, and have someone to talk with that understands your challenges and opportunities.

Mentoring is the new management: You still need to manage your team to deliver all of the tactical performance metrics – that is a given – but you must raise your game. Begin to think of yourself as a mentor to the organization. This mind set reminds you to think more strategically about the people in your organization. It is all about the people.

Be in the moment. Thank people for a job well done – a simple note will do. Recognize the people in front of their peers and bosses. Feed people when they are working long hours or have an ice cream social to celebrate a success. By the same token, point out when something could have been handled better – everyone wants to know what they can do to be the very best – don't wait for the annual review.

You are in the talent management business – stay focused on your vision for your future state organization. Develop your future leaders. Think about the high potential person two steps up the "ladder" and develop an action plan to help them get there – give them stretch assignments and opportunities to raise their visibility – even outside of the technology division. Partner with and hold people accountable for their career development. Ensure you are matching your training programs and hiring to your architectural vision. As you retool your technology, take a three-pronged approach – train your domain experts, hire technology experts and start an intern program – this will energize your organization around change. This is the easy part. While it is uncomfortable, you must address performance problems. I was once asked if I had ever fired anyone. I answered, "No, they always fire themselves." Your goal should be to give people the feedback and tools to choose to be successful and if they aren't, they are making the decision to select out of the organization.

Consider being a mentor outside of the organization to better appreciate the challenges your team faces but probably won't tell you about. It also feels good to give back.

Innovate or perish: We all know about the sticky note – it was discovered by accident. Is that really true? Could the accidental discovering have happened if there wasn't an R&D department? I believe that innovation in any field comes from investment and hard work and involves a thoughtful and structured process – and sometimes a little luck. Innovation requires a multifaceted plan of attack. Harness the ideas of the entire organization – suggestion programs, ideation sessions about the opportunity technology trends provide your organization and how to leverage your existing IT assets in new ways. Out of the ideation sessions create projects to evaluate and pursue the best ideas. Don't wait for customers (internal or external) to ask for enhancements, adopt a mindset of "solving our customer's problems before they know the problem exists."

Invest in the innovation process and track success. Consider setting a goal of one innovative product/project per quarter. Track the amount of investment you are making and set a goal to spend a percentage of the IT budget on R&D for the future. Adopt a philosophy of always saying yes to questions about whether or not IT can do something – after all, IT can, it is only time and money.

Celebrate and reward innovation in the organization and understand that to be an innovative organization not every idea will be a home run.

I hope the lessons I learned along the way are helpful to you. The key is to go beyond delivering tactical results and become a strategic leader. Good luck and best wishes for continued success in IT.

SUE POWERS is responsible for Travelport Airline IT Solutions which provides innovative technical and application solutions, as well as data intelligence products for today's leading airlines.

Travelport Airline IT Solutions manages the mission-critical reservations and related systems for United Air Lines and the combined Delta/Northwest airline, as well as eight other airlines. The Company estimates its IT services were used in the handling of up to 560 million boarded airline passengers in 2009.

Previously, Sue was Chief Information Officer (CIO) of Travelport GDS, overseeing global product, application development and initiatives of the Worldspan and Galileo GDSs and in addition, airline services.

In 2006, the Georgia CIO Leadership Association (GCLA) awarded its top honor to Sue, the Global CIO of the Year Award. In 2003, The American Business Awards selected Sue as Best Product Development or Engineering Executive. Also in 2003, the Technology Association of Georgia named her Woman of the Year in Technology, and she was named one of the 100 Most Powerful Women in Travel by *Travel Agent Magazine*, making her a seven-time recipient of this honor. Travel Agent also named Sue to its People of the Year Winner's Circle in 1994 and 2000.

She received a Bachelor of Science degree in Mathematics from Southern Illinois University and an MBA from Northern Illinois University.

TRAVELPORT is a broad-based business services company and a leading provider of critical transaction processing solutions to companies operating in the global travel industry. Travelport is comprised of: the global distribution system (GDS) business that includes the Worldspan and Galileo brands; GTA, a leading global, multi-channel provider of hotel and ground services; Airline IT Solutions, which hosts mission critical applications and provides business and data analysis solutions for major airlines. Travelport also owns approximately 48% of Orbitz Worldwide (NYSE: OWW), a leading global online travel company. Travelport operates in 160 countries, reported 2009 revenues of $2.2 billion and has approximately 5,400 employees. Travelport is a private company owned by The Blackstone Group, One Equity Partners, Technology Crossover Ventures, and Travelport management.

My Lessons to Help You Achieve Your Dreams

by Latha Ravi

Chief Information Officer

PEACHTREE CITY, GEORGIA

My Lessons to Help You Achieve Your Dreams

My professional journey has been incredible and enjoyable working in Engineering and Technology fields mostly in the U.S. and briefly in India. I grew up in India, completed my Bachelor's in Engineering and then moved to the U.S. to complete my Master's and work professionally in the U.S. I have worked for American, Japanese and Indian companies and led, designed and delivered embedded products for worldwide markets. The environments I studied and worked in included men and women from many cultures. I am grateful for the Blessings in my journey and I would like to share some of my learning to help you in your career and life.

Lessons that help you realize your passion and dream: Discover what you enjoy and love to do and do it most of the time. When you start your career, this may not be very clear. After you work for few years, you will realize that you love some things, naturally excel at them and do not like some things. Pursue your dreams always and never settle for less. Your dreams may change over time.

Your dreams will be fulfilled as long as you can find a way to pursue your passion, deliver exceptionally to your commitments and stay true to your values. Learn constantly from others and from your own mistakes and successes. Keep a journal of your experiences so you can constantly learn from them and teach others too. Recognize immediately if you get complacent or start doing average work. Correct it quickly. Admit your mistakes, learn from them and move on. Set clear goals for yourself and strive to achieve them.

Lessons in leadership: This is one of my favorite subjects and I love to lead and learn from leaders. Everyone is a leader in the organization and their title does not matter. Believe in this and you will climb the ladder with no effort. Since this is such a vast subject, here are some key principles to remember.

- Have passion for your work and show it openly. Enthusiasm for your work is contagious and will motivate and empower those who work with you.
- Be honest, upfront and have very high integrity. Learn constantly from everyone.
- Understand, set and communicate the organization/project vision and goals. Communicate effectively and frequently. Learn to communicate at all levels and to people of diverse backgrounds. Surround yourself with diverse people and views.
- Truly care about people. Understand and help people be successful. Pitch in and help without being asked. Give your 100% to every project. Be willing to work on projects that will make the company successful. Turn every setback into an opportunity. Give credit and show gratitude to everyone who contributed.
- Don't play politics. Stay true to your values. The bad guys will finish last and you will be able to sleep like a baby at night.
- Over deliver to your commitments and practice excellence in your work.
- Treat your customer like a king and your supplier like a partner.
- Build teams whose strength and weaknesses complement/offset each other.
- Hire the best and always hire people with great attitude and who have the potential to be better than you. No one is perfect and everyone makes mistakes including you. Practice humility. Watch your "EGO" and do not let it control you.
- Deliver great quality every time.

- Focus on solutions to problems and provide a solution for every complaint.
- Observe and learn that leadership from different cultures has many common threads and some unique ones too.

Lessons as a woman in the technology world: My grandfather, who was an engineer and one of my important early mentors, encouraged me to join the engineering field. He and my family always used to teach me as a young girl that men and women were equal. He also taught me that if someone has a problem with me being a woman, it is "their problem and not mine." This important lesson has helped me all along in my journey. Remember to treat everyone with respect irrespective of their gender and your gender will not in any way hinder you. "Be confident" in who you are and "speak up" if someone does not give you or someone else professional respect.

Plan ahead and prepare for your feminine needs while working, traveling and attending late night meetings. Follow your "woman's intuition" and walk away from people or situations that make you uncomfortable.

Remember: You are a *human being first and foremost* and a woman only after that. Forget about your gender when you walk into the workplace. You will shine automatically.

Always have an open mind to learn and understand people. Avoid judgment and stereotypes. As women, we have a softer side that helps us empathize and understand employees, team members and situations from different perspectives. If you harness these skills, they will help you and your organization. Learn techniques and skills like stress management, Yoga breathing to manage your energy and emotions so they enhance and do not diminish your work experience.

Seek out industry organizations like WIT that give you an opportunity to learn from others.

Lessons to balance work and life: 'Work and life balance' is a very challenging puzzle that needs constant attention and planning. I made some mistakes along the way in taking my spouse and family for granted as I focused too much on work. If I had to do this all over again, I would spend more time with my spouse and family. My husband constantly encourages, motivates me and is my friend and mentor for my life and successful career. Your career involves some compromises and sacrifices from your family members. Remember to consult with them about their expectations and how your travel and work hours impact them. Remember to appreciate and communicate to them what they do for you to have a successful career. Look at life in 5 to 10 year time frames and see how your situation affects this time frame. Plan what legacy you would like to leave behind.

Striking a perfect balance between work, family, personal and community is an art that you have to learn and practice constantly. Stay healthy by eating right while working or traveling and working out regularly. Yoga and meditation help me manage stress. Meditate daily for few minutes. Have some hobbies and pursue them no matter how many multiple time zones you have to support globally. Taking time for yourself is very important to constantly stay at full potential. Enjoy life and "Be present" in every moment since life is a true gift.

LATHA RAVI is an executive with recent experience as Chief Information Officer (CIO) leading the Information Technology Organization and leading the software design center for Panasonic Automotive Systems Company of America in Peachtree City, Atlanta area in Georgia, USA for the past seven years. Prior to these roles in Georgia, she has held management positions leading software, systems and other engineering disciplines in product design engineering organizations for Ford Motor Company and Visteon Corporation in Michigan, USA. During her 23 year career, she has held leadership positions in technical and management areas of Information Technology, Design engineering, Software engineering, Product design, Automotive engineering, Multimedia,

Navigation and New technology designs. She has four US patents. She holds a Master's in Computer Science and Engineering from Oakland University, Michigan and Bachelor of Engineering in Electronics and Telecommunication from Anna University, Chennai, India. Her hobbies include mentoring professionals, women, immigrants and children, reading, practicing and teaching yoga and meditation.

Rules to Live By

by Denise Reese

Strategic Relationship Manager
Wipro Technologies

BANGALORE, INDIA

Rules to Live By

I'VE BEEN THINKING ABOUT how I would approach this piece for nearly three weeks now. Each time I would sit in front of my computer ready to type, I got through one or two paragraphs and would end up deleting everything I'd typed! There were even a couple of sleepless nights where I'd awaken with what I thought was an "Ah-ha!" moment. I ran downstairs to my laptop and I don't know what happened, but somehow, I achieved a major case of writer's block in the two minutes it took to walk from my bedroom to my computer!

It's difficult to think about a defining moment that shaped me in to the person I am. Not because I haven't had such an epiphany ... but there's just so many! My journey is comprised of numerous experiences that have collided to develop me to be the person I am today.

So, as I sat in front of my laptop one last time, I pondered about the advice I would impart to the next generation of great women in business. I realized that I had some key nuggets that I wish I had grabbed hold of earlier in my personal and professional journey.

Be yourself – I bet you've heard this at some point from your parents, teachers or someone close to you. As I think back in retrospect, I realized that I spent far too much time during my high school and college years trying to be the person I thought everyone expected me to be, instead of focusing on just being me! What I realized as I progressed in my career is that I was hired because of the unique qualifications I possess. By being something/someone other than who you are, you're doing yourself a disservice. More importantly, those around you are missing out on the uniqueness of *you*!

Don't be afraid to ask for help – Whether it's in your academic or professional career, use the resources around you and don't be afraid to acknowledge when you need assistance. You'll be better off for doing so!

Seek out a mentor – This is somewhat in line with asking for help, but it goes a step further. Sometimes, we all need someone to share ideas with, ask for advice, or help with key decisions we have to make. As a woman navigating the sometimes difficult landscape of Corporate America, my mentors (I have more than one ... which is also a great idea!) have been invaluable to me! Each of the women that I call a mentor has various experiences that I can glean from. They help to keep me on the right track and ensure that I'm working to my full potential.

Be a woman of your word – I can't stress enough how important this is. Always do what you say you're going to do, and if you can't deliver on something you've promised, be honest about your limitations. Your name and reputation are everything. Have integrity at all costs and do what it takes to preserve your character. My Grandfather used to have a saying that I adhere to until this day – a good name is better than having all the money in the world.

Be fearless – Fear only holds you back; so don't allow it to control you. There will always be obstacles to overcome, and that's OK! Don't let those difficulties deter you from reaching your goal. More importantly, don't allow others to transfer their fears onto you. Be bold and strong and never let anyone tell you what is not possible.

Be tenacious – Success doesn't come overnight, but it does come! Persevere and stick with your plan. There will be roadblocks that come your way and sometimes, you might even stumble and get side tracked. That's OK! What is most important is that you stay the course and be patient!

Explore the world around you – There is a big world out there and it's waiting for you to explore it! If you're in college, look at study abroad programs and internships that can provide you with international work experience. If you've already entered the job market, consider working at locations for your company outside the U.S. International exposure is rewarding, exciting and enables you to appreciate the uniqueness of other cultures.

Most importantly, take advantage of every opportunity available to you. Many women have come before you and paved the way for you to walk in greatness. Be true to yourself and never let anyone tell you what is not possible! Walk tall, walk strong and blaze a trail for those that will come after you.

DENISE REESE is a Strategic Relationship Manager for Wipro Technologies and Secretary for The WIT Foundation Board. Based in Atlanta, GA, Denise has spent 15 years in technology sales for several major IT services and software organizations and has held positions both in The United States and Europe. Denise holds an MBA in Strategic Management from The Henley Business School in The UK and in her spare time, she enjoys singing, reading and volunteering in the community.

WIPRO TECHNOLOGIES, a division of Wipro Limited (NYSE: WIT), is amongst the largest global IT services, BPO and Product Engineering companies. In addition to the IT business, Wipro also has leadership position in niche market segments of consumer products and lighting solutions. The company has been listed since 1945 and started its technology business in 1980. Today, Wipro generates USD 6 billion of annual revenues. Its equity shares are listed in India on the Mumbai Stock Exchange and the National Stock Exchange; as well as on the New York Stock Exchange in the US.

Be Yourself

by Renee Reyes

Entrepreneur/Inventor
Co-founder/Dry, Inc.

ATLANTA, GEORGIA

Be Yourself

Be yourself. Sounds easy, right? It's not. In fact: when you stop and think about it? Most of us invest a preponderance of our life trying to become everything we're not already: better educated, more attractive, financially independent – you name it.

Of course, there's a difference between bettering ourselves and *being* ourselves. Unfortunately, change blurs that thin line. If you create a novel technology, start a new company, raise money from strangers, grow a business – you'll likely discover that parts of your persona go missing in the whirlwind of those changes. Change is the basis for opportunity in technology. However, when everything is changing around us? We tend to change a bit, as well.

Thus, being you isn't quite as easy as it's cracked up to be. Here are a few thoughts to perhaps illuminate your path to self-discovery.

Be Your Vision. The first step to being you is taking advantage of your natural vision. I call mine my "Runway Sweet Spot": where the lights hit me just right and I look good from every angle. Trust me: that's a rare vantage point and it took me lots of treks down some lonesome catwalks to find its light. Some gals get lucky and their God-given expertise is quickly identified through aptitude testing, a musical instrument or an athletic contest. For the rest of us? It takes a bit more digging. In my case, I discovered I had a gift with emulsion-based organic chemistry after mixing my own haircare products. I could literally see impossible mixtures on my natty mane – but nobody informed me the components were completely incompatible. I found ways to combine elements that were novel at that time. This was my undiscovered knack and I've since found that everybody's got their own. The secret to finding yours is paying attention to what comes easy versus beating yourself up over what seems hard. Remember: your vision is a natural gift. Keep your eyes open – and you will eventually "see" it.

Become Yourself. Ironically, I got my best lesson in working with emerging technologies on a golf course. Ever played golf? It's an inherently simple yet ridiculously complicated game. A links tutor once convinced me to "become the ball". I never quite mastered golf, but I did learn a lot from that experience. Like many young people, I first tried directing myself to a hot new industry. I later attempted to jump in front of an exciting new technology. Both instances were a disaster – I had not yet "become the ball".

Technology can be likened to your various choices in golf clubs. Each exists to make every work application easier. Technology is not a solution: it's a means to a solution. If you view various opportunities from your own position first – in the face of life's fairways, roughs or sand traps – you're halfway to the green from the onset. Technology is the servant. You are the master. You … are the ball.

Finish Yourself. Most people stop short of truly finishing anything. It gets boring. It gets frustrating. We're not making any money. All we see are the problems and the grass starts looking much greener in the adjacent pastures. I made that mistake more than once in my early-entrepreneurial career. Know what I finally realized? It's only after you are totally aware of all the negative issues associated with a technology that you're finally in a position to develop viable solutions. Until that time? You're just an armchair critic.

People asked how I came up with my product and technology for cleaning "dry clean clothes" at home in household clothes dryers. It happened because I stuck with something for the first time in my life. I had followed the advice of a mentor and gotten into the retail dry cleaning business, as it seemed a fertile opportunity and one of the only retail markets not dominated by large chains. The problem was two-fold: that retail vision was my mentor's vision – not mine. Second, I discovered through trial and error that I literally hated the business of dry cleaning. That's usually not the sort of recipe one finds with success. In the past, I would have moved on to something new at that critical juncture. However, experience finally taught me to stay focused and find a profitable opportunity within the mess. It worked. Keep in mind: starting things is easy – but all the money is found at the finish.

Laugh at Yourself. A more difficult aspect of remaining authentic is learning to accept your weaknesses and literally laugh aloud at your screw-ups. I struggled immensely in this department because I was sensitive to criticism and internalized those emotions. This sensitivity carried over into my R&D efforts – a most confining condition.

Making mistakes is the heart and soul of technological breakthroughs. It's only after we fail from going too far that we become aware of how far we can really go. I discovered the key to overcoming a critical nature is laughter. I also found it that it's easier to laugh at yourself when you're in the habit of laughing. To this day, if I don't find a reason for a good belly laugh over the course of a twenty-four hour span, I tune in for some on-line comedy to fulfill the bill. Incidentally, a key aspect of my most valuable patented technology came after making a joke about what to name my new product. Don't ever underestimate the value of a good laugh on your road to success.

Love Yourself. Sometimes, loving yourself is the greatest challenge associated with being you. That was the case for me. Guess what? Although I was born a woman, I started my journey in a man's body. Thus, I was clinically termed a transsexual-woman. I was also called lots of other things. Most of them weren't very fun. This condition and those circumstances made it doubly difficult to love myself. I tried to run away from all I was: big mistake. There are many facets to every life journey but just one constant: *you.*

Never live a lie and never lie to yourself. You are exactly the person you are supposed to be: period. Learning to love myself was the greatest technological achievement of my life.

Be Yourself. Who are you, really? Do you know? If you're like many people starting their career you're perhaps more in tune with all that you're not versus everything you are. That's to be expected. Your calling is just beginning. However, if you don't stay in touch with your center it's easy to get caught up in a draft of current trends versus sailing your own current.

Be your vision, become yourself, finish yourself, laugh at yourself, love yourself … whatever! Just remember: be yourself – and your success will already be on its way.

RENEE REYES is an Atlanta-based entrepreneur and inventor. She is a co-founder of Dry, Inc. and holds ten patents relating to the process of cleaning "dry clean only" clothes in the home. Her technology saved American consumers over $1 billion in dry-cleaning costs since 2000. She also founded Presstine Cleaners in Atlanta, GA – one of the single highest volume dry cleaning stores in the United States. Previously, Ms Reyes was president of Moby Dick Seafood Restaurants National Company. Moby Dick was the nation's fourth largest fast-seafood chain at that time.

DRY, INC. is a privately held consumer packaged goods firm based in Portland, OR specializing in laundry additives and fine fabric cleaning solutions. The company's products are available at Wal-Mart, Target, Publix, Costco and other fine retailers across the US, Canada and Australia.

My Journey from Success to Significance

by Karen Robinson Cope

Managing Partner
Atlanta Technology Advisors

NORCROSS, GEORGIA

My Journey from Success to Significance

As the first women of the year in technology, I felt so honored. The year was 2000 and I was the President and CEO of Enrev, a battery charging company that had recently completed a $25 Million capital raise which brought our total capital raised to over $41M. I was told repeatedly that this was the most money raised by a woman for an early stage company. We were in the final stages of taking of taking our company public and our bankers were the darlings of the IPO crowd. My husband, Richard Cope, and I wondered what we would do with all of the money we would soon have in our bank account as the analysts were said to be valuing our company at over $1B.

Fast-forward 180 days and like many pre-IPO companies in 2000, the market imploded and our dreams of riches also went up in smoke. We ended up selling the company for a fraction of the IPO value and I learned a few valuable lessons:

1. Raising a significant amount of capital is not an end but merely a means to an end. What matters is building a great company where all of your investors get a good return.
2. Timing is everything....
3. As the CEO, you need to make the decisions. Even when you don't have all of the information, any decision is better than no decision. Even a bad decision that is corrected quickly is better than indecision.

With the sale of Enrev, I took time for reflection – to think about what I had done wrong that I could correct the next time, to recognize what I was good at and what I wasn't good at and to think about the things that I am passionate about. Though I had planned to take some time to contemplate my next opportunity, an old friend asked me to consider running his company. When he told me the company sold advertising on payphones, I laughed and told him "I don't believe in advertising and payphones are disappearing."

So why did I end up joining the company as CEO? My priorities and the market had both changed and it felt like it was the right place for me. From a personal perspective, my husband and I had just had a baby girl who we were crazy about. I planned to take her to the office with the nanny and wasn't sure if any "traditional" angel investors or venture capitalists would support a CEO that brought her child with her to work. Prime Point Media did not require much capital and I was sure that I could raise the startup capital from some of my mentors like Dan Parker and Bert Ellis. I had also realized that my expertise was in building companies, not necessarily managing them, so wanted a venture that I could sell in a 3–5 years. When I researched the outdoor advertising market, I realized that over 300 acquisitions had occurred from 1998–2001 and that the average sales price was an attractive multiple of revenue and EBITDA. And finally, I recognized that I was best at sales and marketing – no black box of technology to manage.

In summary, I found a company that fit my skills, passions and stage of my life completely. We were able to raise the necessary capital, hire the right team, build a "game changing" technology that we used to market the products and then sell the company in less than five years. And in the process, we made all of our investors and employees a fair amount of money.

From Prime Point Media, I learned the following:

1. Love what you do and do what you love. For me that included balancing my work life with our family life. Life is too short to be in a place you don't love or working with people that you don't admire.
2. Good technology can make a mediocre company in a poor economy excel. The outdoor advertising industry in 2002 was known for providing advertisers with "cheap eyeballs"

By developing a geo-based mapping system, PPM was able to give advertisers very targeted advertising.

3. Timing is everything ... again. We were able to sell PPM to a public company just before the market crashed at an exorbitant price. Had we waited, not sure we would have ever been able to sell.

For the last three years, I have been able to spend even more time on the causes and people that I love. This includes spending time with my husband and helping him with Nanolumens, a leader in building lightweight, flexible displays and with our daughter, Alex, who is in the 3rd grade at Wesleyan. I also get to spend time helping entrepreneurs, especially women, who are building and growing the next generation of great companies. By sharing some of my trials, I am optimistic that they won't have to make some of the same mistakes that I made.

On a more formal basis, I have also enjoyed being a mentor or judge at the many business competitions or awards programs or being a Director for either private or public companies. Being on the other side of the process (as opposed to the CEO who has been nominated) has given me insight on how Atlanta can better prepare our mid-market companies. To that end, we have started a non-profit that will help privately held companies grow by providing board level advisory services. We also hope that this will help build "community" as we are able to retain more of our executive talent who often move out of state when they retire or have a liquidity event.

It is also clear to me that as it says in the Bible in Luke 12:48, "From everyone who has been given much, much will be demanded; and from the one who has been entrusted with much, much more will be asked." As one who feels very blessed, my main focus has been on finding non-profits that we can put our time and talents into. In particular, I have become very passionate about micro lending or the practice of making small loans to people who are generally outside of the traditional banking system. As an entrepreneur, I understand the concept and as a Christian, I have seen it change families and entire villages all over the world. Working with Opportunity International (www.opportunityinternational.org), we have seen how these loans are helping millions of people rise out of poverty, their independence and self-respect intact. I am on a mission to help educate my fellow entrepreneurs and women executives on how we can help make a difference by giving back, especially with programs like micro lending where a few hundred dollars can change a life.

When I look over the last 10 years, the community of women entrepreneurs who have supported me and the other women executives encourages me. Being the first Women of the Year was exciting but it is even more exciting to see all of the powerful and accomplished women who have followed me.

ATLANTA TECHNOLOGY ADVISORS works with technology companies to: determine the continuing competitive advantage, identify and validate the revenue model, articulate these in a business plan for fundraising and an operations plan for running the company, identify the management needed to execute the plan, raise the money required to fund the plan, assist in the execution of the business, and then plan and execute the liquidity event for the shareholders.

Strategic Volunteering

by Heather Rocker

Executive Director
Women in Technology, Inc. (WIT) & WIT Foundation

ATLANTA, GEORGIA

Strategic Volunteering

As the executive director of WIT, people often ask me, "how did you end up with this job?" It was definitely not a direct career path – though I'm not sure that the "direct" career path exists for many these days. My current role came about from a combination of taking calculated risks, working hard, following my instincts (and my heart), and taking ownership of my own professional (and personal) development.

Taking calculated risks: I was a good student that enjoyed a variety of subjects ranging from Spanish to economics to chemistry to dramatic arts. Though I was taking advanced physics and calculus as a high school student, almost no one even suggested that I pursue higher education in the female-scarce fields of math or science. There were two very important exceptions – and both were men. One was my high school chemistry teacher. He was the first person to speak with me about career options in science and even went so far as to suggest scholarships with schools where he had influence. The other was my father who had studied civil engineering at Georgia Tech. His message to me was simple and clear: you are good at math and science, and if you get a degree in engineering you'll be able to do just about whatever you want in life. So, even though I knew it was the most challenging of my educational options, I went for it. It was this experience that fuels my current advocacy for getting young women interested in technology and science-related career options. My most game-changing risk was taken at the age of 30 and is detailed a bit later in my story.

Working hard – sounds boring, but it's true: I believe that having a strong work ethic will help you in almost any role. My ability to graduate with an engineering degree was not just a result of studying, but also a combination of scholarships, student loans, and several part-time jobs (one semester I had four simultaneous part-time jobs on campus). In my first full-time job as a consultant for the electric utility industry, I consistently volunteered to be on project teams and even to lead the projects that no one else wanted to take. Not only did this position me as a valuable resource to the company, but also it allowed me to learn new skills that I would have otherwise overlooked. I don't believe that you prove your value by being the first in the office or the last to leave. It's very much about being a good team member, proving you're consistently dependable, and embracing a challenge (otherwise known as an opportunity) when it arises.

Follow your instincts and be true to your career aspirations: I was good at my first full-time job in technology. I enjoyed my organization and my co-workers. I made good money. I had opportunities for advancement. That said, I knew in my heart that though this was a fantastic *job*, it wasn't my desired *career*. I spent much of my free time in both school and work volunteering with nonprofit organizations. Not only did I enjoy working toward a result that benefitted others, but also I had the opportunity to enjoy a variety of leadership positions and learn new skills that were not available to me at my job. Through these experiences I learned that I was rather good at leading nonprofit organizations to success and that I had a knack for engaging volunteers. After two years of soul-searching and research, I followed my heart and made my most rewarding calculated risk – the decision to translate my technical and consulting experience to the nonprofit sector and eventually serve as an executive director. I had a newfound faith in my abilities, both technical and managerial. My first non-profit role was leading a technology project, collaborating with IBM, many product and service providers, and the leading nonprofit organizations in Georgia. Two years later, a colleague handed me a job description for a new executive director position for an organization called WIT, and thus, my desired career was born.

Take ownership of your professional development: I can say with 100% certainty that I wouldn't be where I am today if I had waited for my employers to spoon-feed me professional development (training) opportunities. I wish that someone had said to us at college graduation:

- Don't sit at your desk and wait for your manager to send you to some industry conference.
- Don't assume that attending a "networking" event and collecting business cards is going to propel your career.
- Don't let a lack of budget dollars or managerial support derail your need to consistently learn and grow outside of your current role and responsibilities.
- And don't you dare blame others or circumstance when you sit on your hands and wonder why you don't have your dream job.

It's important to remember that professional development doesn't only happen in a training class. Some of my most valuable leadership experiences and new skills were honed in a volunteer capacity. I'm a firm believer that your best opportunity to spread your wings in a variety of ways is through a volunteer role. Think about it – it's a way to try out skills that don't get to hone in the workplace … and they can't dock your pay if you try something and fail! These volunteer roles are typically a "safe place" to try something new and then translate those new and/or enhanced skills to your workplace. For example, I became very skilled at running successful fundraisers as a volunteer – something I would have never gotten to do in my day job. I was able to translate those skills in the areas of financial management, marketing and fund development. In fact, the ability to utilize strategic volunteering roles is one of my favorite components of WIT. We allow women (and men) to jump into a role that will not only grow their skill set but also their network. It's a fantastic way to get outside the four walls of your office, give back to the community, and gain experiences that enhance your professional value.

HEATHER ROCKER joined WIT in 2007 as the organization's first-ever executive director. A graduate of Georgia Tech, Heather holds a bachelor's degree in Industrial Engineering. Prior to joining WIT, Heather was the Product Manager at Georgia Center for Nonprofits, steering the implementation of Nonprofit Marketplace. Previously, she was a senior consultant for EnerVision, Inc where she led projects such as rate/pricing strategy, power supply, and strategic and business planning for the electric utility industry.

Heather currently serves her community as Immediate Past Board President of Atlanta Women's Alliance, Executive Team Member & Past State Chairman for the Distinguished Young Woman of Georgia Scholarship Program (formerly Georgia's Junior Miss), Trustee and Past Committee Chair for Georgia Tech's Board of Trustees, and Volunteer Training Director for the Junior League of Gwinnett & North Fulton Counties. Heather was named to the *Atlanta Business Chronicle's* "2008 Top 40 Under 40", awarded the honor of "2009 Outstanding Young Alumna" by Georgia Tech, and selected as the winner of the 2009 Turknett Leadership Character Award in the "Inspiritor" category. Heather's story and advice are profiled in the book *Change Your Career: Transitioning to the Nonprofit Sector*. She currently authors a blog about strategic volunteering and speaks to nonprofit and corporate groups about incorporating this concept into their leadership development plans. (http://strategicvolunteering.blogspot.com)

Heather and her husband, John, reside in Roswell and are the (brand new) parents of a baby boy, Will.

WIT's mission is to serve as passionate advocates for advancing women in Georgia's technology community. Each year, more than 1,000 thought leaders and professionals attend WIT Forums, WIT's leadership and networking series. WIT delivers professional development programs, such as WIT Executive Coaching and WIT Careers in Action, to enable members to hone their leadership skills and achieve visibility within the business community. WIT's philanthropic and educational programs, such as Girls Get IT, provide outreach to educate and encourage girls and young women to pursue careers in science and technology.

What is the Gender Variable? Reflections on Leadership that Makes a Difference

by André Schnabl

Managing Partner
Grant Thornton LLP

ATLANTA, GEORGIA

What is the Gender Variable? Reflections on Leadership that Makes a Difference

In the year 2010, our society is well past the point of the early emergence of women in leadership positions. Although women are still underrepresented in the board room and "C" suite, we are surrounded by many visible examples of women in all kinds of leadership roles; from those in early-stage startups to those within Fortune 500 multinationals.

So what is it that women bring to leadership?

There is no more in common between Indra Nooyi, current CEO of PepsiCo, and Carly Fiorina, former CEO of Hewlett-Packard, than there is between Atlanta's own Bernie Marcus and Robert Nardelli. We are being "fooled by gender" if we somehow conclude that there is a female brand of leadership. Leaders of both genders are enormously diverse in terms of their character, performance, style and cultural background.

The dilemma specifically facing women is that *the road to success and to leadership positions is far more perilous than it is for men.* This road presents a totally different set of obstacles for women. Reams of research have shown us that this journey is tougher for professional women than for their male colleagues, and that these hurdles can put the brakes on women's ascension to leadership. The reason we admire women CEOs is not because they are better than men, but because they had to overcome greater challenges to get there.

Supporting the aspirations of women on this journey is what WIT is all about. I have had the opportunity to work with many organizations with lofty mission statements, but few have delivered as convincingly as the group of energetic people who are WIT. Among the people of WIT is a sense of ownership, collaboration, esprit de corps, mutual support and celebration that makes WIT effective in its mission. The leaders of WIT attract women who are prepared not only to come to meetings, but also to roll up their sleeves and execute.

Consider Marci McCarthy, who got involved in WIT, helped build the Women of the Year awards, and then created two businesses out of what she learned during the process. It is rare to see an organization so driven by the same volunteers who actually make its work happen. WIT has always been this way; back in 1999, when I first became involved, I remember the energy, enthusiasm and commitment of WIT volunteers that is still strongly displayed today.

In 1999, I was the partner leading Grant Thornton's Atlanta office technology industry practice. Our firm was in the early stages of organizing a committee to promote and support the success of our professional women, and at the same time one of our women partners in the Chicago office was helping to lead the creation of an awards event celebrating women leaders. In the midst of this, I met with Sonia Lucas, then-president of a young and growing organization called WIT. Over lunch we talked about how WIT and Grant Thornton might work together. Our resulting vision was the creation of an awards program honoring Georgia women who are making extraordinary contributions in their communities as business leaders and technology visionaries.

I recall that first awards event in April of 2000 as a self-serve breakfast of eggs and croissants. It was a humble setting, but we were thrilled that our vision of the awards event – dreamed up only one year prior – had come to fruition and had drawn a crowd of several hundred filling the room. My client, Chris Jacobs, CEO of Theragenics, was a nominee, one of a truly elite group chosen by a judges panel made up of leaders in the Atlanta technology community.

I have met so many wonderful individuals through WIT events. I remember meeting Karen Robinson and her husband, Rick Cope, at the very first event. At the time, Karen was the CEO of Enrev, an early-stage, venture-backed company focused on developing battery technology. Karen had established relationships with investment bankers and analysts, and had licensed the technology to a number of consumer product companies. She had also raised over $41 million in private equity and Enrev had been recognized by Frost & Sullivan as one of the top technology companies of 1999. Karen was one of our finalists and not surprisingly, that morning she was honored as WIT's very first recipient of *Women of the Year in Technology*.

My strong first impression of Karen was based on her connection to the venture and private equity world – very much a man's world, and one which she'd very successfully navigated. Karen had convinced this world that she would make it, and that the company she led would be successful. I remember Karen being strong and confident – a person who doesn't let the common wisdom drive perception because she is prepared to drive it herself.

Over the years, I've had opportunity to interact with Karen at a variety of business and social events, and my wife and I have grown to be close friends with Karen and Rick. The impression I had of Karen as the first Woman of the Year in Technology has been reinforced by many subsequent interactions with her, both in the boardroom and socially. Karen has a terrific sense of what is right and wrong, both ethically and in making decisions about leading and driving a business. As a serial entrepreneur, Karen distinguishes herself with her unique leadership style. She is a good listener, and she knows how to build a team. A woman of faith, Karen consistently demonstrates a willingness to make a difference – to devote an enormous amount of time, energy and financial resources to those causes she feels are important. Her husband, Rick, is also a technologist and entrepreneur who serves as the CEO of an exciting startup called Nanolumens. Karen is deeply interested in his business and a great supporter of his ventures and success.

As I have already mentioned, I have met many wonderful leaders though my interaction with WIT. More importantly my interaction with many of these women has enriched my business experience and has given me the opportunity to take this experience and create an environment at Grant Thornton that supports the development of women at our firm.

We all know that WIT has played an important role in the development of women in our technology community, but it is also possible that its influence may be far more significant. As we look further afield and consider those societies that best demonstrate "innovation," we see societies that are progressive and where women are accepted as being powerful parts of the business reality. Those societies that have isolated women and consider leadership a job for the men alone live with their old traditions, resisting innovation and the better life it affords, and pay a dear price.

Advice to young women

The advice I give to young women – whether embarking on a college education or at the beginning of their careers – are points they've probably heard before, but they are important points that bear repeating.

Focus on developing meaningful relationships. Relationships are everything. Invest in relationships at home, at work, outside of work, with your customers, with your boss and in your community. Developing the right key relationships has an enormous influence on what ultimately becomes of an individual. Surround yourself with people who are successful, and their positive attributes will rub off on you, inspire you and set a high bar for your own aspirations and the type of person you become. The old cliché "birds of a feather flock together" holds a great deal of truth. Be an eagle.

Be an optimist. Optimism is a critical function of attitude. For those people who are optimistic about life, good things happen. The opposite is also true.

Take risks. This is especially important for women. Although goal setting is important, don't forget to take risks. Very, very few spectacular accomplishments were ever planned. Taking risks increases the chances that highly impactful things will happen to you.

Be intellectually curious. The most successful people I know take great pleasure in asking questions, understanding systems and problems, and keenly observing everyday events. Take the time to figure out what you are passionate about, because this passion will fuel your intellectual curiosity and ultimately, your success.

Respect others. We all know that treating others as you yourself would like to be treated is a cliché. Even so, those who truly follow this behavior every day will create powerful lifelong assets.

Use technology wisely. Technology has changed our lives in so many ways, providing us with new ways to communicate and tools that increase efficiency, and revolutionizing life. However, always remember that through technology, we have more knowledge, but less common sense; more acquaintances, but fewer friends; more conveniences, but less time. Use technology, but be wise about it, as technology does not provide you judgment; it simply provides you data.

Make a difference. Use your talents and skills to make a difference in the lives of other people. Whether you impact your family, your colleagues, your clients or your community at large, making this your focus from the very beginning of your career will bring true abundance to your life.

ANDRÉ SCHNABL began his career with Grant Thornton LLP in 1974 and has served as the Atlanta office managing partner since 2002. His involvement with WIT in creating the *Women of the Year in Technology* awards was a natural progression of a longstanding career of supporting women to achieve leadership roles and success. Schnabl was one of the first partners in Grant Thornton to embrace the importance of developing the firm's professional women, and in the early 1990s was a part of the firm's leadership focused on this goal. As a client serving partner, he has served a large number of women CEOs, and has also worked closely with many successful women leaders in the community a board member. With this experience as a backdrop, Schnabl partnered with WIT to help create the Women of the Year in Technology Awards.

Schnabl's dedication to the Atlanta community is deep and includes serving as past president of the Canadian American Society of the Southeastern United States, a founding trustee of the Atlanta International School, and immediate past Chairman of the American-Israel Chamber of Commerce. He is also a member of the advisory board of the M.I.T. Enterprise Forum, a Kennesaw State University Foundation Trustee, a member of the Junior Achievement Board of Directors, and a member of the American Institute of Certified Public Accountants and the Georgia Society of Certified Public Accountants.

Women Entrepreneurs: The Gifts & The Sacrifices

by Karen See

Co-Founder, ClarityClose
Former CEO, Abovo Group

ATLANTA, GEORGIA

Women Entrepreneurs: The Gifts & The Sacrifices

IT STARTED OUT AS A WORKING MOMMY'S BUSINESS. With two small children (ages five and two at the time), the phone call from a former boss and a former colleague (both at different companies, but now in conspiracy together) was a shock. They were calling to convince me it was time to start my own marketing agency. (I'm pretty sure now, they really called just to get me to do some work for them, but whatever!) At the time it seemed like divine intervention from God. And it was. But with great gifts, come great sacrifices.

So here are a few Gifts & Sacrifices I experienced over the 11 years serving as CEO of Abovo Group, a B2B integrated marketing services firm for technology companies. I hope by opening my "kimono," I can help you avoid some of my sacrificial lambs as well as encourage you to give yourself a fantastic gift ... your own company!

GIFT #1:
No glass ceiling

During my days as a marketing communications professional at companies like Gerber Alley & First Data Corporation, Health Systems Division (enterprise hospital software), I had a lot of latitude and support. But while I had plenty of opportunities to learn and grow, it only took one boss to slowly slide that invisible glass ceiling over my head.

I knew it when I hit it, but didn't see it coming and couldn't figure out how to break it. No matter how much I stressed my interest in learning strategy, pricing, competitive analysis ... he would just tell me I was "too good" at my current job and therefore, it would be detrimental to the company if he moved me out of that position. So, let me get this straight, "I've done *such* a good job that my reward is to go *nowhere*!"

Clearly, that response didn't work for me, so after a few more stops along the corporate boardwalk, I finally took the entrepreneurial plunge. What I thought was going to be a nice little "hobby/business" turned into the wildest ride of my life. And guess what, there were no glass ceilings because I'm the one that built the house! Take that (name withheld)!

SACRIFICE #1:
No blueprints create a crazy house

If you are an over-achiever like me, sometimes it's good to have boundaries. But since I built that house without a ceiling (in fact, I built it without permanent walls, let alone a blueprint or foundation), it became the house the market built. (Some might think that's a good thing. It is until the market decides to move elsewhere!)

Within the first three years of business, we moved offices four times; each time because we needed more space (or so we thought). The deal is, when you don't have a master plan, you don't know what you're building. It's like you have a plot of land and then all sorts of contractors, plumbers, electricians, interior decorators show up and start doing their thing. That's what Abovo was like.

We took clients faster than we could staff. We hired people faster than we could assimilate. We bought stuff faster than we could think. During this time, there was no strategic plan, no financial reporting, no sales forecasting, no accountability, *no sanity*! (I realize today's market will probably never present such a crazy situation for an entrepreneur, but I've met a lot of struggling companies since then who don't have their house in order either.) Good times or bad ... you gotta know where you want to go or you just might end up in a crazy house yourself.

The sacrifice came when all that good dot.com business went

away practically over night. I found myself stuck with too much office space, too many employees, too much useless equipment and office furniture. The pressure to survive was the worst experience of my life (OK, second worst, but still way bad). It impacted my health, marriage, children, relationships … everything! (The good news … I'm alive, my children are as normal as one could expect, and many damaged relationships have been mended. The marriage … well, that's another story.)

GIFT #2:
When the money is good, it can be very, very good!

I was blessed that during the go-go-days at Abovo, I enjoyed compensation I never dreamed possible … certainly more than I could ever make as an "employee". The very possibility of accomplishing financial success is what motivates most entrepreneurs (that and getting their brilliant idea/service accepted by the masses). It's the engine that drives our capitalistic society; why so many people flock to the U.S. every year. (Alright, enough flag-waving!)

Having a middle-class, small-town Kansas background, I was taught greed was a sin and true Christian values required sharing (especially with those less fortunate). We did well enough that everyone at Abovo during those days received pretty nice compensation (at least in my perception). In fact, one day I actually gave an executive a $50,000 raise. (Now let me be clear … that was *stupid*! In hindsight, it should have been a bonus, not a salary increase. When times get hard, try taking part of someone's salary! It is much easier to say, "sorry, no bonuses this year.").

Despite occasional acts of stupidity, I was reminded once by a former employee (through an unexpected e-mail), how many families I supported financially and how many dreams (like home ownership, new cars) I helped people achieve. (That note was sent during one of my darkest moments and regardless of how much I may have done … and I certainly couldn't have created any of those opportunities by myself, it moved me to tears.)

More importantly, we were able to financially support a lot of not-for-profit organizations … either in cash donations or in-kind pro-bono services. It felt really good … and I consider that a true gift.

SACRIFICE #2:
… and when the money's bad, it's downright wicked!

Let's say you have a $1 million/month payroll, a $50,000/month office lease, plus another $100,000/month various other expenses. *and* you have $150,000 in contracted revenue for just the next month. Oh, and there's no secret slush fund, no investors to cry to, no bank loan waiting with your name on it. Now *go*! (By the way, that was my reality one day.)

Welcome to the hell side of entrepreneurialism! If you're the lead dog, you've got a couple of options:

1. Cower in the corner, whimpering and licking your wounds. Of course, that behavior will ensure you are on the "adopt me" list at the pound.
2. Panic and take high interest-rate financing on your AR and/or wrack up debt on your personal credit cards (with 18% interest). That will probably lead to personal bankruptcy.
3. Suck it up, get in there and fight for your company's survival. That probably means making *really* hard decisions about any and every cost you have: people, office space, benefits and perks, training, your salary … yup, that probably needs to go to $0. Mine did!

And guess who everyone looks at with deer-in-the-headlight expressions? That's right, *you*! *You* are the leader, so *you* need to be the calm, cool head of reason and reality. Don't over-promise, but don't freak everyone out either (even if your insides are on fire). Sometimes I handled these crisis's really well … sometimes I sucked air like a beached whale!

No matter the "rah-rah," effort mustered, you just hope your team will have the same passion and commitment to fight the good fight. Unfortunately, my experience has been that only a very small and loyal group will actually fully engage in the struggle. Most will tell you to your face "we're on board," but in reality … it's self preservation time. (Remember the guys who dressed like women to get off the Titanic. Yup, their DNA has successfully passed down over the generations. Not that only men bail. I've seen the best and the worst of people facing adversity and x/y chromosomes don't matter.)

It's easy to get your feelings hurt (as this is your baby, doesn't everyone love it as much as you?!). And it's discouraging to find out that those you thought were made of strong character and grit were really made of Swiss cheese and marshmallow.

Like any sea-worthy captain … get the right people on the right size boat. Let loose those that are going to take you down (and don't look back). Lift your chins and stroke … stroke … stroke! When you land on shore, you will be a stronger, more connected team than you ever thought possible. And you'll be amazed at what a sleeker, passionate team can do after they've faced adversity together and survived!

GIFT #3:
Working moms – no guilt needed

Starting that "hobby" business so I could have quality child-rearing time … and finding myself in the vortex of the heady dot.com extravaganza was surreal. But egos being what they are (or at least mine), I lavished the attention, got high off the adrenaline rush of decision-making and competitive selling, and basked in the glory of all that was Abovo.

But every evening (when there wasn't some networking event), I'd come home to these two cute little kids … who'd run up and grab my neck, my legs and squeal in excitement just to see me. Pangs of selfishness and guilt, you bet!

Then one day I heard my young children discussing their titles for when they went to work at Abovo. My daughter said she'd be Vice President of Crayons and her brother could be Vice President of Pictures. (If you think hard about this, she was already setting herself up for commerce, as you can't make pictures if you don't have crayons!) I realized that my children were already visualizing themselves as successful … and that's a fantastic gift!

The point of all this is today my children (Rachel, a freshman at UGA studying bioscience and salutatorian of her graduating class; and Kevin, a sophomore at North Springs High School, the youngest section leader in band and an honor student) are mature past their years, self-reliant (they do their own laundry), confident and comfortable in their skin.

While I certainly sacrificed a lot of mommy quality time, I also (unknowingly) educated my children about work ethic, responsibility, compassion, and perseverance. I am pretty sure they would not have been as well prepared for the world had they not watched me with their all-absorbing eyes and brains. What better gift than having your children blossom into self confident, successful young adults! (Of course, you can check back with me after they've reached 21 to see how the story really plays out.)

SACRIFICE #3:
It's not what you think

You probably expect me to say my marriage. Nope, not going there! Marriages work or not for lots of reasons. Was being the CEO of a successful (then not so successful) company a contributing factor, yes. Was it the only reason, no. So no pity party allowed!

The final sacrifice is really about relationships with men (and

I'm talking to heterosexuals for a moment). Once you climb into the driver's seat as a female business owner (assuming you're not running a true hobby business), 80% (that's my estimate) of men will find you intimidating at some level. Especially if their careers are a few grades down in terms of responsibility and/or appearance. (Interestingly, I find many gay partnerships don't seem to have this issue. That's probably a topic for another day!)

So, go into your role as "chief-of-everything-by-day" with eyes open and sensitivity on high. Know that your dream (and success) may sound good to your partner … until it's reality. He'll either find your new role exciting and a source of pride … or stifling and emasculating. I hope it's the former!

Conclusion

In reflection, I wouldn't change a thing! I share some of the greatest rewards and deepest pain that comes with being a female entrepreneur … particularly in technology and even more so in the South.

My greatest hope is that I haven't scared you off, because if you have a burn in your belly like I did, you're destined to do this. I personally never wanted to look back at my life and wonder "what if?" I had no female mentors … no one to show me the way. So I plunged head first in a pool I hoped was deep enough. Luckily it was … and the water felt great!

KAREN SEE has started her second entrepreneurial venture as co-founder of ClarityClose. She and her partner, Michael Taylor, were intense competitors for almost 11 years before they put their daggers away and decided to join forces. Today, ClarityClose provides executive-level "win" consulting for those responsible for selling products, services, companies or causes. In less than a year, the firm has amassed an impressive list of clients including North Highland Group, National Commission on Orthotic & Prosthetic

Education, Florida Municipal Power Authority, Prenova, Capre' Group, ThanksAgain and Carefx.

Karen was a board member of Women in Technology for two consecutive terms in the early 1990s. She was a finalist for the annual *Women of the Year in Technology* award and has served on numerous for-profit and not-for-profit boards.

CLARITYCLOSE is a strategic win consultancy for those responsible for selling services, products, companies or causes. Focusing on the most critical steps of the sales process, the firm helps improve the win to loss ratio by working with executives on assessing, articulating, demonstrating and packaging their unique value propositions.

Can't Win Without You

by Bob Stargel

Vice President Global Nonwovens
Kimberly-Clark

DALLAS, TEXAS

Can't Win Without You

I BELIEVE THAT THE FUTURE GROWTH of industry and the world in general will require the innovative application of science and technology. I am talking about true innovation that actually improves the quality of life for people and makes a difference in the world, not the innovation of creative financing that has led to the current world recession we are in. Identifying, nurturing and progressing talented technologists is critical for driving that innovation success. We need the best and brightest from all demographics, especially women.

I am involved in several initiatives that are aimed at inspiring others and the early identification of talent towards technology and economics. One of those organizations is the FIRST (For Inspiration and Recognition of Science and Technology) robotics program that encourages students K-12 to develop an interest in the technology and planning associated with building a robot and competing in a national challenge against other teams in a game format. Through this initiative, I have been introduced to multiple students, including females, who have developed a passion for technology. What is most rewarding is to see the female students who had no interest in engineering or robots develop a keen thirst for pursuing a degree in the area of science and technology. I have been involved in this organization over 10 years and I have easily seen over 200 female students that have shared a very similar story of not having much interest in science and math until they were involved with this program! This is the same program that initially introduced me to Women In Technology and they have continued to be one of the strongest sponsors of this program in the state of Georgia. It is because of my knowledge of WIT that I met Sandra Hofmann, the current President of this organization.

Here's a funny story: one evening a friend was sharing with me a holiday party picture book. At the end of the book was the WIT logo. I asked my friend, "Is this the Women in Technology group?"

She said she didn't know, but that she would ask the owner of the book. Turns out that it was the WIT I knew and it was Sandy Hofmann's book. She introduced me to Sandy (you will have to ask Sandy where we first met!), and I shared my interest in helping to promote science and technology with females at a young age. It wasn't long before we were chatting away about becoming more involved in WIT. It wasn't long before she had convinced me to be a silent auction candidate at the upcoming WIT Connect! From a chance encounter, I was introduced to Sandy and I have found her to be a beacon for promoting and inspiring women in technology. She does fantastic work that has made a real difference in not only the women's lives but also society.

Women: we cannot win without you! The female population in North America is over 50% of this country. We must have access to this vast talent pool in order to solve the problems of today and tomorrow. To increase the possibility of building a greater nation and world, we need to tap into this valuable resource pool and inspire and drive the active pursuit by women of science and engineering-related fields. We cannot solve the problems of today with the thinking of the past. We need to identify talent in women early and encourage that talent in programs like FIRST Robotics and organizations like WIT.

Promoting the advancement of women matters to me. I am a past winner of the Rodney Chip Award from the Society of Women Engineers. This award celebrates the work of a man or company who has made a significant contribution to the acceptance and advancement of women in engineering. I am very proud of that achievement and remain humbled by the consideration that my team members and the Society of Women Engineers bestowed on me by selecting me as the recipient in 2007. The best part of the award was that I had not even been aware of some of the things I had done in helping women advance – I had simply been selecting and promoting the *best* people for the job! I guess I shouldn't be surprised that women were the best people for the job in a lot of the cases. After all, my wife, an engineer by profession, constantly reminds me that she is the best person for any job at home!

BOB STARGEL is Vice President of Global Nonwovens, Kimberly-Clark Corporation. Global Nonwovens is sector internal to Kimberly-Clark. In his role Bob overlooks the development, commercialization and supply of materials used to support Kimberly-Clark's branded personal health and hygiene products. The Sector consists of seven manufacturing facilities, including 29 different nonwovens machines, a centralized research and engineering team, as well as planning, finance and staff manufacturing operations.

Bob was born in Cincinnati, Ohio and attended the Georgia Institute of Technology in Atlanta. He graduated in 1983 and worked with the Lockheed-Georgia Company prior to joining Kimberly in 1984 as an entry-level electrical engineer.

KIMBERLY-CLARK is leading the world in essentials for a better life. Every day, 1.3 billion people trust Kimberly-Clark products and the solutions they provide to make their lives better. With well-known family care and personal care brands such as Kleenex, Scott, Andrex, Huggies, Pull-Ups, Kotex, Poise and Depend, we hold the No. 1 or No. 2 share position globally in more than 80 countries.

Achieving Career Success – a Continuous Journey

by Jannet Walker Thoms

Executive Consultant, Government Practice
HealthNovation

ATLANTA, GEORGIA

Achieving Career Success – a Continuous Journey

In carefully thinking about what the most appropriate as well as insightful message to share with the next generation of women leaders should be, I reflected on the diversity in my career decisions and roles, key lessons learned, the mentors that guided me through out my career, family and friends that provided support and the obstacles along that way that served to strengthen me over the years, though at times it was difficult to see their value. All these factors have indeed led to the makings of a successful career in information technology.

I would like to begin by sharing how I made the decision to pursue a career in information technology, which was largely influenced by my college professor, the Computer Science department head at the time, during the sophomore year of my college experience. I was a political science major with plans to pursue a career as attorney and to practice family law. I had wanted to be an attorney since I was a teenager, having provided babysitting services for a successful attorney and his family. However, not too longer after beginning my college career, my professor said something that made a profound impact on my college and professional career. He challenged me to consider a career in information technology, as it was frankly a time when very few women were employed in the field with even fewer minority women.

Sadly, the number of women entering college with determined majors in Information Technology was not increasing either. Not surprisingly, he had a clear agenda to increase the number of women and minorities in the Information Technology field to ensure diversity and inclusion for the future in an industry that would one day soon, affect every aspect of life both business and professional. My professor felt that my solid performance in math, sciences and a variety of computer programming courses made me ideally suited for this fascinating and evolving new field. I was enticed by the idea as I was always up for a good business challenge and quickly changed my major. I also realized that pursuing a career in technology would have unlimited potential for opportunities across every industry. The good news here is, he was right.

My lesson learned here would be to always remain open to further exploring and cultivating your career choices based on experiences and changes in the competitive landscape that may guide you to a fulfilling career. In my opinion, being successful in ones career requires many of the areas previously discussed but also includes the essential elements of continuous professional and personal growth, dedication and commitment to your passion to achieve your dreams. I would like to share the top 10 elements to career success that I believe will remain relevant throughout your career.

Top ten suggestions for achieving career success:

1. Lead with integrity in all that you do. Strive to make consistent and thoughtful decisions and actions in your day-to-day activities whether it's directly related to the business of IT, personnel decisions such as hiring, terminations, promotions and reorganizations or interacting with staff, peers and superiors. Being described as a leader with integrity is one of the greatest compliments one can receive and will assist in influencing business decisions and building consensus. Losing this valuable leadership quality is difficult if not impossible to regain. Also, others are watching how you lead, set a strong leadership example for others to follow.
2. Seize the opportunity – be willing to take on that challenging project. Demonstrate leadership and willingness to accept a challenge. This opportunity may provide you with the unique leadership experience and proven ability to manage difficult projects as well as provide increased visibility of your skills and talent.

Be willing to try something that is outside your comfort zone while ensuring you have the resources and support to be successful.

3. Follow your passion in life and your career. A common thread today is finding your passion in your career. A key element of having a successful career is truly finding something that you love doing and build a career around it that allows you to achieve your career goals. It is always easy to identify people that have arrived at a place in their career that allows them to be passionate about what they do … there is a certain lift in their voice and level of energy that is undeniably due to a person that has found their passion. A key to getting to success is finding this wonderful state in your career.

4. Identify and obtain strong mentors in and outside of your organization, as these people are critical to your success by providing invaluable guidance and perspective, lessons learned and constructive feedback throughout your career. Be open in your search considering mentors diverse in experience, age, gender, ethnicity and industry, Also, keep in close communication with you mentors and keep them apprised of your career progressions as they should serve as trusted members of your virtual support team. It is important to understand that mentors can also be your champion at work by provide a positive voice and perspective for you when you need it most, when "you're not in the room." Mentors may change over the years as you change career paths or corporations, be willing and ready to quickly adapt as necessary.

5. Be a strong mentor to others in your company and community as it is just as important to provide mentoring, as it is to receive. At every stage in your career, you have a responsibility of mentoring and sharing of experiences that will benefit others in the corporate pipeline. It is often said that as one succeeds, she should be surrounded with others that move along with her. Be sure to pull others along as you move forward.

6. Hire the most talented and hard working people available that possess the qualities and attributes necessary to building a

high performing, committed and passionate team. Ensure that you aggressively seek diversity in your hiring decisions, as it will promote a more creative team with diversity in thought and problem solving and creates a corporation that is more globally competitive. This approach should also be applied to working with vendors and suppliers.

7. Identify and promote top talent within your organization. Be willing to look beyond the group of folks that you interact with regularly and that seem to be in the spotlight. Continuously search for that hidden talent that may need a little mentoring to become your next star performer. I have found this to be the case in my experiences and when properly mentored these folks can become the shining stars of any organization. Many people in an organization are starving for mentoring and reorganization, I suggest you find them.

8. Develop a plan for continuous career and personal development. One should strive for a life long learning experience which includes continuing education beyond undergraduate studies, professional certifications and courses, awareness of current technology and social networking trends and remaining current on relevant publications and thought leadership books to ensure that you remain informed.

9. Embrace change in your professional and personal life, as it is inevitable that there will be changes. It may sometimes difficult to understand changes in directions at your company but do not resist the change, instead look for ways to effectively and positively support the change in your organization. In today's competitive environment, companies are frequently restructuring to meet the needs of their customers and to achieve performance goals, recognize that change is necessary to improve the way service is provided. Set the example for how to embrace change and achieve the expected results.

10. Volunteer. Participate actively in the community and support organizations that promote women and careers in information

technology such as Women in Technology as well as other business organizations. Give back – volunteer time to provide mentoring to young girls and women, as this will have significant impact on their future career choices and overall development. Participation in the community also leads to productive networking opportunities. Relationships developed as a result of community involvement and volunteerism may lead to future career opportunities and/or identification of talent for your organization.

Thank you for allowing me to share my perspectives with you. I do hope that these recommendations for success have been meaningful and resonated with you. Clearly these suggestions are based on real world experiences in my diverse career, key lessons learned and the positive impact of strong mentors which all have been critical influences that have shaped my career in information technology and led to my continuing success.

I would like to close by sharing my final thoughts on leadership. I believe that passionate leadership inspires employees. I am convinced that as a leader, if you strive to instill the positive qualities in your employees that motivate them to perform exceptionally, create excitement about coming to work and create a rewarding environment that allows them to excel and to attain passion in what they do, you will be successful.

Congratulations on your current successes. Godspeed as you continue your journey of achieving life long career and personal success.

JANNET WALKER THOMS, a technology executive and former CIO, is currently an Executive Consultant for HealthNovations where she consults with government, private and public sector clients to provide strategic technology solutions to meet their business needs. Previously, she was the Vice President for First Data Corporation where she served as the national Transportation Practice Lead for the Government Solutions Division delivering innovative financial technology strategies and solutions to government agencies in transit, parking, education and tolling. Prior to joining First Data, Walker Thoms was a Principal with Booz Allen Hamilton where she was responsible for leading the San Francisco Bay area and Southeastern state and local transportation consulting practice while serving as an frequently sought after executive advisor to top transit executives.

Walker Thoms was formerly the Deputy General Manager/ Executive Vice President for the Metropolitan Atlanta Rapid Transit Authority. Prior to being appointed as Deputy General Manager, Walker Thoms was MARTA's Chief Information Officer and Assistant General Manager of Technology. During her tenure at MARTA, she provided leadership for some of the Authority's most forward thinking technology initiatives including a $50 million business transformation program that upgraded MARTA's business systems to a contemporary state and the design and installation of the Breeze Program, a $200 million state-of-the-art all smartcard based regional fare collection system which is the first in North America.

Walker Thoms' background includes over 20 years of diverse leadership and Information Technology experience in public and private sectors with proven success in effectively implementing technology solutions, organizational restructuring strategies and business development initiatives. Walker Thoms obtained a Masters of Science with a major in Business and a Bachelor of Business Administration with a major in Management Information Systems. She has also completed significant coursework toward her Doctorate of Information Systems.

In 2006, the Technology Association of Georgia's Women in Technology named Walker Thoms as the Woman of the Year in Technology (Public Sector) and the National Black MBA Association named her the 2006 Outstanding MBA of the Year among 7,000 members. Walker Thoms has received numerous recognitions including being named by the *Atlanta Business Journal* as One of the 50 Most Powerful African-Americans in Business.

She has also been continuously recognized as one of Atlanta's Most Influential leaders by Who's Who Publishing, honored by the *Atlanta Business Journal* as one of Atlanta's Most Influential African-American Women and named to the *Atlanta Business League's* list of "Atlanta's Top 100 Black Women of Influence."

A member of the board of the Women of Technology for the last three years, Walker Thoms is the current Vice President of the WIT Foundation, the philanthropic arm of Women in Technology Inc. WIT is responsible for bringing awareness of Science, Technology and Math (STEM) studies and future career pathways to middle and high school young women.

Walker Thoms is a member of the IT Senior Management Forum, Women's Transportation Seminar, and the Atlanta Chapter of the National Black MBA Association. She also previously served on the Board of Directors of the Atlanta Chapter of the National Black MBA Association and as President (2004–2007) winning national chapter of the year twice during her presidency, Georgia CIO Leadership Association, Georgia Chamber of Commerce, Atlanta and the Board of Advisors of the Metro Atlanta Chamber of Commerce.

Jannet has been featured in a variety of publications, some of which include – *Atlanta Business Chronicle*, *Atlanta Tribune*, *Black MBA Magazine*, *Atlanta Business Journal* and *Shape Magazine*.

HEALTHNOVATION is a consulting and services company focusing on the Health IT (HIT) and High-Tech Markets addressing healthcare. For half a decade, HealthNovation and its executives have been a leading provider of information management and strategic business process outsourcing services to government agencies, Fortune 500 companies, education and healthcare organizations.

Take Care of Yourself

by Cindy Tierney

CIO and SVP
Beazer Homes USA, Inc.

ATLANTA GEORGIA

Take Care of Yourself

Early in my career I was excited to accept a job with a major company. My new position involved moving to a different city where I knew no one but I was thrilled to have been given the opportunity. I felt good about what I was accomplishing as a young businesswoman and proud to have been selected over the other candidates for the job.

I'd been in town less than twenty-four hours when the senior management person who hired me invited me to join him and his wife to go fishing. Having grown up fishing with my family I was glad to accept the invitation. I looked forward to meeting his wife, seeing more of the area and learning about the job. Of course I wanted to make a good impression on my boss, too.

Unfortunately, when I arrived at the boat, 'Mr. Boss' told me that his wife wasn't feeling well and wouldn't be able to join us. I was disappointed but didn't even consider not going ahead with our plans. After all, he was much older, a fatherly figure and he was my boss at this well-respected company. I was totally surprised to spend the next few hours being chased around the boat!

When I got off the boat I called the recruiter who had helped me get the job. Here I was in a new town with a new job at a recognized company. I had already purchased a house. My parents were in another state and I was alone. I wondered what to do. After talking with the recruiter I thought, "Toto, I have a feeling we're not in Kansas anymore!"

Back in the office on Monday, I chose to ignore it. My midwestern family – from Kansas City, Kansas – had instilled in me a blue-collar work ethic. I just kept on working and doing a good job. I acted as though the boat adventure had never happened. I was determined to be stronger and never let my boss think that he could ever cross that line with me again. I just kept doing my job. Patience paid off, but it was hard. Eventually he was moved out of the position and no longer my boss.

I always wish I had handled this differently. I did what I thought I was 'supposed' to do, the 'right thing,' what a "young lady" would do. Rather than stand up to him, I dealt with it internally and worked even harder to make sure I was recognized for my intelligence and my contribution to the company. I wish I had reported him immediately. That's what I would have done had I been true to myself and listened to my inner voice.

Later in my career I did stand up. Coming up through the corporate ranks I've seen company cultures that were dishonorable, inequity in pay and promotions and people being treated unfairly. The things you read about in books and see in movies – they really happen!

Once I went to the Human Resources department to get resolution around some issues. They launched an investigation that resulted in a couple of executives being fired. One time I was on maternity leave and learned that my job had been given to an employee who worked for me. When I returned I had to defend why I should get my job back. Another time I saw things in a company that needed to be changed and I was determined to work to make things right for the organization and make things right for the people, and then leave. That's what I did! After stirring up a commotion that resulted in positive changes, I negotiated a package and left the company.

Looking back I realized that I left out an important step. In addition to taking care of the company and the people, I wish I'd taken better care of myself. Hindsight tells me that I could have handled things a little differently and stayed until getting another job.

I was true to myself in standing up for what I believed was right. I learned that being true to yourself also means that you can't always help everybody. You have to remember that you are there, too. You have to take care of yourself in the process. Airlines have it right when they tell you to put the oxygen mask on yourself first before tending to others!

Being an executive, especially a female executive is hard. You will go through different phases in your career. You may start out focusing mostly on being a successful executive. Then at some point you may marry and decide to become a mother. You are expected to be 100% a successful executive, 100% the perfect wife and 100% the perfect mother. Realistically, priorities shift constantly and you must work to *integrate* all aspects of your life and not go crazy trying for a 'balance'.

The words of wisdom that I can share are simple – be true to yourself. You have an inner voice. Listen to that inner voice. Be self-aware. You cannot be successful in your work if you are not true to yourself. In order to do this you can't be owned by money and material things. You have to define what success means to you. Only then you can make decisions strategically about what you are willing to do to be successful. Along with strategy you are going to have to make sacrifices. Only you can decide what sacrifices are right for you to make based on your own priorities. And you are going to have stress. It's up to you to take care of yourself and make sure you manage the stress rather than allowing it to tear you down.

A few years ago, on Monday, July 11, 2003 I found out that the company I was working with was going to pay out my contract. On Tuesday I went in and completed the paperwork to finish things up. I had promised a young woman at the company that I would take her to a businesswomen's networking meeting that I'd been invited to attend. I didn't really want to go but she had also been let go from the company. She had no contract so she had no payout, no job and three kids to support. I'd been invited several times to the networking meeting, but hadn't yet attended. Up until that point I focused only on my job and my family. I wasn't involved in the community and didn't attend business or organization events outside my job. That evening I went to the meeting, but mainly to take her. I didn't think I needed it, but I thought it would be good for her to go.

We sat in the back of the room. Everyone was asked to go around the room introducing themselves telling their name, company and a hobby. They started in the back of the room. I stood and said, "Hi, I'm Cindy Tierney. This morning at 7:00 I was CIO of a company. At 7:10 I was not." Of course everyone laughed. I continued, "For my hobby I ride ATVS (all-terrain vehicles) and dirt bikes for the love of my husband and my girls."

A few rows up a little woman with dramatic grey hair stood and said, "Hi! I'm Sandy Hofmann and I'm CIO of MAPICS." Everyone in the room seemed to know this woman.

The next day I got a call from the president of WIT (Women in Technology.) One of my vendors had told her about me. We talked for three hours and she said, "I want you to help us." I went to a WIT meeting and in the big room filled with women in the technology industry there stood this little woman with the grey hair. I went up to her and said, "I'm sure you don't remember me, my name is Cindy Tierney...." She said, "Oh yeah, I met you at the other meeting. You do the dirt bike thing."

A few months later I saw her again at an event. I said, "I'm sure you don't remember me..." and she said, "Oh, you're Cindy Tierney!" At this point I still was not working, the girls were in second and third grade and my vocabulary was becoming all 'mommy and me.'

After meeting three or four times, Sandy and I went to lunch. We talked about everything and nothing. From then we met once a month, usually for dinner. It was through the relationship with Sandy and WIT that I got my current job at Beazer Homes where I've been for over five years now.

Sandy introduced me to Pathbuilders, an organization that pairs young female executives with mentors for a formal mentoring program. Here I was able to use my experience to give back by mentoring young executives. My first mentee was a young woman with KPMG. She wanted to figure out how to balance her life and career. She wanted it all – a successful career and a husband and children. My goal was to help her see that in order to have it all you have to first be true to yourself. I worked with her for several months. Now she is a partner in the company, is married and has a child. The irony for me in this is that now I am a divorced single mother to my two daughters.

We all want to have it all. Life is about continuous little successes and little setbacks. You can have success with strategy, sacrifice and stress. That's how life is. I don't think anyone has a formula. Ask the right questions. Examine yourself all the time. What do you need to do to be true to yourself? What sacrifices are you willing to make?

In my professional life, sometimes I had to stand up as a leader and as an executive and tell my organization. "We have to make some changes here." In my personal life sometimes I have to go home as a mother and as the head of a household and tell my family, "We have to make some changes here."

You can successfully "have it all" if you define what "having it all" means to you. Stay true to yourself. Listen to your inner voice. Make decisions strategically as to how to have your own version of success. Choose the sacrifices you are and are not willing to make. Realize that there will be stress. And remember to take care of yourself.

CINDY TIERNEY's career encompasses more than 20 years of experience in leading and energizing the key strategic and operational facets of organizations to higher levels of performance.

Currently serving as CIO and SVP of Beazer Homes, she is responsible for assessing the relative impact of emerging technology to strategic business needs and interprets their meaning to the organization's senior leadership team. In her current role, she participates in overall business technology planning, bringing a current knowledge and future vision of technology and systems as related to the company's year over year double-digit growth or to a downturn industry position. She provides key strategic, people and crisis management while continuing to deliver day-to-day operation execution.

Cindy's career highlights include being honored as *Women of the Year in Technology* Enterprise Business Nominee, 2006; Georgia CIO of the Year Awards Enterprise Finalist, 2006/2008; Atlanta CIO Executive Summit Best in Practice Speaker, 2006; Georgia Southern University College 2007 Alumni of the Year; Georgia State Bergeron Mentor Advisor; Pathbuilders Mentor Program and Digital Ball Co-Chair 2009/2010. Professional memberships include Builders Homesite Inc. Board Advisory Council, GCLA Advisory Board Member, Georgia CIO Leadership Association, TechBridge Board, Chair and Georgia Southern University College of IT, Board Member.

Cindy has a Bachelor of Science from Georgia Southern University and is a native of Atlanta, GA. She has two wonderful daughters, Chase and Reese.

BEAZER HOMES USA, INC., headquartered in Atlanta, is one of the top ten homebuilders in the United States. Having built homes for America's families for over 50 years, Beazer Homes has been listed on the New York Stock Exchange since 1994.

Those Who Do – Get to Do More!

by Terry Trout

Vice President, Customer Experience
Cbeyond

ATLANTA, GEORGIA

Those Who Do – Get to Do More!

I CAME TO TECHNOLOGY VIA A VARIED PATH. My first job was building a Personnel department for an Appliance Parts Distributor. (And yes – I just aged myself … we did not call it Human Resources back then.) My favorite part of the job was meeting with employees to find out how we could improve their quality of life at work – and it almost always revolved around what they wished we would fix about their job. It began a long career of looking for ways to make it "smarter, better and faster." I eventually left my corporate role to assume leadership of an acquisition of a company in bankruptcy in Tampa and over the next 17 years led another acquisition and managed 22 locations of what would become the nation's largest distributor. I loved this job because it uncovered a passion for logistics and taught me my first lessons in leadership – creating a vision for teams that would drive their commitment, enthusiasm and creativity.

My story takes a turn when I met Jim Geiger, my now CEO, as we volunteered together to build a Catholic Church in Tampa, Florida. I went to work with Jim at Intermedia Communications; a billion dollar integrated Communications Company and then eagerly followed him to Atlanta to build Cbeyond. As an early employee in a start-up, I had the gift of many roles (translation … utility player) and the opportunity to design a customer experience that we could be proud of as well as create a culture where we were good to each other, to our customers and to our communities. A decade later, I define my role as being a catalyst for customer-centric change.

I eagerly share with my 23-year-old daughters and with other women what I learned as I look in the rear view mirror: *That ordinary people get to do extraordinary things generally because they raise their hand.* Ironically, most of the greatest successes in my life have come from people who had greater confidence in my abilities – than I had in myself. I have now learned to just say *yes*. I am embarrassed at the number of projects, jobs, opportunities, etc that I have been pulled into reluctantly because I did not think I could do it – only because I had never done it yet. I know now that all that generally separates achievers from others – is that achievers start by saying yes.

Fear, unfortunately, it a strong suit for us as women and with age and wisdom, I have come to recognize what a fake obstacle it can become. In fact, I keep a plaque on my desk with one of my favorite sayings – *imagine what you could do if you thought you could not fail.*

That I need to set my own unreasonable goals – not wait for someone to do it for me. I have learned that by creating a plan that tackles obstacle by obstacle, holding myself and my team accountable and measuring progress will lead to results – no matter how daunting the task appears. I have also learned that success is not determined by some "big bang" of an outcome – but generally by being better today than I was yesterday – and doing it again tomorrow.

That any strength overplayed can become my greatest weakness – my passion – my driving need to accomplish can easily sway over into overwork and emotion. I have had to learn that my energy and my mindset need to be matched at the appropriate equation with my talent.

That I am best served when I am serving others. The world is a great mirror. It reflects back to me what I give. When I am optimistic, generous, and helpful, my world will prove to be successful, supportive, and overflowing. When I am short, spiteful or driven (and I can be that) – I find my world reacts with those same ugly tendencies. *My* world is what *I* am.

I also learned that being active in the community has expanded my world, my network and my energy level. Each of us has *something* to offer – whatever time, whatever talent to the degree the season of our life allows. When the girls were little – for me, it was about engaging at church, with soccer – at their school. Now as an empty nester, I can give more freely. As an executive, I can bring to bear resources, services and networking. Every organization I have ever helped has been eager and grateful for anything I could offer – and I have come to believe that it is incumbent on us to each find that place to raise our hand.

To be brutal on process and gracious with people. I've learned to be maniacal about process … because when things go wrong – most often it is because something needs fixed – not because people aren't trying or don't care.

I know now that it also matters as much "how" I do what I do as "what" I do. My teams will thrive if the environment is one that is stable, encouraging and free from backbiting and politics. I may beat the heck out of process – but I work to remember that people who feel empowered by my leadership become kindred spirits and will follow me into uncharted successes.

Finally, that those who do, get to do more. I have come to recognize that those who see an opportunity to make a difference and seize it are infinitely promotable and endlessly valuable. If I always do what I say I will do – people will rely on me. I need to achieve results and I need to it with a generosity of spirit. And if I embrace challenges with less regard to the title and money – I will be the recipient of opportunity that I could never have planned for when I started my career.

TERRY S. TROUT is VP, Customer Experience for Cbeyond, where she champions the customer experience strategically across the organization aligning cross-departmental initiatives to ensure the highest level of customer satisfaction.

With Cbeyond since 2000, previously Ms. Trout held leadership roles in marketing communications, customer operations and operations training. Ms. Trout also led the development of CbeyondOnline™, the company's online account management tool and launched Cbeyond's community service program enabling Cbeyond employees to give back to the communities where they work and live.

Prior to joining Cbeyond, Ms. Trout was vice president of marketing communications for Intermedia Communications, an integrated communications provider. Previously, she was vice president of East Coast operations and corporate marketing for Marcone Appliance Parts Center.

Ms. Trout is actively involved in a variety of leadership and mentoring activities. She founded Cbeyond's Women's Network, an organization designed to foster professional development for Cbeyond women. She holds board positions at The Sullivan Center, with WIT – Women in Technology and The Aquinas Center of Theology at Emory University. Ms. Trout is an active associate of the Marist School Communications Committee and her parish, Holy Spirit Catholic Church's, Liturgy Committee and a previous mentor for WEDA (Women's Economic Development Association).

Ms. Trout was chosen as one of *Atlanta Women Magazine's* Top 25 Power Women to Watch in 2006, which recognized her contribution to community and leadership activities. She won Women in Technology (WIT) *Woman of the Year in Technology* award in 2010 and in 2010, was inducted into the Circle of Champions by Dress for Success, an honor for women championing others in the pursuit for self-sufficiency.

Ms. Trout has a bachelor's degree from Quincy University in Quincy, Illinois, and an MBA from Southern Illinois University.

She is the mother of twin daughters Lauren and Lindsey.

CBEYOND, INC. (NASDAQ: CBEY) is a leading provider of IT and communications services to small businesses throughout the United States. Recently named as the sixth fastest growing technology company by *Forbes* magazine, and added to Standard & Poor's Small Cap S&P 600 Index, Cbeyond offers more than 30 productivity-enhancing applications including voice, broadband and mobile services.

Lessons from My Momma

by Carolyn (Lyn) Turknett

Turknett Leadership Group

ATLANTA, GA

Lessons from My Momma

My momma was born in 1906. She was Momma to me when I was a little girl. That became Mama a bit later and "Mother" as I got older. Most of what I've learned about how women should lead, and everything I've learned about what women should expect and be in the world, I learned from her.

Mother was born Amelia Clio McQueen Crosby in Brunswick, Georgia, and grew up in towns like Nichols and Fitzgerald in south and middle Georgia. There wasn't a lot of money, but she idolized both parents, both of whom died before I was born in 1944. Her father Samuel was born in 1859 and remembered watching his father come home from the Civil War while perched on a swinging gate. He had a high school education and managed to support the family as a sawmill supervisor and a money lender – or maybe a loan shark. I didn't find out until a few years before she died at ninety that he was a prison guard for a few years. She was deeply embarrassed by that for a reason I'll never quite understand.

Viola, her mother, went to the Georgia Normal and Industrial College, a two-year college for women in Milledgeville Georgia that prepared women to be teachers. She was also a poet and a thinker, and my mother clearly grew up thinking that gender didn't matter all that much.

Viola taught Mother the first-grade curriculum when she was four, so Mother began second grade at five. Mother graduated from high school (there were only eleven grades at the time) in Fitzgerald, Georgia, and went to the same school as her mother. It was now, though, a four-year school, and Mother received her degree (with a major in English and a minor in French) in 1923, at the age of nineteen, from what had become the Georgia State College for Women.

She tried teaching high school English, but that was less than successful. One of the other things I didn't find out until I was much older was that she broke her contract in the middle of the year and left. She told me once that she was mortified when she told a student who needed to be fitted for a graduation gown that he needed to get his bust measured. That could have been the final straw. I know that the guilt over breaking that commitment was deep, and after that I think she vowed to be a model of persistence. That's the person I saw.

Mother took a job in Eastman, Georgia, running the office for a business there, and soon met the brother-in-law of the owner and the man who would be my father. Like her father he had only a high school education. He would spend most of his life as a cattle farmer. They were married for 61 years.

Mother had additional training in accounting at some point, and when my sister and I cleaned out the home she'd lived in for sixty years found a letter from 1943 in which she wrote, evidently responding to a classified ad for a bookkeeper, "I hope that you will consider my application for employment temporarily, until you find the man who suits your requirements exactly." Things were different then.

I was born in 1944, and my first memories of my mother's work were when I was about five and my sister was three. She had taken a job in the business school at the University of Georgia as the editor of *Georgia Business*, a publication of what is then the Georgia Bureau of Business Research. During most of my growing up years she worked two-thirds time (largely as an assistant professor in the business school and assistant director of the bureau) and went to graduate school in the remaining time. It took her seven years to get her MBA and eleven years to get her doctorate – graduate schools weren't really set up for working women with a family. She wasn't a great housekeeper, but she was a great mother, and her priorities were clear.

Lessons I learned:

1. *Women can take care of themselves.* I didn't realize as a child or

as a teenager what a powerful lesson this was, but, looking back, I realize that this was the era when women squealed when they saw a mouse and said, "wait until your father gets home" when children needed disciplining. My mother seemed as feminine as any other woman, but she would have simply set the mousetrap. And emptied the trap when the poor mouse was caught. I don't think it would have occurred to her to leave discipline to anyone else. Interestingly, she didn't spank us, but she was likely the toughest disciplinarian in the neighborhood. When she spoke, you listened. She wasn't unkind, but she meant what she said. A seed for balance of Respect and Responsibility in our Leadership Character Model was the way my mother balanced firmness and warmth as a parent. And my mother took care of herself economically as well. I didn't realize until I was well into my teens that she was the primary breadwinner in the family, nor how unusual that was.

2. *Swallow hard and be brave.* I realize that I don't know whether the things she did really required bravery or whether they came easily to her, but she did things most women of her time simply were afraid to do. When I was about to deliver my first child in 1971 she was travelling alone in Mexico on the way back from a conference out west, timing her return so that she could help with the new baby. As I waved goodbye to my parents as a college freshman – a thousand miles away from home with no one I knew at a school (Mount Holyoke) that I had never visited – I did have to swallow hard, but I never thought I couldn't manage. That lesson has served me very well: bravery is not about being without fear; it's about doing hard things even when you're scared.

3. *Men and women are not that different.* This was an unspoken subtext of my growing up years and I probably believe it somewhat less not than I did when I was young. Nevertheless, that unconscious view served me well. I spent two wonderful years at Mount Holyoke in classes with all girls. When I moved to the University of Georgia in my junior year as a math major, I don't remember ever even thinking about the fact that I was the only

woman in many of my higher math classes. That may mean that I'm simply weird, but I'd like to believe that I just never separated the world along gender lines.

4. *Like it or not, in this society work gives people prestige.* This was a good and bad lesson, and it didn't come directly from my mother. I don't remember it occurring to me explicitly until my sophomore year at Mount Holyoke, but I remember suddenly realizing that I liked and respected my mother more than most of my classmates did theirs. Most of those high-achieving women saw their fathers as their role models, even though many still saw marriage and children as their goal in life. My interest in sociology (my graduate school major) likely began then – I saw how programmed we all are by both our home environments and by society at large. I also began realizing that I needed to take a look at my views of my own father. He was a kind, generous, hard-working man – but I definitely had evaluated him on his "earning power," which hadn't at the time equaled my mother's. An aside – I had also learned that farming is a tough, unforgiving business.

5. *We are all children of God.* We would now use a phrase like "value diversity" or "don't discriminate on the basis of race, religion or ethnicity," but the message I remember as a child was that we are all equal in the eyes of God. I grew up in the segregated South. It was because of my mother that I could actually see the prejudice and not be consumed by it.

One of the first things I remember as a little girl was something she said as we were travelling in the car on a family vacation. We saw another car with a black family, and she talked to us about the fact that while we could stop at any gas station and go to the bathroom, that mother and father had no place to stop for their children. I can still feel the sadness and empathy I experienced at that moment, and there are few lessons that have been as important in my life.

6. *Speak up.* This was a lesson I heard in many ways, but one is most memorable. My mother was not perfect, and she could be

critical. She liked most of the graduate students under her tutelage at the Bureau, but there was one behavior that drove her crazy, and she talked about it often. "If you see something wrong, say something!" Don't let something get finished (a document, a project) and then say, "Well, I thought that looked strange." If I were now coaching my mother as a leader now I would ask her to look at her own behavior – surely she was sometimes behaving in ways that inhibited input – but the lesson I learned at the time was to take responsibility and say what you think. For most women that's invaluable advice.

7. *You are responsible for your community.* And for your church, your school, your world. While her plate was more than full, Mother served as PTA president, taught Sunday school, was active in the League of Women Voters, and served as volunteer clerk of our small town when she retired. Both my parents were active volunteers, and serving the community is not a chore for me but a source of immeasurable satisfaction. I also believe that it's important for anyone's career. Peter Drucker said that volunteering for nonprofits is the best way to learn management skills, and I agree. I have found it also essential for building relationships as you build a business.

8. *Most small businesses fail.* This lesson has given me heartburn throughout my life as a business owner. My mother edited and ran statistics for the *Georgia Business* publication, and I heard more times that I can count how only a small percentage of new businesses last five years. I am probably not cut out to be an entrepreneur by personality or by childhood messaging, but perhaps that's been overcome by the learning that life is only fun if you're doing things that are tough.

9. *Keep learning.* Mother was a master of continuous learning – interested in everything and a voracious seeker of information and knowledge. When I was in my early teens she got up every morning at 5:30 to watch a physics program on that new medium – television. She's probably lucky she lived before the Internet – she

likely would have never slept. I am truly my mother's daughter here, and if you're reading this book you are too. Keep reading, keep learning, and keep enjoying the ongoing challenge of life.

CAROLYN (LYN) TURKNETT is President and Co-founder, with her husband Bob, of Turknett Leadership Group, a 22 year-old consulting firm specializing in succession planning, CEO consulting, executive development, talent management and organization effectiveness. Best known for their work in character-based leadership, Bob and Lyn Turknett are co-authors of *Decent People Decent Company*, creators of the Leadership Character Model™, and hosts of the annual Leadership Character Awards.

Lyn earned a BS in mathematics and an MA in sociology, with special emphasis in organizational sociology, from the University of Georgia. Her consulting centers on organizational assessment and change, executive team development, and ethical leadership in rapidly changing environments. Lyn is an active member of several professional associations, including the Society for Human Resource Management, and is a committed community volunteer. She is active in United Way of Metropolitan Atlanta and served on the board for many years, has served as co-host for the Hearts with Hope ball of the Partnership for Domestic Violence, is an elder in the Presbyterian Church, and enjoys "grandmothering" in any spare time.

TURKNETT LEADERSHIP GROUP is a full service talent management firm with over 25 years of experience working with diverse corporate and entrepreneurial enterprises. We are known for our Leadership Character Model and our expertise in succession planning, executive development, human performance consulting, and organization effectiveness.

WAMBAT: Women as Active Members of Business and Applications Technology

by Indra K. Turnbull

President
Connectics.biz

ATLANTA, GEORGIA

WAMBAT: Women as Active Members of Business and Applications Technology

TODAY WE ALL TAKE TECHNOLOGY so much for granted. Can you imagine not reaching down to that extension of yourself to which you are joined at the hip and not being able to immediately text your BFS with the latest thought to flash through your mind – ending of course with LOL (which for the longest while I thought meant Lots of Love – how silly could I be?); have to write a report without being able to run it through Spell/Grammar Check; or turn on your computer and find that it is running at only 3.0 Mbps and feel that the world is coming to an end because it is slower than the average US broadband speed of 3.9 Mbps (in fact a lot slower than most parts of the world) and puts the U.S. in eighteenth place overall in average user broadband speed. (*Source: Akamai's "State of the Internet Report", January* 2010).

WaD we are in a new world – and that world is accelerating at such a speed that sometimes it is hard to imagine where it will ultimately take us. Every day WAMBAM that is supposed to make our lives easier, commerce more productive and profitable; developers and web designers employed; and MaP shopkeepers weep.

A vast number of doctors hold the Internet in disdain according to a recent study released by Forrester Research more than they despise managed healthcare, controlled costs and insurance companies. Patients no longer blindly accept a diagnosis or treatment regimen in what used to be the mystical world of medicine and the mysteries of the human body; where a doctor was placed on a pedestal and considered to be an oracle and all-knowing of things we mortals could never understand and certainly someone we would never dare question or challenge. In today's information technology driven world, as soon as we experience a twinge, a bout of indigestion or a sudden rash, we run to our computers, search our symptoms and within seconds we get back a whole list of sites out there in cyberspace that will tell us what terrible disease we have been stricken with. Having self-diagnosed, we present ourselves in our physician's office, armed with reams of paper, which we thrust at the poor unsuspecting doctor to support our diagnosis, and requested treatment regimen.

Most of us also recognize that perhaps the greatest single influence on the practice of medicine is technology. Doctors can now in real time conference and share data with specialists across the globe to make diagnoses; perform complex robotic surgeries that once required cracking open chests and intensive invasive procedures; probe or view the body with CT scans, MRIS or the use of radionuclide's (nuclear medicine) in the diagnosis of disease. And, one of the most important advancements in medicine, the mapping of the human genome, could never have happened if it were not for the "super computer."

However, my foray into technology was not so heady or earth shattering as creating the World Wide Web; advancing nuclear and nanotechnology; or making significant breakthroughs in holography science and technology. My entry into the incredible and mind-boggling technology space was some 20 years ago before the Internet was a household word; where having a computer on your desk in your home not only took up most of your desk space and cost around $2,000; and the only way you could find your way from A to B was to stop and ask directions or get the unwieldy and hard to read map out of your glove box.

In the United States in 1990, at the time I became involved in the technology sector, the percentage of women in the computing profession was 35.2% and this declined to 28.4% in 2000. A recent report from the *Computing Research Association* indicated that the number recently fell below 20%, from nearly 40% in the mid '80s.

I was not a computer science major nor had it ever been my intent to enter this most foreign and what I perceived to be "geeks only" industry. In 1990, however, circumstance dropped me into taking over the management of the U.S. operations of a small, British-based yet relatively successful, technology company that was a leader in bar-code and printer graphics technology.

I immersed myself in this newly found world and became addicted to what technology could achieve and how businesses could be so positively impacted in efficiency of process and productivity by its adoption. Two years later, in 1992, after the successful sale of the industrial printing technology company, I founded Innovative Icons – which within two years of its founding was reputed by industry analysts as "revolutionizing the social printing industry – bringing it from the dark ages into the 21st century." In today's vernacular it would be categorized as WAMBAM and WYSIWYG.

The premise behind the business model was very simple. It was to utilize technology to its fullest extent to accept remote orders from stationary stores, transmit them to a centralized production facility and thermographically print invitations, announcements or social stationary without typographical errors (proper names) and exactly as a customer had signed off on with respect to the font, ink color and layout they wanted on that invitation or announcement – with an immediate turn around and at a highly affordable price point.

Technology could achieve all of this – and we did. The two fundamental elements, however, on which the business needed to be built, were diametrically opposed in terms of high versus low tech. The final product was very low tech but it was technology that created the end result. So, the first steps in establishing the business were to hire creative artists who, under my direction, designed a distinctive line of over 400 invitations and announcements called The Isabella Collection™. At the same time we assembled a group of young and very talented software developers to write a proprietary program which would facilitate a customer "designing" their invitation on a computer screen in an off-site location, managing the typesetting, ink color, font choice and layout themselves.

When finished, the program was called "It's Childs Play™," so named as my then 7-year-old son became our chief usability tester and our standard defined as: if a 7-year-old could easily navigate his way through the process from card selection to final order, it was a reasonable assumption that a store owner or customer would be able to. And, it is never too early to get our children involved in the practical business applications of technology.

The two cornerstones of the business well underway, we were now ready to put together our marketing, customer support, operations and production teams. This involved setting up a print shop of seven presses, each with a different color ink; installed quality control and image press production computer stations; set up high powered servers to receive orders from customers/stores across the country; established a customer support desk; designed/built custom in-store point of sale displays and kiosks to house a computer, printer and card catalogue; purchased computers to lease to store owners; bought two trucks to cover the country; and hired technicians who would install the systems into stationary shops across the US and into Canada.

Within six months of first conceiving the idea, we installed our first pilot Isabella Invitation Stations in six metro Atlanta stores. In early 1993, we exhibited at the Atlanta Stationary show and took orders from stores across Georgia as well as South and North Carolina and Florida.

However, Isabella's official debut and introduction to the social stationary world was in May 1993 at the International Stationary Show in New York where she could only be described as "the Belle of the Ball."

Stationary storeowners from across the country flocked to our stand and although the show officially closed at 5:00 PM – we were still taking orders for Isabella two hours later and literally had to be ejected by Javits Convention Center's security personnel. Isabella also attracted greeting industry giants, Hallmark and American Greetings who upon "meeting" her, immediately were making "marriage proposals."

Within weeks, Isabella was residing in stationary shops across the U.S. as well as in Canada.

We were amongst the earliest companies to use on-line, customized ordering via the Internet – not to mention the adoption of "straight to press" image processing technology. A customer's order was on press within 15 minutes of it being received on our servers and shipped out to the customer the same day – no other company in the industry could do that.

From White House Invitations and Christmas cards to American Movie Classic promotional announcements, Isabella established herself as an icon in the industry. She was even featured on NBC's Today Show.

As exciting as all of this was, we had our challenges too. The main one being that our customers (store owners) understood the stationary business, but the vast majority had a hard time grappling with the technology. And their customers were equally challenged. This was something we took into account from the outset in designing our business model and was a primary reason we were in the computer leasing business as well as being in technology development and thermograph printing. As hard as it is to believe today, most of the stores in the early '90s did not have a computer and a vast number of their customers were not computer literate. Therefore not only did we have to supply the computer to get a storeowner to make a decision to buy into Isabella, we had to design the system and the keyboards to make the whole process as simple as possible for the store owner and their customer to easily complete the transaction.

When a computer would go down or communication with our servers would go off line, we would receive panic calls from the store with the pronouncement that Isabella was not well and what should they do. When told to first try "rebooting" the computer, our customer service personnel would have to explain to a very confused and upset caller that it did not mean they should kick Isabella (the computer). She had truly taken on a persona of her own and had become so warmly adopted by these previously technology challenged ladies who had now humanized technology and discovered that it was not so threatening or difficult to use after all.

Being a 'Woman in Technology,' I was able to address the needs of a predominantly female customer base. Although I must tell you that as we set up Isabella Invitation Stations on apple carts in the center of malls, more and more men were placing orders for invitations and announcements than ever before. Announcements for poker nights; Super Bowl parties; baseball playoffs; and college basketball and football gatherings all made their way onto Isabella cards – not to mention divorce announcements, dubbed by some customers as "freedom notices."

I believe the success that Isabella enjoyed was because I knew my customer; understood and respected their timidity regarding technology and recognized their fear that the computer and technology were assaulting their world and comfort zone in general. I did not approach it from a position of superiority or insensitivity as so many developers and programmers tend to when designing applications but tried to take a common sense and practical approach to solving a problem – 45% industry reprint rate; relatively high order cost to customer; and slow turnaround in what was in the early 1990s approaching a billion industry – yet totally underserved by technology.

After selling Isabella in 1995, I embarked on another venture where technology played a significant role in what was traditionally a very low-tech business – the staffing industry. My ApplicantAnalytics™ technology, which is utilized in the evaluation and position specific matching of a candidate against a unique position opening, has dubbed me the "Match.com of the recruiting business."

In the intervening years, we have seen many others introduce technology into the recruiting industry – Monster and Careerbuilder the main players in the on-line job board posting and resume database space; Taleo and Brassring, two of the leading Applicant Tracking System providers; all of whom offer candidate filtering. However my ApplicantAnalytics™ technology and my company, Connectics, is unique in matching candidates position specific – with a dynamic, interactive on-line interview that ranks, rates and matches every applicant against the "ideal" employee for a given position.

I never conceived when I entered the business world that one day I would be running a technology company – it was as foreign to me as the man in the moon. However, it was serendipity that brought us together and it is something I will never regret. It has given me opportunities and challenges I might never otherwise experienced and a chance to make a difference. Not in terms of incredible medical advances or introducing a whole new technological device that will revolutionize how people communicate, but through some relatively mundane practical and common sense applications that have brought efficiency of process, moving an industry from the dark ages to the 21st century in terms of its production; and raising the bar and standards in another that for so long had a reputation of being a revenue cowboy by just throwing resumes at clients and hoping that something would stick.

Science and technology are no longer the exclusive domains of men but today, as exemplified with the exceptional roster of women in Atlanta's Women in Technology, women hold major roles in Fortune 500 companies, academia, start-ups and professional services as senior management executives; information technology managers; application developers; project managers; patent or intellectual property attorneys; computer scientists; etc., but are still under-represented in comparison to our male counterparts in spite of endless opportunities.

I would like to prove the naysayers and pundits wrong when they forecast that teenage girls who are now using computers and the Internet at rates similar to their male peers are five times less likely to consider a technology-related career. As technology continues to advance and change our world, the roles that women can play are enormous and those of us in technology today need to encourage, guide and mentor the next generation of young women to take their place beside their male counterparts and equalize the balance – bringing their own special skills, sensitivities and contributions to a very exciting industry.

So listen well – this is a CTA to all you BACS out there. Technology needs you and through it you can enjoy an incredibly exciting and rewarding career. I have!

P.S. *Following is Indra's Key to Acronyms and Text Message Shorthand for the uninitiated purists amongst us....*

BAC – Bad a** chicks
BF – Best friend(s)
CTA – Call to Action
LOL – Laugh out loud
WAMBAM – Web application meets brick and mortar
WaD – Without a doubt
WYSIWYG – What you see is what you get

INDRA K. TURNBULL has over 25 years of senior level corporate executive experience. After several years in corporate leadership roles, in 1990 Indra took over the management of the U.S. division of a British-owned high tech company which was a leader in bar coding and industrial printing. On the divestiture of the parent company to a privately held venture owned by Larry Ellison, CEO of Oracle, in 1992 Indra founded Innovative Icons, a technology driven printing company that was reputed by industry analysts as revolutionizing the social printing industry.

The company was purchased in 1995 by Williamhouse Regency, who ranked alongside Taylor Corporation as one of the pre-eminent players in the social printing industry. Indra continued on as president through the transition but left in 1996 to once again turn her talent of using technology to power another historically low tech business, executive search and recruitment. This time through the development of ApplicantAnalytics™, the ability to match candidates position specific for each unique job opening through an adaptive and advanced on-line interview process, she has changed the paradigm in yet another business sector. Indra has been recognized as a highly intuitive and professional businesswoman and for her talent in improving business processes through bringing together the very best management talent and the adaptive use of technology. Her extensive experience in management and technology has gained RBO Solutions and Connectics.biz the company she now heads up, reputations of leading the way in providing innovative, quality solutions to traditional business services.

CONNECTICS.BIZ practices the Art and Business of Connecting People, Products and Services. We empower companies to connect, partner, and profit in today's Global Economy by providing an integrated solution for companies to enter new markets and grow through providing practical services that encompass marketing, outsourced sales, business services and staffing solutions

WIT President 2007 and 2008

by Judi Vitale

Vitale CFO Consulting

VININGS, GEORGIA

WIT President 2007 and 2008

I JOINED THE BOARD OF WOMEN IN TECHNOLOGY (WIT) in early 2004, on the suggestion of a business acquaintance and after talking with two exceptional ladies who were on the board at that time. Prior to then, I had dedicated my time between work and home, leaving little time to even think about volunteerism or giving back to the community that had treated me well for many years. My sons were in college or high school, so they needed less of my time. I had been a member of WIT for years and had attended a few meetings and several of the annual events, but to join the board meant more time commitment on my part. Was I ready for that? And, was I ready to make that commitment to a women's organization?

I had grown up in a corporate world full of men. There were few times when there were any other women in the board meeting or on the management team. My first instinct about joining the WIT Board was that the meetings would be gossipy sessions, with lots of talking and very little getting accomplished. Sure, I might be giving back to the community, but how could I endure all the disorganization? I finally agreed to be a guest at a board meeting to get a sense of the organization. Sure enough, the meeting started five minutes late and everyone started gossiping and talking. I thought, "I'm glad I didn't commit to this yet." Then, five minutes later, everything changed and now almost seven years later, they will have to throw me out to get rid of me!

I had never been involved in anything so organized, with such dynamic women. After that first meeting, I immediately joined the Board of Directors and became Director of Finance. That year, WIT negotiated with TAG and became an independent society. Beginning the next year, I was Treasurer, then Vice President, and then President for two years. Currently, I am in my second year as Chair. Has it been a lot of work? Yes, especially during the early years and the two years as President. Has it been worth it? Yes, definitely.

WIT has changed dramatically over the past few years. From an independent organization, to a founding society of TAG, to an independent society, to being both a 501(c)(3) and a 501(c)(6), to being the premier organization in Georgia for the recognition and advancement of women in the field of technology. And, I have changed over those years as well.

When I joined the Board, I was CFO of a software company and had been there almost twenty years. The next year, I resigned and joined a larger software company, which was acquired within a year and a half. In 2007, my first year as President of WIT, I joined a consulting firm providing CFO and accounting services to small or mid-sized companies. Today, I am an independent CFO helping small companies with their financial and accounting needs. During my time on the Board of WIT, I moved from a company where I had been twenty years to being in my third position since that first software company. I definitely have gotten my 'sea legs,' but more importantly, I have learned how crucial having a network of trusted individuals, both friends and business associates, can be in business.

Building a network, especially without an intention to do so, has been the most rewarding aspect of my tenure on the Board of WIT. For the first three years on the Board, I was situated well professionally and did not need help in that area. I spent my time helping others, as part of my WIT responsibilities and on my own. I mentored a few women managers, and fulfilled my responsibilities in the community promoting WIT and finding supporters for the organization. In 2007, after three years on the Board, I was leaving the company that had been acquired. With the intention to take a couple of months' time before looking for a new position, and without sending a notice to my network that I was doing so, I started receiving calls and emails offering support, help, introductions, and anything else needed to get me to the next position. Wow, was I amazed and delighted! Without realizing it, I had acquired a network of business associates and friends who were coming out the woodwork to help me. I still get 'goose bumps' thinking back to those times. Friends, all I can say is that it is important to build your network when you don't need it. Then, when you do need it, your supporters will be there.

Another reward I have received while working with WIT is the delight and appreciation I see and hear from the women attending the various WIT coaching programs. These women feel they have been given a chance to open up with their thoughts and dreams, an opportunity to receive feedback and help in putting together plans, and guidance in how to tackle those plans to further their careers. I remember one manager who had been in her position for several years, who was not quite confident enough to go for that next opportunity with her company. After the program, she very meticulously started working on her plan to get to that next level. Sometime later, I ran into her at an event and she was so excited to report she had gotten a promotion and was working on the steps to get to the next promotion. Our hearts skip a beat and our mouths smile when we hear these stories!

Over the years I have been on the Board of WIT, there have been many changes. We have added coaching programs, such as Careers in Action Leadership Foundations for female managers or associates looking to advance their careers, and Reinventing Your Career for those women wanting to get back in the workplace or wanting to change their career. We have increased our community programs for our next generation of women in the field of Technology. We have increased our sponsorships and scholarships for other programs, such as FIRST Robotics, and with job shadowing and mentoring programs. Through all of these initiatives, I am struck by the women who are energized or re-energized by what we 'can' do, by what others before them have done and what they see can happen for them, and by what they can do if they just believe in themselves.

JUDI VITALE is an independent CFO, providing part-time and interim CFO services to small or mid-sized companies. She has over 25 years of experience in financial and operational leadership. Judi has moderated technology panels and has served as a judge in business launch competitions in Metro Atlanta. Prior to this, Judi was a partner with AcuityCFO, a financial services and consulting firm, Prior to AcuityCFO, Judi served as Vice President and Chief Accounting Officer of Indus International, now known as Ventyx, Inc., a service delivery management software company. Before Indus, she was with Firstwave Technologies, a customer relationship management software solutions provider, where she served as Senior Vice President and Chief Financial Officer. Judi also serves as Chair on the Boards of Directors of Women in Technology and Computers for Youth, and sits on the Boards of Directors of the WIT Foundation and TechBridge. She is also on the Advisory Board for Startup Chicks. Judi was Turknett's Leadership Character Award Nominee in 2009. Judi graduated summa cum laude from Shorter College with a B.S. in Management.

Judi provides CFO financial and accounting consulting services to small or mid-sized companies needing help on a part-time or interim basis.

Swans

by Richard Warner

CEO
What's Up Interactive

DUNWOODY, GEORGIA

Swans

Back in 2003, Kasie Scott Palmer approached me about helping with a program that WIT was about to launch called "Executive Coaching." The idea of the program was to create an intensive multiple-week program that targeted things like public speaking, personal presentation and networking. Only senior women executives would be eligible to participate. The feeling was that these promising, high profile women could uniquely benefit from this type of training.

Because I'd been on camera or in front of a radio microphone since my early college days, including many years at FOX5 and Georgia Public Broadcasting, Kasie's team felt I would be a logical candidate to handle media training. Their format called for me to go over some of the basics about how the media works and then, one by one, interview the women on camera. We would play back the tape for the group so each participant could see how she came across on the TV screen.

I attended the initial Executive Coaching session where each participant stood up, told a little about themselves and what they hoped to get out of the program. I would say that, while I was impressed with their accomplishments and the role they played in their organizations, none of the women had much presence as they addressed the group.

Fast forward a few weeks and now it's my turn to lead the Saturday media training session. I was a little nervous about it, frankly. Speaking in front of a camera comes easily for me. I don't give it much thought because I never equate the camera lens with TV viewers. Instead, I'm always thinking about the guy who's operating the camera. If he laughs at something I say, I feel great. If he's off doing something else and seems to be bored with my presentation, I feel uneasy. Doing live television, the only people I'm talking to are the three or four crew members in the studio.

Speaking in front of all these women for several hours, well, that's disconcerting.

I decided the first part of my presentation would be about local media gossip. They'd have fun hearing my opinion about who hates whom in Atlanta (channel 5 hates channel 2), which TV and radio stations are the leading competitors, and even what the media landscape might look like in years to come. I talked about how each type of media operates and described the pressure that all reporters are under. They learned how to give answers on TV (talk in one sentence answers) versus the newspaper (quote lots of facts and figures) and how to make a reporter's job easier so you might come across better. By the end of all that, I was beat.

Now it was their turn. Each of these high-powered women executives got to sit in front of the camera for five minutes and answer my questions about their companies and their careers.

It never occurred to me how intimidating this was. Without exception, these women approached my interviews like I was a dentist about to perform a root canal. Some said they had been dreading the whole thing for days. Of course, we weren't actually going to put the interviews on the air and only Executive Coaching participants would see each other's performances. I also promised to burn the tape as soon as we were done.

No matter. The thought of being in front of the hot lights, on camera, answering questions – just one on one, with nowhere to escape, was very intimidating.

They all came through fine, but as Dan Rather said, "the camera never blinks." Watching themselves on a TV monitor, participants learned how they come across in person. Each woman was her own worst critic, but everyone else in the room gave encouragement. Several said they were amazed how gestures like not looking someone in the eye when you talk to them or bobbing left to right in a chair while talking were distracting and took away from what they were saying.

As promised, I burned the tape.

OK, now fast forward again. Ten weeks after the Executive Coaching participants first gathered, WIT held a graduation, where each participant gave a presentation about what they learned. One by one each woman stood and talked, off the cuff, to the audience of about 30 people that included family members, consultants like WIT's leadership team and myself.

Attending their presentations remains one of the most memorable days I've ever spent. Each woman had developed greater poise, presence and clarity. The improvements were nothing less than stunning. One woman explained that she had given this moment a great deal of thought and decided to focus her remarks on something intensely personal. She decided not to talk about her job, her career or what she learned from Executive Coaching, and focus instead on her spiritual journey. She spoke from the heart about the challenges she faced in her personal life and how religion had become a positive force at a difficult time. By the end of her remarks, there wasn't a dry eye in the room.

Attending the first and last Executive Coaching session and seeing the impact the program had on the participants gave me greater appreciation of the value of WIT.

RICHARD WARNER is CEO of What's Up Interactive. He leads a team of 30 professionals who provide web, video, social and mobile services to companies that rely on interactive marketing strategies. Since 1980, he's also interviewed hundreds of CEOS and covered business for television and radio stations across Georgia. Richard serves on the Georgia Film and Video Commission and serves on the Board of Trust at the Henry Grady School of Journalism and Mass Communications at his alma mater, the University of Georgia.

WHAT'S UP INTERACTIVE specializes in website design and development, video production and search and social media marketing. In business since 1990, we partner with our clients to develop innovative strategies and technology that grow their influence and impact online.

The Idiot Savant of Relationships

by Patricia Whitley

Teacher
Veritas Classic Schools

ALPHARETTA, GEORGIA

The Idiot Savant of Relationships

TODAY, I AM A MATH AND SCIENCE TEACHER at a private school and additionally oversee the workings of my home and family. But, from 1984 to 2005, I worked in the business/technology sectors of Atlanta – first, in corporate educational services and later in sales and marketing.

And, from 2004 to 2005, I was also the vice-president of Women in Technology (WIT). During these years, my career evolved and both my work and volunteer positions became more intertwined. My responsibilities and visibility increased in both. My duties at home grew along with those at work. I had children. My parents got older. And, as home changed, so did I. My priorities shifted. My heart went home.

So, I left a great firm and a wonderful opportunity with WIT to be nearer my children and to become more available to Mom and Dad. I became a member of the "sandwich" generation actively involved with both my children and my parents. The change impacted our personal finances terrifically and it changed the way I saw myself, too. But, through it all, I learned excellent lessons. Some were brilliant and others embarrassing and painful. But blended they became something rich – like fudge chocolate. And, today, from that richness, I create emphatic lecturettes for the young people in my care – the girls *and* the boys of the generation *you* will write letters to. Here are two of the stories I tell most frequently – both from the corporate division of my life. I call them: "The Idiot Savant of Relationships" and "Why Disorganization Seals Your Feet in Concrete and Throws You off a Bridge."

STORY I:
The "idiot savant" of relationships

An idiot savant is someone with extraordinary abilities in one area. When Richard called us into his office that day, he told each of us what he perceived our extraordinary abilities to be. He emphasized his point by calling us each "idiot savants" of something. For instance, to him, one of us was an idiot savant of marketing; another – the idiot savant of details; a third, the idiot savant of writing. Me? I was his "idiot savant of relationships."

While I could argue with his choice of metaphors, it highlighted a great point: Figuring out where you have extraordinary or exceptional abilities and then using them at work can help advance your career. And, certainly, being recognized for those strengths can help you enjoy your work even more. (We'll talk about the importance of neutralizing the impact of your weaknesses later).

The process of identifying what someone is especially good at and then giving them the chance to use it on the job has been called "strengths-based" development. Studies find that people are more emotionally involved at work when they can use their strengths there and this leads them to being more productive and satisfied, too. These emotionally-engaged people make more overall contributions to their places of employment than those who see no opportunities to use their strongest suite of skills. Books like *Now, Discover Your Strengths* by Marcus Buckingham and *Strengths Finder* 2.0 by Tom Rath and the Internet-based *StrengthsFinder® Profile* have become popular tools for those wanting to identify their talents and to turn them into employable strengths. Organizations like Gallup Consulting, a global consultancy firm, have strengths-based development programs as part of their functional practice areas.

In my case, Richard had labeled me correctly. I *was* an expert of sorts in relationships. My degrees were all in communications-related fields. Multiple experiences granted me access to some of the country's leading experts in the field of nonverbal communication and with practice and feedback I refined a unique sensitivity to these types of cues. Richard often asked me to use this latter skill set and it impressed me that he recognized the significance of this form of communication and that he valued my expertise in it. (The book, *Blink* by Malcolm Gladwell provides an exceptional description of nonverbal communication and its role in how people relate to one another.)

Did using these strengths help me? Yes, they did – listening and nonverbal skills in particular. They helped me forge strong, trusting relationships and to understand concepts that intellectually, I simply could not get excited about. For example, I humbly admit I am no technical maven. So, while other managers at Digital were phenomenally gifted and much more experienced in technological applications than I was, I was gifted in listening to my staff. They were the talented and creative technologists – many of them still rank as some of the most brilliant people I have ever known. Through listening to their words and attending carefully to the messages their facial expressions, postures, and sighs added to the words they said, I learned what made each of them happy and satisfied with their work. And then, I determined to give them access to that very thing. For some, it was huge projects to be challenged with. Others needed support and intervention and through listening, I learned the better way to handle this until they could become productive again. Others were so confident that they became their own manager – I just gave them air cover. I believe it was listening and attending to them in the way that I did that allowed me to find their strengths and to let them loose in our unit. This created strong loyalty between us and consistently high productivity amongst my team. In the end, when Digital was going through the last of its dreadfully painful lay-offs, it was this loyalty and subsequent productivity that held my team of 40 together and left us the last unit standing in what had been a most vibrant and successful department of hundreds.

So, though my 7th and 8th graders laugh at me for being called an "idiot savant," they do get the point: Find what you're good at and build your career on that. Please consider doing the same.

STORY 2:
Why disorganization seals your feet in concrete and throws you off a bridge

If one of the most important things required to be successful is to focus on your strengths, then an equally important task is to neutralize your weaknesses. Earlier, I promised we'd talk about that necessity and so, let's do that now.

Unfortunately, like acne can scar an otherwise pretty face, my difficulties with time management, organizational skills, planning, and administrative details left deep pits on an otherwise satisfying and engaging career. Nothing strained more relationships, cost me more opportunities and money and produced more stress than this inability to get organized. So hateful were the repercussions of this on my family, my career, and me that I eventually sought professional help and discovered that I had Adult ADHD. After a couple of unsuccessful trials, my doctor and I eventually found a medicine that works perfectly for me and that calms most of the noise in my head. I can for the first time in my life, focus – as one of my managers used to admonish me to do.

I suppose it was all the admonishments, the corrective criticism, the gentle and not so nice reminders about my forgetting this or being late (chronically) for that or not completing this project on time (again) and yes, the seldom but dramatic pronouncements of my inherent stupidity that caused me to put so much energy – most of it negative, in trying to fix this aspect of myself. Each time I'd renew this process, I became depressed because it seemed I could never get it right. That's why a proper diagnosis and treatment plan helped me so much. And, it's why I emphasize this lesson to all my children. I don't want them to suffer from underestimating the power of order. I tell them it doesn't matter how smart they are, how pretty, how cute or charming people say they are – disorganization will eventually steal from them every time. They have no excuse. They must be at least "good enough" at this to reach a comfortable measure of success.

Organization comes naturally to a lot of people and it develops clearly as some people age. But in many children and adults, it is a skill that never fully arrives. So, I teach an organizational skills course that explains its value and then gives practical tips on how to set up agendas, establish margins, etc. There are great books on the subject like *The Organized Student* by Donna Goldberg and *Lost, Late and Unprepared* by Cooper-Kahn and Dietzel. Drs. Russell Barkley and Edward Hallowell are significant writers in the field of ADHD but their work provides guidance to all people eager to improve their productivity and peace of mind through greater organization. Dr. Daniel Amen has many thought-provoking books on developing the more focused brain. I use these resources and more in my classes.

The point is if you are not an organized person, get that way. And, if you've tried numerous strategies to become organized and you are still out of control, then consider being evaluated for a biological reason for your chaos. If you are just confused about how to get started, find a mentor, read a good book or give yourself permission to ask for help. Find an "idiot savant" who loves details and pay them to set up a turn-key system for you. Regardless, get good enough at this so that disorder doesn't steal from you any more. And, then turn toward your strengths and enjoy what you do best.

Remember: life is a forward march; there is no retreat! I'm sure life has already taught you major lessons, too. And, as you continue to move forward, take good notes. Remember your lessons. Organize them. And, write back. Tomorrow's children will be very interested in what you'll have to say.

PATRICIA KIRBY WHITLEY began her corporate career in 1984 with Digital Equipment Corporation and left in 1994 to become the first sales manager of ETEC, the Microsoft Training and Consulting arm of McCall Consulting. She later joined the venture capital firm, Technology Ventures, as its Communications and Marketing Director. While at Technology Ventures, she joined the board of directors of WIT as its first public relations director and that same year became involved in public relations for the inaugural "Digital Ball." She stayed involved with both organizations until her retirement in 2005 concluding her career with WIT as its vice-president.

In 2004 while working at Grant Thornton, Patricia also joined the board of the Greater Atlanta YWCA and for two years co-chaired the TGI Tech program ("Teenage Girls in Technology"), an after-school program encouraging middle school girls to consider careers in science, technology, engineering and mathematics. She served as a state-wide board member for the Future Business Leaders Association (FBLA) of Georgia – a position she completed in 2010.

Patricia began teaching math and science in 2007 in various public and private schools and for the last two years, has been a member of Appalachian State University's (ASU) Mathematics Education Leadership Training (MELT) program participating in a corporate grant designed to study the best pedagogical practices for middle and high school science and mathematics students. She and her husband, Jon, have two sons, Joshua and Jace.

VERITAS CLASSICAL SCHOOLS provides a classical Christian model of education and is used as a unique compliment to home schooling families. Veritas Classic Schools was incorporated in the mid 1990s and has grown into numerous campuses across Alabama, Georgia, Mississippi, South Carolina and Tennessee.

Building the Next Generation of Women in Technology

"Our work is not just a passion, but a vocation to help young people – young women in particular – be educated about their choices and to find their best direction with the confidence they need to pursue their goals."

— MARGOT KING, *President* of The WIT Foundation, 2010

THE STATISTICS ARE ALARMING – according to the National Science Foundation, America lags behind other nations in the number of students majoring in science and engineering at colleges and universities. Additionally, women make up just nine percent of those receiving engineering degrees. WIT, Inc. and WIT Foundation are changing all that!

Opening the pipeline

Founded in 2004, the WIT Foundation is a 501c3 non-profit organization that supports the philanthropic aims of WIT, Inc. The WIT Foundation focuses on pre-career programs, awarding cash grants to area organizations and non-profits focusing on girls and science, technology, engineering and math (STEM).

WIT starts early guiding women in technology toward success, and the WIT Foundation is an important component in reaching out to the next generation of women. The objectives of the WIT Foundation and associated programs are:

- To create a pool of young girls and women that will enter into a career in technology
- To help bridge the gap between the education and the business communities to establish a firm link between choices for STEM curriculums and careers in technology
- To provide exposure and interaction with various users and uses of technology as well as female role models
- To provide opportunities for Georgia companies to showcase their use of technology, their favorable work setting, and successful female role models within their organizations
- To provide opportunities for WIT partners to collaborate on program execution
- To enable participants in hosted events and workshops to answer technology-related career questions such as:

> "What types of jobs are available in IT if I major in science, technology, engineering or math?" or "What is it like to work in a company that depends largely on technology?

The story of the WIT Foundation and how it all began is inspiring. Even more exciting are the wonderful stories of girls experiencing the world of technology and volunteers sharing through their mentorship.

Remembering the beginning

Children are often asked, "What are you going to be when you grow up?" In today's world of technology advances and global connectivity, more career choices are available than ever before – and that question is relevant to children and adults alike.

Sue Miller, President of WIT in 2000 and President of The WIT Foundation from 2007 through 2009, considers herself part of the small core group – consisting of Kasie Scott Palmer, Victoria Albee, Joan Herbig, and others – that created the Girls Get IT program. Coming into Information Technology from another industry, Miller was passionate about helping others make that transition. After learning the startling statistics about how few girls enter technology-related fields, she wanted to make an impact to improving the number. Miller saw how the efforts to help women interested in IT careers could be extended to reach high school and middle school girls. The statistics suggested that the girls typically decide not to pursue technology in middle school, so the WIT group was determined to target their first events to reach middle school girls.

A mentorship program had been a part of Women In Technology since its early days and so the group was well aware of the benefits of being able to talk with others about career or educational decisions. With the help of Joan Herbig, who had been engaged with the mentoring program, WIT held what would be now called a "Behind The Scenes" workshop for a group of girls from the Atlanta Girls' School. As CEO of XcelleNet, Herbig had access to both their front- and back-office operations. She shared with the girls an insider's view of both the technical and non-technical roles within the company. The girls were intrigued and excited! Their school already had interest in supporting technology-related careers and this tour led to subsequent discussions. It also sparked requests from the students and administrators alike to hold more events along the same topic. It seemed that the timing was right to build on the success of the XcelleNet visit and to create a formalized program for girls. The Girls Get IT program, along with the WIT Foundation, was born.

"In establishing The WIT Foundation in 2004, we expanded our mission to encourage younger women to enter technology. We wanted girls to see that technology is cool," says Kasie Scott Palmer, the first President of The WIT Foundation. "Girls don't often understand that a career in technology does not necessarily mean you need to be a technologist."

Collaborating for tomorrow

Today the Girls Get IT (GGIT) program is a collaboration, between the Women In Technology Foundation and the Georgia business and academic communities, to inspire girls in middle and high school to choose careers in science, technology, engineering and math (also known as STEM). The program name has a double meaning: girls get it because they understand the academics behind these fields and they also recognize the impact which technology has on our daily lives.

As the first chair of the program, Vicky Albee coordinated the first official GGIT program event with The Weather Channel. This two-hour field trip for 11–15 year old girls featured interactions with senior executive women, including Vicki Hamilton, senior vice president of the Weather Channel. The girls toured satellite and server facilities at The Weather Channel. They observed an active television studio where they learned about technology operations, software support, meteorology, and quality assurance. The popular field trip was quickly followed by other events and the program continued to grow in scope and substance.

The GGIT workshops and events expose girls to real working situations and provide them with guidance on training and skills necessary for those roles. "It's our responsibility to grow the next generation, to show young women what options they have if they chose STEM-related studies," says Margot King, 2010 President of The WIT Foundation.

Giving the girls a chance to interact with professionals helps them to understand if a particular role or industry may be a good fit for them – instead of relying on what they've heard or seen on TV. "Kids are not making major decisions based on good information. If you've made the wrong decisions early on, changing your mind can be costly from a financial and emotional perspective later," King continues. "This is our chance to impact that historical trend to inform girls – as well as parents who pay for it – and to assist them in making their first critical decisions: where and what they're going to study."

In short, these events reinforce connections between what girls study now and how that can be applied to a future career.

Endless Possibilities

by Susan Solomon

Co-founder
Sherpani Partners
ATLANTA, GEORGIA

THE WIT FOUNDATION PLAYS A CRITICAL ROLE in funding the GGIT programs that are already making a difference. In these programs, girls see and hear about exciting new possibilities in technology from strong, successful female role models. Sherpani Partners assists with the design, development, and delivery of the programs with many enthusiastic WIT volunteers managing and staffing the programs.

Sandra Schumann and I met Sue Miller for breakfast one morning to talk about how Sherpani Partners and WIT might partner in creating career exploration programs for girls. Sherpani Partners is a non-profit organization providing career guidance and education to the community. Children are learning about careers as early as elementary school, and we are passionate about helping young people make the best academic, school and career choices. The ideas started flowing, breakfast became brunch and we knew the possibilities were endless.

We began with workshops for girls in the FIRST Robotics teams that The WIT Foundation sponsored. Building on their success, we worked with Sue to create the first GGIT Job Shadow Workshop, based on the Career Reality Experience™ that our company conducts in local high schools. That first year, most girls were from Cool Girls, Inc., and they were very excited to have this opportunity to learn from seasoned, top-level executives.

Sandra and I are amazed at the commitment of the WIT volunteers and we appreciate the opportunity to partner with them. Sherpani Partners' challenge in working with WIT in the future will be to help create additional opportunities for these wonderful women to impact the lives of young girls.

ESTABLISHED AS A NONPROFIT ORGANIZATION BASED IN ATLANTA, SHERPANI PARTNERS provides direction and focus for career exploration and planning to students and adults. For more information, visit www.sherpanipartners.org.

Growing the Girls Get IT Program

THE GIRLS GET IT PROGRAM creates the context for discovery moments. In welcoming environments like their schools or host companies, the girls mingle with technology professionals who are ready to recognize and encourage technology-related inspiration.

Bolstered by contributions from partners and collaborators, the GGIT program participation has grown four-fold in recent years. Program content has been strengthened with standard practices, including use of assessment questionnaires.

"These assessments help the girls understand, early on, what their proclivities are, what they are interested in, where their strengths lie, and what areas of study may be available – as well as how all of this translates to career later on," says Margot King. "Often, these exercises are the first time the girls have been asked about different career choices. Working with Sherpani Partners was a huge benefit because they added additional structure to the program and provided recommendations for the assessment tools."

The program has been enhanced further with valued input from host companies like AutoTrader.com, Intercontinental Hotels Group, McKesson, and The Weather Channel. Premier academic institutions like Georgia Institute of Technology and Georgia State have also participated. Program activities now include Behind The Scenes workshops, the Job Shadow program, and Career Exploration workshops, all of which are hosted free of admission charge.

Making a difference

Technology has become an integral part of everyday life, and future development is becoming more dependent on it. The Girls Get IT programs are especially important now for a variety of compelling reasons.

Our need for technology professionals is growing.

According to the Bureau of Labor Statistics, technology job opportunities are predicted to grow 22 percent by 2018, a faster rate than all other jobs in the professional sector. Computer and mathematical occupations are expected to add 785,700 new jobs from 2008 to 2018, and, as a group, they will grow more than twice as fast as the average for other occupations in the economy, according to projections. Further, women currently comprise only 24% of the workforce in technology.[1] Women – particularly young women – trained for STEM careers can increase the overall percentage and help to meet this increasing need.

Technology innovation is more in demand than ever, especially in the areas of computers, telecommunications, and medicine.

In the 30 years prior to 2006, male patent holders amassed a total of 1,286 patents compared to only 92 patents secured by women scientists. Female academic scientists patent at about 40% the rate of men.[2] Against worldwide competition, stronger industries can be built with more inventions and innovative processes patented by women in STEM careers.

Balanced leadership will engage strengths of both men and women.

Technical men are significantly more likely than women to be in high-level positions. The odds of being in a high level position are 2.7 times as great for men than women.[3] Young women, groomed early on for leadership roles will be better equipped to contribute when they take on these roles.

Female support networks and role models

---

1 2008 National Employment Matrix. Bureau of Labor Statistics, Monthly Labor Review, November 2009. http://www.bls.gov/opub/mlr/2009/11/art5full.pdf

2 Ewing Marion Kauffman Foundation Sponsored Study: "Gender Differences in Patenting in the Academic Life Scientists." www.kauffman.org/details.aspx?id=920

3 Climbing the Technology Ladder: Obstacles and Solutions for Mid-Level Women in Technology. Simard, C., Davies Henderson, A., Gilmartin, S., Shiebinger, L., &Whitney, T. http://anitaborg.org/files/Climbing_the_Technical_Ladder.pdf

encourage career development.

Factors leading women and minorities to STEM *careers included: Supportive family members (69%); "inspiring and dedicated teachers" (66%); a challenging curriculum and/or an abundance and variety of* STEM *courses (33%); extracurricular activities (24%); role models (22%) and financial assistance (19%). Seventy-seven percent (77%) said they thought the* STEM *workforce in the U.S. is lacking women and underrepresented minorities owing to a lack of early encouragement and nurturing.*[4] Mentorship programs and personalized attention will yield high results as more and more young women enter STEM fields.

Equity in compensation is important to recruit and maintain qualified professionals.

Among 18 civilian STEM occupations, women's earnings as a percentage of men's earnings ranged from 80–94%. Women are not currently filling 50% of any roles except as biological scientists.[5] Equivalent salaries will encourage young women to consider these occupations, and, once in, will consider staying in them longer instead of leaving for another industry that pays better or is more fair.

---

4 Bayer Sponsored Study: "Facts of Science Education" and resulting article "Colleges, Professors Discourage Women from Pursuing STEM Careers." 2010. http://campustechnology.com/Articles/2010/02/23/Colleges-Professors-Discourage-Women-from-Pursuing-STEM-Careers

5 U.S. Census Bureau, American Community Survey, 2008. U.S. Department of Labor, Bureau of Labor Statistics, 2009. Women in the labor force: A Databook (Report 1018) (Washington, DC) Table 11.

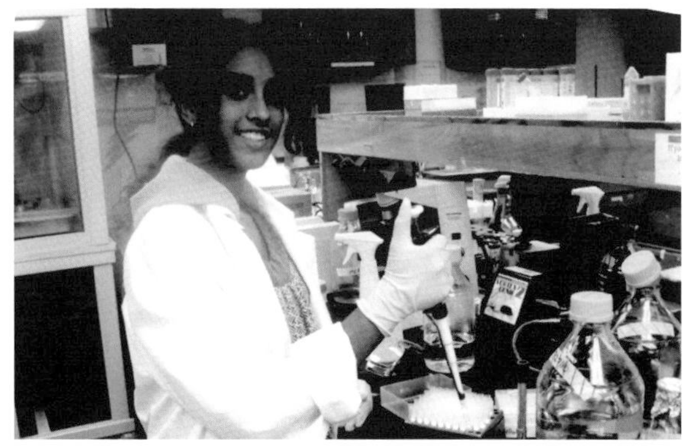

Behind the Scenes Workshops

Insights

"It was fun to see how nanotechnology works in something like sunscreen. I never knew it was so important. I thought the super powerful microscope was cool, too!"

— CALEIGH HEBERT, GGIT Member

Looking backstage

DISCOVERING HOW TECHNOLOGY serves as the backbone in corporate, academic and healthcare strategies can be the spark that sets a young girl on the path to a technology career. Behind The Scenes (BTS) workshops provide business, educational, and medical entities the opportunity to showcase their operations. These organizations typically provide a tour of their facilities and give girls a hands-on presentation of different technology-related careers there. When the girls meet the executive women and see first-hand how technology makes a company successful, it creates awareness and interest which can inspire these young girls to look further into technology-related careers.

Through the BTS workshops, the girls can experience the inner workings of what might be an otherwise off-limits organization. For example, the Georgia Tech Nanotechnology Research Center opened its doors to 32 girls, aged 11–14. The Center's scientists started off the girls' visit with a quick lesson in Nanotechnology and its growth potential in the next decade.[1] Then, the girls participated in a laboratory activity, where they tested different types of sunscreens to determine what level of protection was offered. The exercise was meant to demonstrate the value of nanoparticles in everyday products, like sunscreen. Later, over a pizza lunch, the girls talked one-on-one with Georgia Tech undergraduate students who were participating in a summer program at the research center. The visit wrapped up with a quick tour through the center and the state-of-the-art Nanooze Children's Exhibit.

Girls participating in these workshops have an opportunity to see firsthand how the technology employed in our everyday lives is created, applied, and distributed. Taking tours of the facilities

---

1 The National Science Foundation estimates that by the year 2015, there will be a need for two million workers worldwide in the fields of nanoscience and nanotechnology. At that time, nanotechnology is expected to be a $3T industry.

and talking with employees helps the girls envision themselves in a variety of new environments and new career opportunities. By attending these Behind The Scenes workshops, they are able to explore the possibilities of being involved in these tech-related endeavors.

Career Exploration Workshops

Insights

"Oh, so that's how doctors have the right bandages to put on their patients. I always wondered, and now I know."

"It must be so cool to say 'I work with the Department of Defense.' I only thought they worked with men in the Army."

"You mean I could tie in my love for music with science? I thought I had to pick one or the other! I'm hearing about music recording, music therapy or working in digital communications."

Exploring a career

THE CAREER EXPLORATION (CE) WORKSHOPS are designed to introduce girls to a variety of career options in a single setting, usually in a short afternoon or evening session. Girls participating in the workshops have conversations with professional women currently working in technology fields. These women share their jobs and educational experiences. The range of professions represented is wide: for example, at one CE event, girls shared experiences and questions with a biochemist in product development for products used in surgeries, a project manager on a worldwide software implementation, and a telecommunications researcher working with the Department of Defense. The girls talk to these impressive professionals within a comfortable "round-table" setting, changing tables after a short interval to talk to other professionals that are present.

According to facilitator Sherpani Partners, typical conversation topics from the girls might include:

- How long have you been working in your field?
- What do you like best/least about working in your field? What would you do differently in your career path?
- Would you have chosen a different college major or are there other majors you would have liked?
- What other kinds of certifications or education are required in your career?

These conversations provide special "insider's insight." To complement this learning, the girls are given the chance to discover their own interests, preferences, and personality styles through standard assessment tools. The results are shared with them during the same day so that the girls receive immediate feedback. As the young girls face decisions about their education and future, they will hopefully be able to incorporate the learning from these exceptional women as well as their personal interest assessments to help determine their next academic or professional steps.

Job Shadow Program

Insight

"What surprised me was the fact that there are so many different parts to the IT world and that there are more opportunities than just coding. IT encompasses many different opportunities and this experience has shown me that I can be in the IT world without having extreme IT knowledge."

— TRINITY FREEMAN, GGIT Member

Revealing the world

EXPERIENCING A PROFESSIONAL ROLE before actually taking on a job is the golden opportunity provided by the Job Shadow program. In this weeklong event, girls follow a professional woman who is in a technology role. They shadow this woman to observe and to understand the day-to-day happenings in functions such as development, product innovation, project management, operations, support, and human resources. By pairing girls with career women in technology fields, the girls can learn more about what a career looks like if they were to hold a diploma in science, technology, engineering or math.

The intent of the Job Shadowing program is to demonstrate:

- What it's really like in the workplace
- What career opportunities exist
- What it means to be a woman in a technology role
- How to present yourself in a business context
- How individuals and teams work together.

The program begins with an orientation to the site, a review of the agenda, and Mentor Matching. Girls are paired with accomplished women who guide them and encourage their participation while accomplishing their regular objectives through the week. In one-on-one conversations, the girls learn how their mentor achieved their career goals, how they made their educational choices and how they may have overcome career obstacles. The girls participate in personality and interest questionnaires, and then discuss their findings with their mentors.

During lunches, the girls gather to listen to guest speakers (who are often in senior-level positions like CIO, Vice President or Program Manager) and compare observations. Like the real world, the Job Shadow program comes with responsibilities: each girl is asked to write down Daily Reflections on what she experienced or learned; to interview her mentor on duties and job training; and to prepare a one-page presentation of her learning, likes and surprises. At the end of the week, each girl gives a presentation to her peers, which allows the entire group to benefit from her time "on the job."

The Job Shadow workshops provide a detailed glimpse into real achievements and challenges in the workplace. Girls experiencing this program will be better equipped to make education and career choices based on what they learned and how they felt. Many of them will be able to take advantage of newly formed relationships with their mentors, reaching out to them as academic and career transition points arise throughout their lives.

Experiencing the Ah-ha Moments

THE GIRLS WHO PARTICIPATE IN THE WIT programs depart with memories of a rich experience and a new excitement about the possibilities of their life. These are some of the "ah-ha" moments experienced:

HALEY BOWERS – "(At AutoTrader.com) I learned about something that I will probably never forget, and I feel like a geek for saying so, but when my mentor taught me about the Project Life Cycle, I was enchanted."

KAYLA DIXON – "(At SunTrust) I really enjoyed seeing the trade and stock center, how it works and what they do on 3 or 5 different computer screens. I also liked seeing the data base center where I saw all the wires and servers that keep all the computers in the building working and on point."

MORGAN MCCALL – "(At SunTrust) I learned that I am a good organizer which would make me very good at creating portfolio responsibilities for projects. My list of future career possibilities has absolutely grown."

MADISON MCCALL – "SunTrust, being so technologically-advanced as a company, arose in me an even greater interest in the [technology] field the minute I entered the workspace. I was surprised, though, to find out that the schedule of an employee is booked almost every day with meetings and team gatherings."

MEGAN MCCALL – "I liked the way they (SunTrust) organized their notes for a project status. I witnessed a reviewing of the Stoplight report. I learned that I like to be busy and active so being a Project Manager or a Client Engagement Consultant is a possibility for me."

HARITHA PAVULURI – "Two things I liked most about what I saw or heard this week (at GSU Biology) were dissecting calf hearts and the Bio-Bus Program's Site Visit to Redan-Trotti Library. I really like Biology and Lab Work, and learned I can combine various interests into one career."

Overheard comments

Over the program's history, other girls' comments have been captured and reflect the new insights obtained:

"I was sure I wanted to be a math teacher, but after being in a dot-com company where everything is tied to technology, I can't think of being in a career *not* using technology."

"Who would have guessed these little things could do so much? Nanoparticles are going to be very important to our future."

"I didn't know there was so much technology in health careers. It's almost like you can't take care of patients without it."

Changing Futures

by Jenni Crenshaw

Executive Director
Jabian Consulting
ATLANTA, GEORGIA

JOINING WOMEN IN TECHNOLOGY provided me with a group of women mentors and furthered my passion for mentoring others and giving back to my community. Exploring that passion brought me to the Girls Get IT program where I have the chance to give to young girls the same hopes and dreams that were given to me.

Growing up in a small town, it was the mentoring I received

that opened my eyes to the world of technology and the opportunities for women. My mentors taught me that no matter where I was born I could truly do anything. They taught me that just because it wasn't what everyone else was doing, didn't mean it wasn't the right thing to do.

This year, I have the honor of serving as Chair of the Job Shadow Program. The experience was amazing for the mentors, mentees and me personally. Not only did I get to network with amazing women, but I also have been able to take some of the experiences back to my company, Jabian Consulting, to improve our internal mentoring relationships. I now look at my daughters with a better understanding of how they see the world. I know that I can open their eyes to their endless possibilities.

I look forward to continuing to work with Girls Get IT. Seeing the responses in the girls' faces, hearing their stories and hearing them say, "I now know that I can do *anything*," confirms that by participating in Girls Get IT, I am changing futures.

JABIAN CONSULTING is an Atlanta based IT and management consultancy that applies senior level consulting specialists to our clients' top priority projects. Jabian takes an integrated approach to creating and implementing strategies, enhancing business processes, developing human capital, and better aligning technology – ultimately helping clients drive business value by increasing revenue and decreasing operational costs. Jabian Consulting is a division of Jabian, LLC, a privately held corporation based in Atlanta, Georgia.

And More Rave Reviews!

IT ISN'T JUST THE GIRLS WHO GAIN INSIGHTS. The programs also impact the employees and volunteers:

JUDY BOWERS – "It's a joy to watch the girls stand up in front of 40–50 individuals, really synthesizing data they learned and applying the logic. The Job Shadow program is a great experience for young minds: it gives the girls an opportunity to engage in technology in an active working environment, creating interest in both. They may even come back to work for our company at a later point in their lives."

LETITIA CLARK – "In fourth grade, one of my teachers brought in computers and taught us to use them. She moved with me through 12th grade and has become a lifelong mentor. In the

Job Shadow program, I got involved to give back. I knew this was a way to help shape the girls' directions, as my mentor has helped shape mine."

LAUREN EDELSTEIN – "There's no program like this but 'Bring Your Daughter to Work Day.' The Job Shadow program is more robust because it's longer than one day. The girls see the corporate environment, and their mentors show them different roles and explain the different functions. Sometimes tech learning comes on the job, and it's important to realize that."

SABRINA JOHNSON – "As a project manager, I was given the opportunity to grow professionally through the Job Shadow program. Every day, there were announcements to give and information to share, and people counted on me for them. This helped enhance my public speaking skills while doing something great for the girls."

KRYSTINA MORRISON – "The internet is not that old – maybe twenty years, and our company is 13 years old. We're still expanding, still learning. There are changes every day in a technology-driven business, and we're able to show some of that in the Job Shadow program."

BELVA PORTER – "I've been involved in information technology for over 20 years – in the areas of computer programming, systems and business analysis, quality assurance and testing. Being a mentor in the Job Shadow program gave me a chance to be part of a larger initiative, getting young women involved in technology."

MICHELLE SMITH – "The Job Shadow program is a great way to show how the different groups interface. Being in IT doesn't mean you're alone at your computer all the time. You interact with others and can really make a difference."

FIRST Robotics Partnership

Insight

"Being involved in these programs has really brought me to that solid ground of being completely sure that I want to pursue a career in technology. Since the summer I have been looking up a lot of scholarships for girls going into a technological field and I've pushed for the highest position on my robotics team: CEO."

— HALEY BOWERS, GGIT and FIRST Robotics Member

Finding a perfect fit

As part of its charter, The WIT Foundation provides opportunities for WIT partners to collaborate on program execution. Although one of the challenging aspects of actively involving girls in technology is the lack of programs or competitions for them, The WIT Foundation may have found a perfect fit with FIRST Robotics organization. According to its website, www.gafirst.org, "The FIRST Robotics Competition (FRC) combines the excitement of sport with science and technology to create a unique varsity sport for the mind."

In these competitions, high school students form teams to build robots that scrimmage each other in a game – but the stakes are a little higher, says Bob Stargel, Judge Advisor for the FIRST Robotics Peachtree Regional Competition and Chairman on the Peachtree Regional Planning Committee. "The robot competition is bigger than building a robot. It is focused on building lifelong skills and interest in science and technology that eventually will be used to help with real-life business problems, like sustainability programs and water filtration programs for Third World countries."

Competing in the real world

The six-week competition is much like the RFP (Request For Proposal) process in the business world, says Suzy Crowe, National Board-certified teacher of math and AP computer science at Milton High School, as well as the coach of the robotics team. "The teams are given specs – sometimes 200 pages or more – which they must adhere to in building the robot or be disqualified. The kids read them and think about strategic and tactical things like what will make the robot work? Which things will earn the most points? What materials should we use? Then they come up with different ideas and debate the merits of each design. The kids work on the engineering design and build plan. They get the parts they need and learn how to build – inventing something that will meet challenge of that game. Then they take the prototype to the competition to play against other teams."

Awards are given not only to teams scoring the most points, but also in specific areas such as innovative use of materials, best design, and entrepreneurial awards for best business approach. Teams can advance through regional, national and international levels, where over 250 million kids participate.

Building life skills

The FIRST Robotics' competition organically folds in life skills such as working in teams, writing plans, building a budget, coordinating logistics, and marketing their efforts. The kids also must seek out business mentors, technical advisors, and sponsors to help pay for expenses – areas that naturally fit with WIT and The WIT Foundation.

"We try to focus on bringing girls into the technology area, and we get a lot of help from WIT in doing that," says Crowe. WIT volunteers are very involved – they actively recruit girls for these teams, assist during competitions, and serve as mentors and board members.

The WIT Foundation supports the FIRST Robotics programs through sponsorship dollars. The WIT Foundation has sponsored the FIRST Robotics Peachtree Regional event in Georgia for a number of years. At this past year's event, WIT featured a speed-networking event for student attendees wanting to talk with successful technology professionals. The girls packed the room all day! In addition, The WIT Foundation has designed a grant to support teams. To apply, teams must submit a profile describing which students serve in which roles and, most importantly, describe what they've done to encourage enrollment of girls in the program.

"The intent is to diversify – to have the girls actively be part of the technical and business aspects of the project, not just designing the T-shirts," says Crowe. "I think a country's strength depends on equity. As women feel more and more comfortable with what they think about and what they can do – and have encouragement to bring their ideas and thoughts to life – we will see a stronger environment in general. You should never want to work with ideas from just one group: there's strength in diversity for solutions to our problems."

Building a Continuum

Insight

"This program has definitely given me a better understanding of how careers really work. I have learned things about myself through this program (like my likes and dislikes) that I believe will affect my career choices. I would recommend this program to anyone that may think they're interested in technology because it helps you learn a lot not only about IT, but also about yourself."

— ZOE CANARAS, GGIT Member

Accelerating successes

FORGING A BROAD RANGE OF EXPERIENCES, the Girls Get IT program is well positioned for continued success. The WIT Foundation leadership will expand relationships with those companies and educational institutions already involved and will seek out partnerships with others across the state. By tapping into even broader resources, WIT Foundation hopes that even more females can be given the opportunity to be exposed to different industry and academic experiences.

"Through their involvement in the Girls Get IT program, companies have a rare opportunity as well," says Margot King. "This is the future workforce of America, and also its future consumer base. Not only do our partners have branding and public relations opportunities working with these young people, but they get immediate feedback from them which can impact product design or approaches to reaching a diverse audience."

The partnerships with academia can be mutually beneficial as well. College level administrators can work with students and their parents in curriculum planning to foster interest in science, technology, engineering and math, attests Suzy Crowe, who actively connects her students at Milton High School with Georgia Tech and other schools. Knowing STEM classes and majors exist in these schools attracts higher enrollments. "A lot of my students attend these schools, continue advanced studies, and choose to be TAs (teaching assistants) for the university," she says.

Traveling the path to self-discovery

These programs are like checkpoints on the path of self-discovery. As these girls travel on their journey – becoming young women and then adults – the influences they have had on their education and career choices travels with them. With programs like Girls Get IT, they can become productive, professional, and successful women in technology. Along with this core objective lays the intention of an "inspired continuum," which fosters a hope that as these girls mature, they too will become mentors and contributors, and will assist in strengthening existing WIT programs and in creating new ones for young women who follow them.

"WIT's legacy in this community is multi-faceted," says Sue Miller. "It's not only in what we've done to showcase women and to be the place where women in technology can thrive, learn, gain visibility, etc., but it's also about the programs we have created and the financial support The WIT Foundation has given back to the community to support the next generation."

Next Generation Acknowledgements

The list of contributors to WIT Foundation grows larger each day, but a special thanks to those WIT volunteers who assisted in telling this story: Donna Cobb, Wendy Kemp, Emily Ping, Katie Tucker, Patti Wagner, Lila King, Sandra Schumann and Valerie Streit. Thank you for the inspiration and perspiration!

Thank you to the organization and employees of AutoTrader.com, Grant Thornton, IHG, Kimberly-Clark Corporation, Sherpani Partners, SunTrust Bank, The Weather Channel and Turner Broadcasting for your sponsorship, your guidance, your talents and your advocacy in delivering the WIT Foundation programs.

A special thanks to the teachers who are nurturing the next generation of women in technology:

Alpharetta High School, Centennial High School, Kell High School, Milton High School, North Cobb High School, Roswell High School and Walton High School as well as Georgia State University Department of Biology and The Georgia Institute of Technology Department of Nanotechnology. You rock!!

— BONNIE BAJOREK DANEKER

The Branding of the Book
How *Climb* came to be

ONE OF THE BIGGEST CHALLENGES we faced in planning this book was figuring out how to brand it. How do you gather all of these stories under one theme? What's the overarching message? What about the title? The look? Essentially, how could we treat the book itself as a brand?

So we turned to brand consultancy West Reed for help with these questions. They presented a number of different creative directions, including various title concepts and cover designs. In the end, we went with their recommendation to build our message on the simple, bold, one-word statement "Climb".

Thanks to West Reed and others, Climb is now an important brand in itself that will help support and promote the work of WIT – and of women in technology around the world.

WEST REED is a brand consultancy that helps B2B firms define their brand message and communicate it more effectively – both visually and verbally. The firm has worked with a number of Atlanta-based technology companies as well as national and international brands. Learn more at www.westreed.com.

About Women in Technology (WIT)

WIT'S MISSION IS TO SERVE as passionate advocates for advancing women in Georgia's technology community. Each year, more than 1,000 thought leaders and professionals attend WIT Forums and WIT's leadership and networking series. WIT delivers professional development programs, such as WIT Executive Coaching and WIT Careers in Action, to enable members to hone their leadership skills and achieve visibility within the business community.

WIT's philanthropic and educational programs, such as Girls Get IT, provide outreach to educate and encourage girls and young women to pursue careers in science and technology. WIT has two annual premier events, WIT Connect, WIT's annual fundraiser event, and WIT's *Women of the Year in Technology Awards* honoring the women who lead Georgia's technology community. WIT is a founding society of the Technology Association of Georgia, an umbrella membership organization that serves the Georgia technology community. For more information on WIT and the WIT Foundation, WIT's philanthropic arm, visit www.mywit.org.

A NOTE ON THE TYPEFACE

This book is set in Adobe Caslon Pro – a typeface designed by Carol Twombly as a revival of William Caslon's classic types from the 1700s. In addition to its being a timeless, beautiful typeface, we felt Adobe Caslon Pro was particularly well-suited for a book about women in technology – as it was created by a woman.